CW00669949

PENGUI

# SACRED ANIM

Nanditha Krishna is a historian, environmentalist, and writer based in Chennai. A PhD in ancient Indian culture, she is the director of the C.P. Ramaswami Aiyar Foundation and C.P.R. Environmental Education Centre. She has pioneered the documentation of the ecological traditions of India, restored over fifty sacred groves, and established schools, a research institution, and a museum of folk art. Her published works include *Sacred Animals of India*, *Book of Demons*, *Book of Vishnu*, *Madras Then Chennai Now*, *Balaji-Venkateshwara*, *Ganesha*, *Painted Manuscripts of the Sarasvati Mahal Library*, *Arts and Crafts of Tamilnadu*, and *Art and Iconography of Vishnu Narayana*, besides numerous research papers and newspaper articles. She is a professor and research guide for the PhD programme of the University of Madras and has received several prestigious national and international awards.

# PRAISE FOR THE BOOK

'*Sacred Animals* . . . is not a coffee-table book. It requires that you read, not just glance through it. The book evokes the vision of an ancient civilisation—ours. From Vedic to historic times, it chronicles the dynamics of man–animal interaction in India down the centuries'—*The Hindu Business Line*

'A good read at a time when the world as we know it is in the throes of an increasingly contentious debate on the future of our environment'—*Mail Today*

'The book, written in simple, straightforward language, treats the complex subject with the confidence that is born out of meticulous and thorough research and strong convictions. Tribal lore, folklore, ancient scriptures, traditional tales, history, scriptural texts, cave paintings—no source seems to have been left uncombed in the effort to chronicle the history and progress of the Indian's attitude towards animals'—Book Review Literary Trust

# SACRED ANIMALS
of INDIA

## NANDITHA KRISHNA

PENGUIN BOOKS

PENGUIN BOOKS
Published by the Penguin Group
Penguin Books India Pvt. Ltd, 11 Community Centre, Panchsheel Park,
New Delhi 110 017, India
Penguin Group (USA) Inc., 375 Hudson Street, New York, New York 10014, USA
Penguin Group (Canada), 90 Eglinton Avenue East, Suite 700, Toronto,
Ontario, M4P 2Y3, Canada (a division of Pearson Penguin Canada Inc.)
Penguin Books Ltd, 80 Strand, London WC2R 0RL, England
Penguin Ireland, 25 St Stephen's Green, Dublin 2, Ireland
(a division of Penguin Books Ltd)
Penguin Group (Australia), 707 Collins Street, Melbourne, Victoria 3008, Australia
(a division of Pearson Australia Group Pty Ltd)
Penguin Group (NZ), 67 Apollo Drive, Rosedale, Auckland 0632, New Zealand
(a division of Pearson New Zealand Ltd)
Penguin Books (South Africa) (Pty) Ltd, Block D, Rosebank Office Park,
181 Jan Smuts Avenue, Parktown North, Johannesburg 2193, South Africa

Penguin Books Ltd, Registered Offices: 80 Strand, London WC2R 0RL, England

First published by Penguin Books India 2010

Copyright © Nanditha Krishna 2010

All rights reserved

10 9 8 7 6 5 4 3 2 1

The views and opinions expressed in this book are the author's own and the
facts are as reported by her which have been verified to the extent possible, and
the publishers are not in any way liable for the same.

ISBN 9780143423201

Typeset in Dante MT by InoSoft Systems, Noida
Printed at Akash Press, Okhla

This book is sold subject to the condition that it shall not, by way of trade
or otherwise, be lent, resold, hired out, or otherwise circulated without the
publisher's prior written consent in any form of binding or cover other than
that in which it is published and without a similar condition including this
condition being imposed on the subsequent purchaser and without limiting
the rights under copyright reserved above, no part of this publication may be
reproduced, stored in or introduced into a retrieval system, or transmitted in
any form or by any means (electronic, mechanical, photocopying, recording or
otherwise), without the prior written permission of both the copyright owner
and the above-mentioned publisher of this book.

*For the many animals who are part of our everyday world and bring us joy, and for those that suffer needlessly as a result of human cruelty.*

*vidyāvinayasampanne brāhmane gavi hastini*
*śuni caiva śvapāke ca paṇḍitāḥ samadarśinaḥ*

(Those who are wise and humble treat equally,
the Brahmin, cow, elephant, dog and dog-eater)

*Bhagavat Gita, 5.19*

# Contents

# Preface

'Sacred Animals of India' was planned for the Asia for Animals Conference held in January 2007 at Chennai. However, when I began researching the subject, I discovered a wealth of material that was impossible to ignore. So I decided to cover the subject in greater depth.

This book was first published as a limited edition by C.P.R. Environmental Education Centre (CPREEC), for release during the National Conference on the Environment and Indian History held at Chennai in January 2008. It has been expanded to include many more myths and legends involving animals, and rewritten for a more general readership.

My love for animals was instilled in me by my late father, A.R. Jagannathan, a wildlife enthusiast who took me to so many national parks and sanctuaries that I became an avid environmentalist. He was an ardent Hanuman devotee, while my late Ganesha-worshipping mother Shakunthala Jaganathan and I jointly wrote a book *Ganesha—The Auspicious . . . The Beginning* (Vakils, Feffer and Simons Ltd) in 1992. The seed for this book was probably sown long ago by my parents.

None of this would have been possible without the interest and involvement of Ravi Singh and Udayan Mitra of Penguin, who encouraged me to complete the book quickly, and Archana Shankar, my editor. Thank you, Ravi, Udayan and Archana.

Several people helped me in so many ways: M. Amirthalingam assisted me right through my research, especially in finding the correct names for each animal in various languages. Dr T. Sundaramurthi and P. Sudhakar of C.P.R. Environmental Education Centre, Chennai, and Dr A. Raman of Orange University, Australia, gave the zoological information and ecological role of each animal. G. Balaji searched for illustrations in the private collection of the C.P. Ramaswami Aiyar Foundation and H. Manikandan kept track of all the materials. My husband Dr S. Chinny Krishna, who is also the chairman of the Blue Cross of India, updated me on animal welfare issues in India. He also read, re-read, questioned and edited the book. My sincere thanks to all of them.

Once we decided to illustrate this book with drawings, Y. Venkatesh went through the ardous task of sketching each figure. It was a difficult task to make elaborate pictures of Ganesha and Gajalakshmi into simple sketches, but he did it, I believe, very successfully.

Every animal is introduced with the myths and legends that establish its religious status, followed by a short note on the ecological or social role of the animal, which made it important in people's lives. The problems of its survival and treatment in today's world have also been covered.

I have tried to provide the Hindi, Tamil and Sanskrit names for each animal and/or the local name in the state where it is specially revered, for many animals are restricted to specific geographic areas.

An appendix on Sacred Animals and Animal Divinities of Ancient Mesopotamia and Egypt has been included. While all ancient civilizations revered animals, the similarities between these neighbours and India require special emphasis. Further, although they may be of greater antiquity than the Indian examples, they have been restricted to an appendix so that they do not divert attention from the main topic of the book.

This book is dedicated to the many dogs and one cat who gave me so much love and companionship over the years, and to the many animals who have suffered and continue to suffer at human hands—bullocks pulling overloaded carts, cattle and goats trucked or walked for days without food or water, animals fattened and killed agonizingly to provide man with a plate of rich food, wildlife hunted from fast-moving vehicles with technically sophisticated weapons ... the list is endless. May they find peace in their future lives.

This book does not whitewash the problems faced by animals. Rather, it is a timely reminder of traditions that once gave animals protection from human inhumanity. India had a rich heritage of respect for all life forms. This respect has been destroyed, without being replaced by anything similar or better. Unless we protect our wildlife from hunting and extinction, and our domestic animals from cruelty, we are not fit to call ourselves educated, or even a people who inherited the great legacy of ahimsa or non-violence.

Nanditha Krishna
Chennai

# Introduction

The ancient religions of India—Hinduism, Buddhism and Jainism —have never differentiated between the soul of a human being and the soul of an animal. All life forms are subject to the cycle of birth, death and rebirth. The liberation of the soul depends on one's karmas or actions, and one goes through several births till the soul realizes the truth. Thus a person, an animal and an insect are equally part of the cycle of life, death and rebirth. Finally, when good karmas lead to self-realization, the soul is liberated from the cycle of samsara. This is moksha or nirvana, the ultimate liberation of the individual soul, leading it to oneness with the Supreme Being or Brahman. Everything has been created by the Supreme Being, comes from the Supreme Being and returns to the Supreme Being. Animals are sacred because people identify with them, an identity born of the belief in karma and the transmigration of souls.

Ancient civilizations revered nature in all its aspects. In Indian traditions, the proper balance of the pancha bhuta (five elements) —prithvi (earth), vayu (wind), akasha (sky or space), apa (water) and agni (fire or energy)—is essential for the harmony and balance of life on earth. All life forms contribute equally to the balance of these five elements.

The worship of animals probably began very early in human history, when human beings were struggling to survive in a hostile environment. Man and animal have coexisted since the beginning of creation, sometimes in harmony and at other times in hostility, as they fought over limited resources. The carnivores with their strength, speed and physical prowess were feared and had to be overcome. The human brain created tools to achieve superiority over animals and this led to the development of cultures and civilizations. The respect for a powerful adversary made him into a god, worshipped out of fear.

This was a time when people were still food gatherers. Many Indian tribes believe that eating a portion of the flesh or wearing a part of the animal's body (like the claw or teeth of the tiger) will transfer the qualities of that animal to the person. Animals were revered for specific qualities that the devotee hoped to attain. A tribal shaman may go into a trance and enter the soul of an animal, in which state he can see things denied to a human being, thus giving the animal an omniscient quality.

The Lepchas, hunter–gatherers of Sikkim, believe that everything in the environment is of spiritual significance, that animals and birds share a symbiotic relationship of mutual obligation and trust with humans. Their socio-ethic norm, called bukrup, involves avoidance of unnecessary wastage and destruction of nature. Females of wild animal species may not be hunted. Males may not be hunted during particular periods or under certain conditions. Fishing is prohibited between July and October, the breeding season. A person who cuts a single tree must plant eight saplings in its place and nurture them for six years. Migratory birds, especially cuckoos, decide the agricultural calendar and are therefore sacred. The blood pheasant is sacred, for it saved the Lepcha ancestors from the great flood and guided them to the safety of Mount Tedong (Jha 1998).

The early Stone Age rock paintings at Bhimbetka, in the Raisen district of Madhya Pradesh, belonging to between 10,000 and 7000 BCE, are the earliest known site in India depicting the hunt, fighting animals, honey collection, and elephant- and horse-riders, the presence of the horse being quite a surprise. The paintings belong to the Upper Paleolithic, Mesolithic, Chalcolithic, Early Historic and Medieval periods. The earliest consist of linear representations of huge animals, such as the tiger, bison and rhinoceros. The figures of the Mesolithic period are smaller stylized figures of humans and animals with linear decorations. The weapons included spears and shields, pointed sticks, bows and arrows. The paintings of the Chalcolithic period include scenes of agriculture, while those of the Early Historic period include religious symbols and tree spirits (yakshas?). Several animals have been depicted in Bhimbetka: mammals like tigers, lions, boars, bison, elephants, deer and dogs; reptiles like lizards and crocodiles; and birds like the peacock. One rock full of animals is referred to as the 'Zoo Rock'. Scenes of hunting using bows, arrows, swords and shields are aplenty. In one cave, a bison is chasing a man, whose two companions watch helplessly.

As people progressed to food production—settled agriculture and farming—the gentler and less-threatening species, like the cow, bull, buffalo and horse, and even the largest of them all, the elephant, were domesticated and put to work. There is obviously a correlation between the type of food consumed and the domesticated animal, for all the domesticated species, including elephants and camels, which were domesticated later, were vegetarians. The worship of these animals was different— they were large and strong, yet gentle and hard-working. While many animals were revered for themselves, many became the companions of the gods.

Animals, in the Indian tradition, are considered to have the same feelings and passions as human beings. They can metamorphose themselves at will and understand human speech, thus becoming divine. By recognizing their divinity, Indian religions gave them a unique position which helped to protect many animal species. Some animals were regarded as the abode (either temporary or permanent) of the souls of the dead.

The deification of a particular animal did not depend on its numbers, but on the qualities and uses that made it unique. The deification led to the protection of the animal, a safeguard that was lost in the British period when many animals were described as vermin and people forced to kill them, thus exterminating the cheetah and bringing others like the lion, tiger and leopard to near-extinction.

## Role of Animals in Indian Tradition

Animals were revered for several reasons. The elephant, a keystone species, was recognized as the remover of obstacles, his role in the Indian jungle. The langur was a fellow primate. The tiger was the most feared. The fish was an ecological indicator. The boar was an indicator of rain and ploughed the soil, helping the farmer. The cow was essential for milk. The bull was a draught animal. The blackbuck was essential for the survival of the khejri plant which was the mainstay of the desert. And many others, all of whom had an important ecological or social role.

The elephant-headed Ganesha, the simian Hanuman, the animal incarnations of Vishnu, Vaghdeo the tiger, and the blackbuck were divine. The qualities of the animals were assumed by the associated deities, and an elaborate mythology was built around each.

Some became vahanas or vehicles of the gods, and could be equals, inferiors or companions. The bull and the eagle were originally equal companions of Shiva and Vishnu respectively, but were relegated to minor roles later.

Many were totemic figures who acquired lower positions as they were absorbed into the Hindu pantheon. The totemic tradition was widespread in ancient India: many Sanskrit gotra (lineage) names and names of sages are of animal origin, such as Bharadwaja (owl), Garga (crocodile), Rishyashringa (born of a doe), Jambuka (jackal) and Gautama (rabbit), or of plant origin, like Kaushika (kusha grass), or even water, such as Agastya. Many clan names have animal origins, such as Maurya, More (peacock) and Ghorpade (monitor lizard). The different faiths and belief systems were syncretized into Hinduism.

Some animals were friends and companions. The dog was a wanderer and hanger-on who attached himself to people, characteristics that were replicated in the companion of Bhairava. Some were local chieftains, like Sugriva the monkey king, who built the bridge to Lanka and provided the army for Rama. Jatayu the vulture gave up his life trying to save Sita.

The sanctity of an animal may be derived from its economic value. Cattle are respected by pastoral societies that rely on the animal for their sustenance. The pastoral Vedic Aryans considered cattle as a major source of wealth, and therefore sacred.

Some animals were a part of social history and ended up as demons. Mahisha the buffalo was the ruler of ancient Mysore (Mahisha-ur), who was defeated in battle by Durga. The buffalo was worshipped by the indigenous pastoral tribes of India. The war between the buffalo demon and the goddess replicates the conflict between buffalo-revering tribes and food producers who worshipped the Mother Goddess. When the latter won the war, the former became a demon. But Mahisha lives on as the buffalo god of the Todas, Maria Gonds and as the deity Mhasoba in Maharashtra.

Finally, animals like the lion, the mount of Durga, who was earlier the mount of the Babylonian Ishtar and the Greek Artemis, probably entered India with migrations or travellers.

The interrelationships of terms like 'wild' and 'tame' are complex, since the two live in a continuum (Ritvo 2008). Thus the elephant, a wild animal, is tamed and, in a form of cruel irony, Ganesha's attributes are the goad and noose that are used to control and train the elephant. The buffalo, a tame herbivore, becomes the demon Mahisha when confronted by the Mother Goddess.

There are three paths (marga) to liberation: the highest is gnana or knowledge of the illusory nature of life (maya); the next is karma or action; the third is bhakti or total devotion, even surrender, to one's personal god. A human being has a superior birth for the sole reason that he can consciously choose a path. But there are animals that rise above the limitations of their body and live a life complying with one of the three marga. They need no longer be subject to the cycle of life and death and can attain liberation by passing a human birth.

## Avataras or Incarnations of Vishnu

'Avatara' means 'one who descends'. It is believed that whenever Dharma or the Law of Righteousness is in danger, Vishnu incarnates himself to save the world from evil. Vishnu's incarnations perform all the three roles of creator, preserver and destroyer, for he destroys evil and re-establishes dharma. In the Bhagavat Gita (4.7–8), Vishnu promises to incarnate himself:

*yadā yadā hi dharmasya glānirbhavati bhārata*
*abhyutthanamadharmasya tadātmānaṃ srijāmyaham.*
*paritrāṇāya sādhūnām vināśāya ca duṣhkritām*
*dharmasaṃsthapanarthāya sambhavāmi yuge yuge.*

(O descendent of Bharata, whenever there is a decline in religious practices, and a predominance of irreligion, I descend myself. For the deliverance of the pious, for the annihilation of the miscreants, to re-establish the principles of religion, I appear, millennium after millennium).

This stanza is one of the main tenets of the Hindu religion, and promises divine intervention and the tying together of all creation on an equal footing. The most important aspect of Hindu theology is the association accorded to different species with reincarnation. More importantly, it is believed that the Supreme Being actually gets himself incarnated in the form of various species. *Shrimad Bhagavatam* (1.3.5) says: 'This form is the source and indestructible seed of multifarious incarnations within the universe, and from the particle and portion of this form, different living entities like demigods, animals, human beings and others are created.'

The number of incarnations is generally regarded to be ten, although in some books like the *Bhagavata Purana* the number may go up to twenty-two. However, the popular belief is that there are ten incarnations, of which nine have come and gone. What is important about the ten incarnations is that there is a natural evolutionary process, for Vishnu incarnates as several species, taking progressively developing forms. The first four forms are, in order, the fish or Matsya, who lives in water; Kurma the amphibious tortoise, who lives in the sea and on land; Varaha the boar, the four-legged mammal; and Narasimha the half-man half-lion.

The rest are Vamana the dwarf; Parashurama the wild man with the axe, not unlike 'Stone Age' man; Rama, the perfect man and role model; Krishna the politician-philosopher, a highly evolved being; Buddha the man of peace; and the tenth incarnation Kalki, the future destroyer of this world. Many incarnations are probably local deities who were absorbed as incarnations of Vishnu as they were absorbed into Hinduism and were fitted into a natural evolutionary ladder, preceding Charles Darwin. However, only the first four incarnations, who appeared in the Satya Yuga, the first age of the world concern this book. By incarnating himself, Vishnu reiterates that all creation—animal and people—are equal.[1]

## Samudra Manthana

The story of the samudra manthana or the churning of the ocean first appears in the epic *Ramayana*: many of the sacred animals are among the sacred nine gems (navaratna) that were churned out of the ocean.

---

[1] Jayadeva, a great poet of medieval India, composed the *Gita Govinda* about the ten incarnations. The relevant stanza has been translated and quoted in the sections on the Fish, Tortoise, Boar and Man-Lion.

According to the *Mahabharata*, the asuras or demons had become very powerful because of their knowledge of the sanjivani vidya, the ability to rejuvenate the dead or dying, taught to them by their guru Shukracharya. Scared, the devas or gods asked Brahma for advice, and the latter advised friendship with the asuras. So the devas invited the asuras to jointly churn the ocean for amrita, the nectar of immortality. The cosmic tortoise Kurma—also an incarnation of Vishnu—offered his back to support the churning staff, Mount Mandara, and the snake Vasuki offered to be the churning rope.

Among the nine gems that came out of the ocean were the divine elephant Airavata, the divine cow Kamadhenu and the divine horse Uchchaishravas, along with the goddess Lakshmi, Prosperity herself. This story may be an allegory for ancient trade, for the mythical Airavata was believed to have been born of the river Iravathi (Irrawaddy) in Burma, home to the sacred white' elephant. The horse was imported from the Arabian peninsula. Only the cow was indigenous. Many other items that were churned from the ocean are among the many items once traded in ancient India.

### Kashyapa

Kashyapa was a divine progenitor or Prajapati. According to the *Ramayana*, he was the seventh and youngest son of Brahma, while the *Mahabharata* says he was the only son of Marichi, one of the six mind-born sons (manasa putra) of Brahma.

Kashyapa plays a major role in creation. He married the thirteen daughters of Daksha, who gave birth to the gods, demons and all creatures. Aditi was the mother of the Adityas (gods or devas); Diti was the mother of the Daityas (demons or asuras);

*Mohenjo Daro seal*

Danu was the mother of the Danavas; Krodhavasa the mother of Kamadhenu and all the cows, as well as of the elephants; Vinata was the mother of Aruna and Garuda the eagle; Kadru of the Nagas or snakes; and Sarama, the Vedic dog of Indra, the mother of all canines. His other daughter were Danayu, Sinhika, Pradha, Vishwa, Kapila and Muni. By making Kashyapa a divine progenitor, the gods, people and animals became siblings. There is an echo of the Harappan horned deity, surrounded by animals, and the Vedic Pashupati, or lord of the animals, in the literary descriptions of Kashyapa.

*Animal Myths*

In all the above roles, animals interact with the human world in myths. This is not unique to India: all ancient civilizations had myths which brought together gods, people, animals and nature. Animal myths may include explanations for

- a physical feature, such as why the squirrel got its stripes,
- the origin of an animal, particularly one with a special status like the cow,
- an animal's behaviour, such as the eagle devouring the snake,
- the ecological role of an animal, such as the elephant who controls field mice,
- a historical event, such as the defeat of the pastoral buffalo-worshippers by the worshippers of the Mother Goddess,
- social functioning, such as the multitasking of the bull,
- social cohesion created by the totem or symbol that binds a tribe,
- a moral order, such as the strength and gentleness of the elephant or the generosity of the cow who gives milk,
- the passage of the soul aided by animals like the owl and the vulture in Zoroastrianism,

- the punishment of evil, like Hanuman does in the *Ramayana*, and
- the control of natural forces, such as the dog who guards the Vedas and the path to heaven.

## Vehicle/Vahana

The word vahana means vehicle, derived from the Sanskrit vah, which means to carry or transport. Animals, in Indian tradition, are generally the vahanas or vehicles of the gods, just as they provided draught power for humans. Often, the vehicle is the only way of identifying the deity. There is usually a story connected with why a deity is associated with a particular vehicle.

In totemism, the suppression of one tribe by another is represented by the deity of the defeated tribe in a position lower than the victor's god, and a myth to explain the incident. A confederation of two tribes or communities was generally represented by combining the deities of both, such as Shiva on Nandi or Vishnu on Garuda. The nature of the animal is also taken into consideration. The dog, for example, is never used as a vehicle: a companion animal, he is the companion first of Indra and later of Shiva.

The vehicle is both an emblem and a symbol. If the bull is the emblem identifying Shiva, it is also a symbol of strength and virility, just as Vishnu's eagle emblem symbolizes the sun and Durga's lion emblem symbolizes fertility. It may represent the forces of evil that are destroyed by the deity, as in the case of Ganesha, who sits on the mouse, described as a demon, in order to control the much-disliked rodent. Some animal vahanas have specific names, some do not. Often a god is associated with different animal-vehicles at different periods and in different books or situations. For example, Indra's original companion was originally the dog Sarama; he later used the white elephant Airavata as his vehicle; sometimes he rides the horse Uchchaishravas. The gods and their vehicles are

- Agni (Fire)—Ram
- Ayyappa—Tiger
- Bhairava (Shiva)—Dog
- Brahma (Creator)—Swan
- Brihaspati (Creator)—Elephant
- Buddha—Horse
- Chamunda (Devi)—Owl
- Chandi (Devi)—Lizard
- Chandra (Moon)—Ten horses, antelope
- Durga—Lion, tiger
- Ganesha—Mouse, rat
- Ganga (River)—Crocodile, fish
- Indra—Elephant (Airavata), dog (Sarama), horse (Uchchaishravas)
- Jagaddhatri—Tiger
- Kama (Love)—Parrot, crocodile
- Kamakhya (Devi)—Rooster
- Kartikeya/Murugan—Peacock (Paravani), rooster
- Ketu—Eagle
- Kubera (Wealth)—Mongoose
- Lakshmi (Prosperity)—Elephant, owl, peacock
- Manasa—Elephant, snake
- Pushan—Goat
- Rahu—Lion
- Rati—Pigeon
- Sarasvati—Swan, peacock
- Shani (Saturn)—Crow, vulture
- Shashti—Cat
- Shitala —Donkey
- Shukra (Venus)—Crocodile
- Shiva (Destroyer)—Bull
- Soma—Antelope
- Surya (Sun)—Chariot pulled by seven horses

- Ushas (Dawn)—Chariot pulled by seven cows
- Varuna (Ocean)—Crocodile, tortoise, fish
- Vayu (Wind)—Antelope
- Vishnu (Protector)—Eagle (Garuda), snake (Adishesha/Ananta)
- Vishvakarma— Elephant
- Yama (Death)—Buffalo
- Yamuna (River)—Tortoise

*Panchatantra*

The *Panchatantra* is a collection of stories written by Pandit Vishnu Sharma in the fourth century CE. However, it is based on much older oral traditions and are perhaps the oldest children's stories ever written. Among the antiquities found in Lothal (about 3000 BCE), is a large vessel on which are depicted birds with fish in their beaks, resting on a tree, while a fox-like animal stands below, reminiscent of the *Panchatantra* story of the crow and the cunning fox. The story of the thirsty crow and the deer—in which the deer could not drink from the narrow mouth of the jar, while the crow succeeded by dropping stones and raising the water level—is depicted on a miniature jar. These well-known *Panchatantra* tales are obviously much older than their compiler-author.

The *Panchatantra* is a niti shastra, a textbook of wise conduct, written in prose. It begins by telling us that King Amarashakti of Mahilaropya in south India had four mischievous sons who were badly in need of discipline. The king employed Pandit Vishnu Sharman to teach them politics, administration and morals, which he did through a series of stories or fables. The *Panchatantra* is a textbook of artha or worldly wisdom, one of the three objects of human desire. The morals of the stories glorify shrewdness and practical wisdom in the affairs of life, politics and government. The five principles illustrated in the five books are the loss of friends; the gaining of friends; causing dissension between friends;

separation; and union. The stories are fables, based on animals, always ending with a moral. The animals portray constant characters, which replicate human nature:

- The lion is the king, always big and strong, but stupid.
- The jackal (or fox) is the clever, cunning hero.
- Small animals like birds, frogs, insects are clever and work in teams.
- Large animals like the elephant and crocodile have brute force but are stupid.

There is a glorification of small versus large, of David versus Goliath, perhaps born of the clever pandit's job of having to teach four dimwits who would become king on the basis of their birth. Thus the small man is clever, while those given size and status by birth are stupid.

While the *Panchatantra* may be dismissed as children's stories, they have also influenced popular opinion about animal characteristics, and are therefore very relevant. Thus the lion is, even today, regarded as a large brute, only interested in food, and without much intelligence; the monkey as clever and witty; jackals as sly, cunning and greedy and birds as good examples of team work. These impressions also impact the extent to which an animal may be regarded as sacred.

*Animals on Flags and Pillars*

In the *Mahabharata* war, each ruler is distinguished by the emblem, generally of an animal, on his flag. This practice continued into medieval and even modern India, where every party is represented by a symbol, some of them of animals (such as the Bahujan Samaj Party whose symbol is the elephant). Likewise, pillars topped by animals, initially constructed out of wood and later of stone, were engraved with edicts. King Devanama Piyadasi, identified with the Mauryan king Ashoka, ordered that his edicts be engraved 'wherever stone pillars were found' (Inscription no. 7), indicating that the pillars topped by lions, bulls or elephants were built before his time. The many free-standing pillars supporting animals found all over the country suggest that they represented various cults of animal worship, and Ashoka's edicts were inscribed on them.

## Rainbow Warriors

In the course of Indian history, certain individuals contributed —deliberately or otherwise—to the elevation of the status of animals. The best-known are Rama, Krishna, Mahavira, the Buddha, Ashoka and Jamboji.

### Rama (about 1000 BCE)

Rama is the hero of the *Ramayana*, one of the two major epics of Sanskrit literature. Rama's wife was abducted by Ravana, the rakshasa king of Lanka, and Rama travelled to Lanka to find her. In the course of his travels he came across several indigenous tribes. Those who were antagonistic were designated as demons and destroyed, while those who were cooperative were assimilated. Among the latter are many 'animals' and 'animal' tribes. Rama's association with several animals did much to elevate them in the public eye.

The Vanaras were the people of the forest, or vana nara, later identified as monkeys. Their hero Hanuman is also one of the heroes of the epic. They were his allies, building the bridge (setu) between the Indian peninsula and Lanka to enable Rama and the Vanara army to cross the sea. They fought against the rakshasas (demons), many laying down their lives. For this deed, they are still protected all over India.

Jambavan, the wise bear, was the chief advisor to Rama during the war. He is also called a Vanara or forest dweller by Valmiki. In the *Mahabharata*, Jambavan's daughter Jambavati marries Krishna. The bear was thus given a special status for his wisdom.

Jatayu the vulture fought the demon-king Ravana in a bid to save Sita as she was being carried away. His soul was liberated by Rama, and all vultures are held to be sacred.

The tiny squirrel contributed to the construction of the bridge to Lanka by carrying the smaller stones, rolling in the sand which he shook off his body and on to the bridge, thus providing the binding material. Rama placed his hand on the squirrel to bless him, and the three stripes on the animal's back are attributed to this action of Rama. Thus squirrels are not harmed even when they eat fruit from the orchards.

Rama was later identified as an avatara or incarnation of Vishnu and became one of the most popular deities of medieval Hinduism. As the cult of Rama developed, the animals he associated with developed their own sanctity, with Hanuman attaining a divine status. Killing them is considered a heinous sin even today.

### Ahimsa or Non-violence

The concept of ahimsa—non-violence in thought and deed—is India's unique contribution to world culture. The Vedas and Upanishads were the first to speak of ahimsa. Although the Aryans were not vegetarians, the concept of non-killing appears in the earliest literature. The Rig Veda (10.87.16), condemns all forms of killing, even for food, preferring vegans to drinkers of milk:

> The yatudhana who fills himself with the flesh of man,
> He who fills himself with the flesh of horses or of other animals,
> And he who steals the milk of the cow:
> Lord, cut off their heads with your flame.'

This was an important admission from a pastoral people who used vast quantities of ghee (clarified butter) for their rituals. The gods were called 'bulls of the Aryas', indicating their twin characteristics of manliness and gentleness.

The *Yajur Veda* (13.47) says that service to animals leads to heaven: 'No person should kill animals helpful to all and persons serving them should obtain heaven.' According to the *Atharva Veda* (12.1.15), the earth was created for the enjoyment of not only human beings but also for bipeds and quadrupeds, birds, animals and all other creatures. The emergence of all life forms from the Supreme Being is expressed in the *Mundakopanishad* (2.1.7):

> From Him, too, gods are produced manyfold,
> The celestials, men, cattle, birds.

These ideas led to the concept of ahimsa or non-violence. Much later, the *Manusmriti* (5.45) says, 'He who injures innocent beings with a desire to give himself pleasure never finds happiness, neither in life nor in death.' The *Shrimad Bhagavatam* (1.7.38) says that a cruel person who kills others for his existence deserves to be killed, and cannot be happy, either in life or in death. The consequences, according to the *Yajnavalkya Smriti* ('Acharyadhyaya', 5.180), are that 'the wicked person who kills animals which are protected has to live in hellfire for the days equal to the number of hairs on the body of that animal.'

In the later Puranas, killing animals and eating meat were considered to be such heinous sins that neither prayers nor pilgrimages or bathing in holy rivers would absolve of it.

Although Sanatana Dharma[2] did not require its adherents to be vegetarians, vegetarianism was recognized as a higher form of living, a belief that continues in contemporary Hinduism where vegetarianism is considered essential for spiritualism.

Around the sixth century BCE, two great religious preachers were born, who took the Upanishadic philosophy of good conduct and non-killing to the people in the common language: Mahavira the Jina (victor), and Gautama the Buddha (wise).

---

[2] The name traditionally used for Hinduism.

Both emphasized that ahimsa or non-violence was essential for a good life.

### Mahavira (599–527 BCE) and Jainism

Mahavira ('Great Hero') was born as Prince Vardhamana, son of Siddhartha, Raja of Kundalpura, and Queen Trishala or Priyakarni, in 599 BCE. He abandoned home in 569 BCE to become a monk. He attained enlightenment in 557 BCE and attained nirvana in 527 BCE. Queen Trishala had fourteen auspicious signs before she gave birth to Vardhamana, foretelling the advent of a great soul. These symbols included the elephant, bull, lion, and a pair of fish, which denote great spirituality in Jainism.

*Goose emblem of Jaina Tirthankara Sumatinatha*

Mahavira was not the founder of Jainism: he was the twenty-fourth and last Tirthankara[3] who revised the Jaina doctrines and established the central tenets of Jainism. *Ahimsa paramo dharmah*: 'Ahimsa (non-violence) is the highest religion' is a tenet basic to Jainism. Violence is the root cause of all crises. Ethical discipline is important and sacred. To liberate oneself, Mahavira taught the importance of right faith, right knowledge and right conduct, which includes non-violence (ahimsa)—not to cause harm to any living being.

Jainism is basically an ethico-metaphysical system. In comparison to Hinduism and Buddhism, ahimsa is the prime

[3] Tirtha means ford, a means of crossing over, and denotes a spiritual guide or philosophy which enables one to cross over the ocean of recurring births in this world. Kara means the one who makes, and the word Tirthankara means 'one who crosses the sacred ford', or a Jain saint.

vrata (vow/discipline) to be understood and practised by both the common man and the ascetic and is equivalent to the realization of the Supreme Being. All other virtues are secondary and subservient to ahimsa. According to Jainism, himsa is not the mere causing of violence; it is the 'severance of any of the vitality in a mobile or immobile being'. Ahimsa, as viewed by Jainism, is very comprehensive and takes into consideration the welfare of all beings on earth. Keeping anything in confinement, without consideration for its freedom to exist or live, is bandhana (captivity). Rearing animals without adequate shelter, air, light, space and food is atichara (bad conduct). Keeping animals, including dairy animals, tied with ropes or chains throughout the day is violence. The simple prayer of the Jainas is 'Let the law of the Jaina give all happiness to all the living beings of the world. All beings desire to live. They like pleasure, hate pain, shun destruction, like to live long. To all, life is dear' (Ramanujam 2006).

Of all religions, Jainism gives the greatest respect to life. Jeev daya—compassion for all living beings or the gift of life —is its prime philosophy and this has extended to the creation of animal hospitals and pinjrapoles (retirement homes for old cattle), most of which are run by Jains. So strict is the need to respect life that Jaina monks and nuns cover their mouths to prevent insects and even bacteria from entering, and sweep the ground as they walk on it to avoid stepping, even accidentally, on an ant or other insect.

While Jainism remained a minority cult, it had a profound influence on Hinduism. The meat-eating Aryans came to shun hunting and killing. Brahmins became vegetarians and non-killing of animals became the highest philosophy. This had a profound impact not only in ancient India but even on several Muslim rulers of medieval India. Much later, in the twentieth century, Mahatma Gandhi adopted the philosophy of ahimsa or non-violence to obtain freedom for India from British rule.

As the images of all the Tirthankaras are identical, their pedestals contain the animal emblem of each, which is the sole means of identification. They include

- Rishabhanatha (Adinatha)—Bull
- Ajitanatha—Elephant
- Sambhavananatha—Horse
- Abhinandanatha—Monkey
- Sumatinatha—Curlew or red goose
- Padmaprabha—Lotus
- Suparshvanatha  Swastika
- Chandraprabha—Moon or crescent
- Suvidhinatha (Pushpadanta)—Crocodile
- Shitalanatha—Pipal tree
- Shreyamsunatha—Rhinoceros
- Vasupujya—Buffalo (female)
- Vimalanatha—Boar
- Anantanatha—Hawk or bear or porcupine
- Dharmanatha (Vajranatha)—Thunderbolt
- Shantinatha—Deer or tortoise
- Kunthunatha—Goat
- Aranatha—Fish
- Mallinatha—Water jar
- Munisuvrata—Tortoise
- Naminatha—Blue lotus or Ashoka tree
- Neminatha—Conch
- Parshvanatha—Snake
- Mahavira—Lion

## Gautama Buddha (563–483 BCE)

Siddhartha Gautama was the founder of Buddhism. He was also known as Sakyamuni ('sage of the Sakyas') who belonged to the Sakya tribe. At the age of twenty-nine, Siddhartha left his palace for the first time. Despite his father's effort to remove the sick, aged, suffering and dead from his view, Siddhartha saw them and was deeply disturbed. He left his palace to become a mendicant. Then, sitting under a pipal tree, now known as the Bodhi tree, in Bodh Gaya, he attained enlightenment at the age of thirty-five. He realized that the nature and cause of human suffering was ignorance, and went forth to preach methods of eliminating it. From then on, he was known as the Buddha or 'Awakened One'. The Tripitaka, a collection of discourses attributed to Gautama, was committed to writing about 400 years after his death.

Among the teachings of the Buddha, the foremost was ahimsa (not causing harm to anyone). Non-violence is not merely refraining from inflicting injuries on others with one's limbs or weapons. Non-violence has to be practised with purity of mind, tongue, and body. There should be no ill feelings, which are a form of violence. To cause harm to others through the body is also violence (himsa). No one should be harmed even by speech. Speech should be sweet, pleasing and wholesome. All actions should be helpful to others.

One day Gautama Buddha saw sheep being driven to be sacrificed. He gently lifted a little lamb on his shoulder and followed the sheep to the special enclosure where the king was to perform the sacrifice. When he heard that the ceremonial sacrifice of the lamb would bring great good to the ruler and the state, Buddha said that since a man, especially one who was a prince and a monk, was much more valuable than a lamb, the king should kill him (the Buddha) and win greater merit. He added that the sacrifice symbolized one's inner weaknesses and vices and the benefits were false desire and attachment. It was enough to pray at sunrise and sunset that all beings should attain happiness. To take another life in order to live longer and with greater fulfilment of one's desires was a reprehensible act, said the Buddha. You must not sacrifice a sheep, but your own lust and greed, hate and malice. If you sacrifice your selfish desires, you earn peace, realization and nirvana.

The eightfold path taught by the Buddha emphasized the importance of abstaining from activities that bring harm to other living beings and non-killing. The Boddhisattva is one who is full of maitri (friendship) towards all animals, for he aspires to achieve buddha-hood. Said the Buddha, 'As a mother would be very good towards her only child, her well-beloved son, so too you should be very good towards all creatures everywhere and to everyone' (Dwivedi, 1989). The Buddha himself sought refuge from his bickering disciples by living among the animals who served him devotedly. The Jataka tales hold up the noble qualities of various animals as examples to emulate.

Many of the earlier births of the Buddha were believed to have been as animals, while his final birth as Gautama Buddha was prophesied in his mother Maya Devi's dream of an elephant entering her womb. The snake is a folk deity associated with the Buddha, who is often depicted being protected by a snake, while the earliest Buddhist sculptures, which do not portray the Buddha except through his symbols, show the snake people—men and women hooded by snakes—worshipping the bodhi tree and the feet of the Master. The deer is another favourite animal in Buddhist sculpture, representing the Buddha's first sermon at the deer park at Lumbini.

Three animals represent the three stages in the life of the Buddha: the elephant represents his birth, when his mother dreamed of an elephant entering her womb; the horse represents his renunciation of his kingdom and embrace of monasticism; and the deer represents his first sermon, which took place in the deer park at Sarnath.

Unfortunately, one Jataka tale of the Buddha's death from eating poisoned pork became reason for the licence given to Buddhists to eat meat. The Jatakas came into existence a thousand years after the Buddha and there is no confirmation for this Jataka story, which may as well be a later interpolation to justify meat-eating by the Buddhist clergy who had sought to fashion the Buddha in the light of their own and their patrons' requirements, much as the Roman Catholic Church reinvented Jesus Christ to suit the requirements of imperial Rome. The Buddha himself was a great champion of ahimsa and sought to remove meat-eating and animal sacrifice from Sanatana Dharma. In fact, it was the influence of the Buddha and Mahavira which converted the meat-eating Brahmins to vegetarianism.

Later, Buddhism developed an elaborate mythology and theology. The Dhyani (meditating) Buddhas and some Boddhisattvas each have an animal vehicle, similar to the Hindu gods. The Dhyani Buddhas and their vehicles are

- Amitabha—Peacock
- Akshobhya—Elephant
- Raktayamari—Buffalo
- Vairochana—Lion or Dragon
- Marichi Ashokakanta—Pig
- Arya Marichi—Pig
- Marichi Pichuva—Chariot of Seven Pigs
- Dashabhujasita Marichi—Chariot of Seven Pigs
- Amoghasiddhi—Eagle
- Ratnasambhava—Lion

The aspects of Boddhisattva Manjushri with animal vehicles include

- Manjughosha—Lion
- Vagishvara—Lion
- Manjuvara—Lion
- Vadirata—Tiger

The aspects of Boddhisattva Avalokiteshvara with animal vehicles include

- Simhanada—Lion
- Harihariharivahana—Lion and eagle
- Vajradharma—Peacock

*Ashoka (304–232 BCE)*

If anybody can be credited with the mass propagation of ahimsa in India, it was the Mauryan king Ashoka. His grandfather Chandragupta is believed to have renounced his throne to become a Jaina monk, so the interest in a theology of non-violence was already a family tradition.

Filled with war and bloodshed, Ashoka's early years were occupied in expanding and consolidating the Mauryan Empire, which included Uzbekistan and stretched up to the gates of Persia. Ashoka was appalled at the loss of human and animal life, especially of elephants and horses, after the battle for Kalinga (modern Orissa), and swore to give up war and violence. His state policies, henceforth, were based on dharma, or the law of righteousness. Ashoka's edicts on rocks and free-standing pillars stand testimony to his adoption of ahimsa as his state policy, to his preaching of non-killing of animals as essential to dharma.

*Ashoka's First Rock Inscription at Girnar*

Ashoka's first major rock edict, from Girnar in Junagarh district, says:

Beloved of the Gods (Devanamapiya) King Piyadasi has caused this dhamma edict to be written. Here no living beings are to be slaughtered or offered in sacrifice. Formerly in the kitchen of the Beloved of the Gods King Piyadasi hundreds of thousands of animals were killed every day to make curry. But now with the writing of this dhamma edict only three creatures, two peacocks and a deer are killed, and the deer not always (not regularly). These three living beings too shall not be killed in future (Sircar 1986).

The edicts of Ashoka, found in northern India, were written on pillars topped by capitals of four majestic lions or bulls seated back-to-back, carrying a large wheel, the wheel of dharma. The selection of the heraldic animals is significant. The lion was a symbol of royalty and power, while the bull was a continuum of the Vedic period, when the gods themselves were called bulls. The base of his pillar capitals also had a ring of lively animals —bulls, elephants, deer, horses and geese— at the base, in an obvious state of happiness resulting from a policy of ahimsa.

*Ashoka's First Rock Inscription at Girnar— Rock Edict 1*

Beloved-of-the-Gods, King Piyadasi, has caused this Dhamma edict to be written. Here (in my domain) no living beings are to be slaughtered or offered in sacrifice. Nor should festivals be held, for Beloved-of-the-Gods, King Piyadasi, sees much to object to in such festivals, although there are some festivals that Beloved-of-the-Gods, King Piyadasi, does approve of.

Formerly, in the kitchen of Beloved-of-the-Gods, King Piyadasi, hundreds of thousands of animals were killed every day to make curry. But now with the writing of this Dhamma edict only three creatures, two peacocks and a deer are killed, and the deer not always. And in time, not even these three creatures will be killed.

D.C. Sircar, Select Inscriptions, *Vol. I*, pp. 15–16

Ashoka spoke out against sacrifice and the killing of animals and spread the philosophy of ahimsa throughout India and Asia. While the Buddha was concerned with returning Sanatana Dharma (Hinduism) to the noble Upanishadic path, devoid of ritual, caste and animal sacrifices, it was Ashoka who turned the Buddha's message into a new religion.

## Shaivism

Bhakti means devotion. The bhakti movement or belief in a personal deity started in Tamil Nadu in the early centuries of the present era, when the Shaivite saints or Nayanmaar spoke out against social evils like the caste system and religious practices like animal sacrifice.

One of the important features of Tamil Shaivism was its total rejection of meat eating and its assertion that the liberation of the soul was to be attained by the individual without sacrificing animals. Respect for animal life became symbolic of an evolved person. The impact of Shaivism on animal life was so great that even today the Tamil word saivam means vegetarian. Southern Shaivism entailed strict vegetarianism and a respect for life. A sign of upward mobility was the changeover from animal sacrifice and meat eating to a more vegetarian lifestyle, both in religion and food habits.

## Vaishnavism

Several tribes—the Vrishnis, Ahirs and Yadavas—were followers of Krishna, who lifted the mountain Govardhana to protect the cowherds and their cattle. If in the south Shaivism spoke out against the killing of animals, in the north it was Vaishnavism, especially the Krishna cult that preached a religion of love for all creation and a special role for cows that gave milk and were, therefore, mother substitutes. This was to have far-reaching consequences.

Vishnu incarnated himself several times, four of which were the fish, tortoise, boar and half-man half-animal. Thus divinity was equal in man and animal, and this gave a boost to the conservation of several species and to the attitudes towards animals.

## Medieval Saints of the Bhakti Movement

Several saints preached devotion to a personal god, equality of man, kindness to animals, and vegetarianism. Medieval Indian saints like Ramananda, Mirabai, Kabir, Tulsidas, Surdas, Jnaneshwar, Namdev, Ekanath, Sant Tukaram, Ramdas, Purandaradasa, Kanakadasa, Vadiraja, Basavanna, Akka Mahadevi, Shri Krishna Chaitanya, Sankaradeva, Narasimha Mehta and Narayana Guru, besides many others, were vegetarians who encouraged their followers to give up meat eating and preached kindness to animals. Guru Nanak, founder of the Sikh religion, also preached vegetarianism. Swamis and gurus of contemporary Hinduism also spread the message of kindness to animals and vegetarianism, reinforcing in every age the idea that animals have souls and sentience.

## Jamboji of the Bishnois

The harsh environment of the Thar Desert in Rajasthan has made the local people conscious about the importance of maintaining the area's ecological balance and wildlife conservation. Bishnoi communities have even sacrificed their lives to protect nature and wildlife.

Guru Jambheshwarji Maharaj (popularly known as Jambhoji, Jamboji or Jambhaji) was born in 1485 CE, in Pipasar, a village near Jodhpur in Rajasthan. In 1519 CE, at the age of thirty-four, Jamboji founded the Bishnoi religion, the name deriving from the twenty-nine principles he preached. Out of these, eight were prescribed to preserve biodiversity and encourage good animal husbandry. Jamboji passed away in 1536, leaving behind guiding principles for his community to save the environment and its animals. Jamboji was a great visionary, who had forseen the consequences of man's destruction of nature for economic development. He saw the need for environmental protection and weaved his principles into religious commandments so that people could internalize those ideas easily. Jamboji preached brotherhood, equal rights for women, preservation of wildlife and trees, and kindness towards all animals. These principles form the religion of the Bishnois who follow them devotedly. Jamboji said he would be reborn in every blackbuck and thanks to his teachings, the Bishnois have never allowed anyone to kill any living being or cut any green trees. So successful have their conservation efforts been that the desert is covered with trees like the khejri, jal, rohida, aak, ber and kair, making the Thar the world's greenest desert. Blackbucks and shy chinkaras roam freely and fearlessly in large numbers in the area. Bishnoi women are known to even nurse orphaned blackbucks. Recently, a famous film star who hunted and killed blackbucks was pursued relentlessly by the community in spite of his popularity and star power. Such is the commitment of this community.

## Vegetarianism

About forty per cent Indians are estimated to be vegetarians who do not eat meat at all. This would be the largest concentration of vegetarians in the world.[4] Indian vegetarians are mostly lacto-vegetarians. However, vegetarianism in India is mainly dictated by religious and caste traditions. Some, like traditional Bengali Brahmins eat fish but are otherwise vegetarian, while others, like the Jains, will not even touch root vegetables like onions and potatoes, considering them to have equal sentience.

Great Indian saints and seers like Vyasa, Panini, Patanjali and Adi Shankara were vegetarians and spoke out against the eating of

[4] This figure does not include those who are vegetarians because of poverty.

flesh, as right thinking and spiritual attainment were not possible with meat eating. The Indian religions believe that eating meat and fish leads to negative karmic influences. Religious duties are prescribed towards the animals and negative karma is incurred from violence against them. Between Hinduism, Buddhism and Jainism, respect for life became all-encompassing. Importantly, kindness to animals and vegetarianism became hallmarks of an evolved human being. Thus these were the goals to aspire for, and killers of animals were relegated to the fourth caste or even designated as untouchables.

The influences of all the Indian religions and cults resulted in most members of the first and third castes—Brahmins and Vaishyas—giving up the killing of animals for food or sport. In Vedic religion meat eating was not banned but was restricted by specific rules. Several scriptures bar violence against domestic animals. The *Chandogya Upanishad*, 8.15.1; *Mahabharata* 3.199.11-12; 13.115; 13.116.26; 13.148.17; and the *Bhagavata Purana*, 11.5.13-14 strongly condemn the slaughter of animals and meat eating.

According to the Rig Veda (X.87.16), 'One who partakes of human flesh, the flesh of a horse or another animal and deprives others of milk by slaughtering cows, O King, if such a fiend does not desist by other means, then you should not hesitate to cut off his head.'

The *Yajur Veda* adds 'You must not use your God-given body for killing God's creatures, whether they are human, animal or whatever.'

According to the *Atharva Veda* 'Those noble souls who practise meditation and other yogic ways, who are ever careful about other beings, who protect all animals are the ones who are actually serious about spiritual practices.'

Chapter 5 of the *Manu Samhita* discusses the killing of animals and meat eating, and is probably responsible for the vegetarianism of Brahmins and entire caste groups who adopted the advice of the sage. The *Manu Samhita* (5.48–52) recommends that since

> . . . meat can never be obtained without injury to living creatures, and injury to sentient beings is detrimental to the attainment of heavenly bliss; let him therefore shun the use of meat. Having well considered the disgusting origin of flesh and the cruelty of fettering and slaying corporeal beings, let him entirely abstain from eating flesh.

Further, it is not only the person who eats the meat but the butcher and even the king or administrator who are equally at fault.

> He who permits the slaughter of an animal, he who cuts it up, he who kills it, he who buys or sells meat, he who cooks it, he who serves it up, and he who eats it, must all be considered as slayers of the animal. There is no greater sinner than that man who, though not worshiping the gods or the ancestors, seeks to increase the bulk of his own flesh by the flesh of other beings. (6.60).

Did Rama eat meat? Valmiki's *Ramayana* does not mention that meat was served either in the palace of King Janaka or King Dasharatha, or in the forest where Rama was in exile. In fact, the epic says 'Sri Rama does not take meat or honey. He partakes every day of wild fruits and boiled rice in the evening. (*Ramayana*, V.36.41).

Meat-eating and hunting were activities perceived as essential for good warriors. The *Mahabharata* says Kshatriyas should hunt and eat meat (13.115.59–60; 13.116.15–18), but opposes the same for hermits who must be strictly non-violent. In the *Mahabharata* both meat eaters and vegetarians present various arguments to substantiate their viewpoints. Apart from the debates about domestic animals, there is also a long discourse by a hunter in defence of hunting and meat eating. Both ritual slaughter and hunting were challenged by advocates of universal non-violence, and their acceptability was doubtful and a matter of dispute.

The *Mahabharata* (13.115) contains a lengthy discussion about vegetarianism between the eldest Pandava prince Yudhishthira and his dying grandfather Bhishma.

> What need there be said of those innocent and healthy creatures endued with love of life, when they are sought to be slain by sinful wretches subsisting by slaughter? For this reason, O King, know that the discarding of meat is the highest refuge of religion, of heaven, and of happiness...The man who abstains from meat is never put in fear, O king, by any creature. All creatures seek his protection...If there were nobody who ate flesh there would then be nobody to kill living creatures. The man who kills living creatures kills them for the sake of the person who eats flesh. If flesh were regarded as inedible, there would then be no slaughter of living creatures. It is for the sake of the eater that the slaughter of living creatures goes on in the world. Since the life of persons who slaughter living creatures or cause them to be slaughtered is shortened, the person who wishes his own good should give up meat entirely...The purchaser of flesh performs himsa [violence] by his wealth. He who eats flesh does so by enjoying its taste; the killer does himsa by actually tying and killing the animal. Thus, there are three forms of killing. He who brings flesh or sends for it, he who cuts off the limbs of an animal, and he who purchases, sells, or cooks flesh and eats it—all of these are to be considered meat eaters.

The dire consequences of eating meat are foretold in the *Mahabharata* through the conversation between Bhishma and Yudhishthira. Bhishma, grandfather of the Kauravas and Pandavas, says, 'He who desires to augment his own flesh by eating the flesh of other creatures, lives in misery in whatever species he may take in his [next] birth.' (XII.115.47).

> The highly wise seven celestial Rishis, the Valakhilyas, and those sages who drink the rays of the sun, all speak highly of abstention from meat. The self-created Manu has said that the man who

does not eat meat, or who does not kill living creatures, or who does not cause them to be killed, is a friend of all creatures (XII. 115.9–10).

Bhishma advises Yudhishthira: 'The man who, having eaten meat, gives it up afterwards wins merit by such a deed that is so great that a study of all the Vedas or a performance, O Bharata, of all the sacrifices [Vedic rituals], cannot give its like' (XII. 115.16). 'O sinless one, there is absolute happiness in abstaining from meat, O king. He who practises severe austerities for a century, and he who abstains from meat are both equally meritorious. This is my opinion' (XII. 115.52–53).

In reply, the Kshatriya warrior and Pandava prince Yudhishthira says, 'Alas, those cruel men who, not caring for various other sorts of food, want only flesh, are really like great rakshasas' (XII. 116.1).

Thus the epic is clear that killing animals and selling and eating meat were equally negative karmas that would result in a rebirth as a lowly being.

The *Bhagavata Purana* (7.15.7, 11.5.14) adds: 'Those sinful persons who are ignorant of actual religious principles, yet consider themselves to be completely pious, without compunction commit violence against innocent animals that are fully trusting in them.'

There are strong differences of opinion between Hinayana and Mahayana Buddhism about meat eating. According to the Hinayana canons, the Buddha refused to institute vegetarianism and even ate meat on several occasions. There were, however, rules prohibiting certain types of meat, such as that of human beings, leopards and elephants. Monks were also prohibited from consuming meat if they had witnessed the animal's death or knew it had been killed specifically for them, a prohibition that has led to a lot of hypocrisy in modern Buddhism.

On the other hand, the Buddha strongly denounced the eating of meat according to the Mahayana sutras. The Buddha, according to the Mahayana *Mahaparinirvana Sutra*, said 'the eating of meat extinguishes the seed of great compassion', adding that the consumption of meat and fish (even of dead animals) is prohibited by him. According to this sutra, the Buddha predicted that later monks would 'hold spurious writings to be the authentic dharma' and would claim that the Buddha allowed the eating of meat, whereas he did not. In the *Lankavatara Sutra*, the Buddha speaks strongly in favour of vegetarianism, since the eating of the flesh of sentient beings was incompatible with the compassion a Bodhisattva should cultivate. Several other Mahayana sutras also prohibit the consumption of meat.

When monks from India migrated to China in CE 65, they met followers who provided them with money instead of food, a practice alien to Indian monks. They used the money to cultivate their own vegetable plots and bought their other food needs from the market, a practice that has survived in Chinese Buddhism where the vegetarian monks cultivate as much of their food as possible.

Vegetarianism in Jainism is based on the principle of non-violence (ahimsa) as in Hinduism, but it is stricter than in the Hindu traditions and mandatory for all Jains. Jains are lacto-vegetarians, and some even abstain from eating plant parts that grow underground, such as roots and bulbs, because tiny beings may be killed or injured when the plants are pulled up. The Jaina canons preach vegetarianism, fasting and many acts of self-denial.

The *Thirukural*, a Tamil treatise of between 200 BCE and 200 CE, has many references to vegetarianism, such as 'How can he practise true compassion who eats the flesh of an animal to fatten his own flesh?' The author Thiruvalluvar implies that there was a vibrant vegetarian society in his times.

Sikhs serve only vegetarian food in gurudwaras and the food eaten during religious occasions in the Sikh faith is always vegetarian. Some sects like the Namdharis still practise vegetarianism. The Guru Granth Sahib says: 'The world eats dead carcasses, living by neglect and greed. Like a goblin, or a beast, they kill and eat the forbidden carcasses of meat.' But, while the original followers of Guru Nanak were vegetarians, Guru Gobind Singh, the last guru, encouraged Sikhs to eat meat so that they could become warriors and defend themselves from invaders. Sikhs believe that they must avoid halal meat or meat killed by any method similar to that of halal meat. The animal must be killed in one stroke, called jhatka.

In modern India, jhatka slaughter, prescribed for Hindus, has virtually disappeared since most butchers are Muslims, and only the Sikhs still follow this method of slaughter.

More recently, Mahatma Gandhi was a staunch vegetarian and promoted kindness to animals. 'To my mind, the life of a lamb is no less precious than that of a human being,' he said. 'I should be unwilling to take the life of a lamb for the sake of the human body. The more helpless a creature, the more entitled it is to protection by man from the cruelty of man. The greatness of a nation and its moral progress may be seen by the way its animals are treated (www.thinkexist.com/quotations).'

## Animal Sacrifice

Animal sacrifice was a part of Vedic ritual. The Brahmanas are full of elaborate instructions for sacrifice. The seers of the Upanishads revolted and, as the Rig Veda (X. 87.16) itself condemns all forms of killing, including animal sacrifice and meat eating, there was sanction in the earliest shruti, against animal sacrifice.

The movement to cleanse Hinduism of animal sacrifice was taken up by the two great reformers, Gautama Buddha and Mahavira Jina, just as Jesus Christ's mission began by stopping the sale of caged birds in the Temple of Jerusalem and throwing away their cages. Followers of Jesus called him the Lamb of God, probably meaning that their Messiah had replaced the sacrificial lamb. Similarly, the mission of the Buddha and Mahavira was also to clean up the Sanatana Dharma of their times, particularly the stopping of animal sacrifice. The efforts of the Upanishadic philosophers, the Buddha and Mahavira paid off: Brahmins gave up animal sacrifice and even became vegetarian.

Unfortunately, central authority has never been vested in a single person or group in Hinduism. A believer may adopt any and every god and religious practice. The bhakti movement took this to a higher plane when sacrifice meant giving oneself up to one's personal god. Thus there could be no edict (or 'fatwa') banning animal sacrifice. Even as it was given up by the upper castes, it has continued among the most backward, scheduled castes and tribes all over India. In east and north-east India, animal sacrifice continues unchecked among all classes and castes.

Animal sacrifice among Muslims (Bakr-Id) is permitted by law and is even celebrated with a public holiday. The Prevention of Cruelty to Animals Act states: 'Nothing contained in this Act shall render it an offence to kill any animal in a manner required by the religion of any community.' This was done primarily to permit the Muslim community to sacrifice animals.

Various states of India have laws that prohibit animal sacrifice including the Andhra Pradesh Animal and Birds Sacrifices (Prohibition) Act of 1950; the Gujarat Animal and Birds Sacrifices Act of 1972; the Karnataka Prevention of Sacrifices Act, 1953; the Kerala Animals and Birds Sacrifices Prohibition Act, 1968; the Pondicherry Animals and Birds Sacrifices Prohibition Act, 1968; the Rajasthan Animal and Birds Sacrifice Prohibition Act, 1975, and the Tamil Nadu Animal and Birds Sacrifices Prohibition Act, 1958 (repealed in 2004). Like all laws in India, these are rarely implemented, especially in remote rural areas, while success depends on enforcement.

The Bodhgaya Temple Act, 1949, a result of the association of Buddha with Bihar, prohibits people from performing animal sacrifice within the temple precincts. In many Indian states, such as West Bengal and Assam, there are no laws prohibiting animal sacrifice. But, when King Gyanendra of Nepal sacrificed animals at the famous Kali temple of Kolkata and Kamakhya temple of Assam, there was a public outcry, although animal sacrifice goes on regularly in these temples.

Dravidian parties in the south claim that sacrifice is central to their religious practices. Maybe it was. It has been so in every ancient religion all over the world. It is essential that religious practices grow out of the limitations of primitive beliefs and evolve to a higher level that does not cause harm in the name of God or religion. After all, human sacrifice was once the norm all over the world. It was banned as a cruel and primitive practice. Animal sacrifice is no less so.

### Animals of Ancient India

The Indus Valley culture extended from western Pakistan to eastern Uttar Pradesh in northern India, and southwards till Maharashtra, from between 7000 BCE and 1500 BCE. The writing on the seals is still not deciphered, leaving a mystery, but the images on the seals and the clay toys have thrown up a variety of animals from which we know what animals lived in that region. Several animals including two varieties of the Indian humped cattle were domesticated by the Indus Valley people. But many animals once known to the people of north and north-western India (including modern Pakistan) are now almost extinct: the tiger, rhinoceros, wolf, bison and river crocodile appear on the seals, although they are no longer found in the region.

### Changing Values in Medieval North India

Until the seventh century CE, when the Chinese traveller Hieun Tsang traversed the country, there were vast forests and wildlife that made travel both dangerous and difficult. When did it change?

Ancient Indian kings were occasional hunters. The Muslim rulers of medieval India changed the rules: hunting became mass killing, and the halal method of killing for meat, by which the animal was bled to death slowly and painfully, replaced the Indian system of jhatka killing (in one stroke). The Muslim invaders were nomads on horseback, in search of fresh pastures for their goats and sheep, which provided them mutton, their staple diet. Indian values of kindness to animals left them cold, except for Akbar who banned cow slaughter during the sacred chaturmas.

Babur, founder of the Mughal Empire in India, wrote of great masses of rhinos between the Indus River and the city of Bhira, thereby confirming the rhino images found on the Indus seals 4,500 years earlier. The Mughal Emperor Jahangir killed 17,000 animals in his lifetime, including 889 nilgai, eighty-six tigers and lions and 1,670 gazelles and antelope, besides many others. In 1634 CE, Jahangir's son Shah Jahan killed forty antelopes in four days at Palam, near Delhi. The Mughal kings wiped out the rhinos and the tigers once encountered on the Yamuna, close to the cities of Delhi and Agra. Apart from hunting animals, they had vast zoos: Akbar kept over 1,000 cheetahs at one time, while Jahangir owned over 12,000 elephants (Rangarajan 2001).

The Mughals, however, also studied the animals. Babur recorded the birds and animals he encountered in Hind. Jahangir was an enthusiastic naturalist who had the wildlife of his kingdom faithfully reproduced in miniature paintings.

The invaders introduced a form of Persian hunting, regarded as entertainment, into India. Cheetahs, hooded, blindfolded and kept on leashes would be taken to forested areas in bullock carts or on horseback. Trained dogs were then sent to flush out the prey. When the blackbuck or deer was near, the hood and blindfold would be removed and the cheetahs released to kill the tired animal.

## Colonial History of Wildlife

In the eighteenth century, the British offered special rewards for every tiger killed, so that forests could be razed to the ground and agricultural land extended, thereby increasing tax revenue. A new image of the tiger was created—its natural shyness was construed as its cunning and savage nature. It was described as having a predilection for human flesh, making it a man-eater and a savage enemy who ought to be killed. Bison and cheetah were regarded as vermin. The British appetite for hunting increased with the facilitation of hunts and trophy rooms in clubs and army messes.

After the Mutiny of 1857, the deliberate disarming of the people led to fearful consequences, for they could no longer defend themselves. The large-scale slaughter of deer and buffaloes by the farmers and the English reduced the food sources for carnivores. In the 1870s, the British were killing 20,000 animals a year. The cheetah was deliberately targeted for extermination— the district collectors paid a bounty of twenty-five rupees for each animal killed. The maharajas were also encouraged to give rewards and some, like the Maharaja of Kota in Rajasthan, also offered twenty-five rupees for the head of each cheetah, more than twice the amount given for a tiger. Similarly, in the North-West Frontier Provinces (now in Pakistan), a wolf was worth more than a panther. Over 80,000 tigers, 150,000 leopards and 200,000 wolves were slaughtered between 1875 and 1925. The last tiger was killed in Bombay in 1929 (Rangarajan 2001).

In England, forests and the wilderness were associated with squalor and poverty, as were their inhabitants. Stories of local heroes like Robin Hood illustrate the battle between forest dwellers and the nobility, which the latter eventually won. The Bible too advises the reader to 'go forth and conquer the wildernesses'. The wolf represented evil cunning and was hunted to extinction. The colonialists, who wanted to increase land under cultivation—poppy in north India, grain in central and south India and tea in the hills, all of which brought large profits—extended this culture to India.

While 'Europe had experienced centuries of state-sponsored carnivore killing . . . it was a new experience in India. In many areas where the confrontation between people and the predators was not so intense, extermination did not work. Religious and cultural factors meshed with self-interest . . . The cheetah's sprint and the roar of the lion became a rarity. If the tiger did survive, it was because much of its home was in the hill forests (Rangarajan 2001).' The Raj left its mark on the natural world. Special hunts were arranged for governors and Governors General by pliant maharajas who vied with each other to provide the best hunting facilities for the white man and, thereby, increase the number of guns that could salute them or the privileges they were entitled to. The erstwhile ruler of Bikaner killed nearly 50,000 animals and over 46,000 game birds, including thirty-three tigers and thirty great Indian bustards. By organizing these hunting parties, the maharajas were treated as 'honorary whites' (ibid).

Their methods were extremely ugly and cowardly: they would tie up kid goats and mongrel dogs to a tree to lure unsuspecting carnivores to an easy kill, hide in a machan in the tree and shoot.

In the 1930s and 1940s, some rulers made a few changes. The erstwhile Maharaja of Morvi protected the rare wild ass while the late Nawab of Junagadh gave protection to the Asiatic lion, limited by now to the Gir forest, to be killed only at his invitation. Only those that were threatening human lives were selected and shot dead, while he gave cash compensations to farmers whose livestock had been killed by lions. In the 1940s, hunting was banned for the first time in India, in the state of Travancore, under the then dewan, Sir C.P. Ramaswami Aiyar.

The conversion of prime forest lands to tea estates in Assam and the Nilgiris, the logging of wood for the expansion of the railways and the planting of commercial species like pine and wattle to feed industries destroyed the natural habitat and carnivores were killed as the forests were cleared. Yet the continued survival of several species, in spite of the shrinking habitats, the large-scale hunting by the erstwhile maharajas and the British rulers and contemporary poaching, was undoubtedly due to their religious associations. People respected and therefore preserved several animal species, such as the elephant, the blackbuck and the monkey. The ecological role of some species like the fruit bat and the birds of prey made them sacred and ensured their survival. Where the tiger was revered, it survived. The cheetah was not regarded as sacred, and perished.

### Prevention of Cruelty to Animals Act, 1960

In 1960, animal activist Rukmini Devi Arundale tabled the Prevention of Cruelty to Animals Bill, 1960, in Parliament 'to prevent the infliction of unnecessary pain or suffering on animals and for that purpose to amend the law relating to the prevention of cruelty to animals'. The Animal Welfare Board of India was set up with Rukmini Devi as its first chairman. Societies for Prevention of Cruelty to Animals (SPCAs) were given powers to arrest and fine people involved in cases of cruelty to animals, but corruption and very low fines made the powers meaningless.

The Animal Birth Control (Dog) Rules, 2001, were notified to control the stray dog population as a means to control rabies and curb cruelty to dogs. Under these rules, the killing of dogs was banned: street dogs were to be sterilized and vaccinated with the participation of animal welfare organizations and the local authority.

### Wildlife Protection Act, 1972

In 1972 a tiger census based on pug marks revealed a shocking figure of only 1,800 tigers in the wild, and the Wildlife Protection Act came into existence, made possible by India's most environmentally conscious prime minister, Mrs Indira Gandhi. In April 1973, Project Tiger was launched and nine (now twenty-nine) national parks set up to protect them. Gir Lion Sanctuary was established in 1992, followed by Project Elephant in 1992, with twenty-five reserves today.

Two million rhesus monkeys were exported in the first three decades after Independence. Prime Minister Morarji Desai banned this practice in 1977. The export of frogs' legs was also banned.

Many more sanctuaries and national parks have been established for the protection of Indian wildlife, but with little success. Today, the thriving international wildlife trade is threatening the survival of wildlife in India. In 2005, it was discovered that no tigers were left in Sariska Tiger Reserve in Rajasthan—they had all been killed by poachers. There are now about 1,300 tigers in the wild. Few tuskers (male elephants) are left, while the rhino is hunted for its horn. The lions of Gir are killed by poisoned cattle carcasses. Every month customs officials catch a few star tortoises that are on their way to Singapore—many more go undetected.

Habitat destruction, unchecked development, corruption and bureaucratic apathy are sounding the death knell of India's wildlife. With hunters adopting sophisticated technologies, the rate of killing has become higher and faster, in spite of the many deterrent legislations. China, East Asia and the Arab countries of the Middle East are the largest markets for the wildlife trade today.

# Sacred Animals

## Ant

| | | |
|---|---|---|
| Scientific Name | : | Formica sp. |
| Common names | : | Chinti (Hindi) |
| | | Erumbu (Tamil) |
| | | Pipilika (Sanskrit) |
| Distribution | : | Throughout India |

Kindness to the ant is regarded as the ultimate form of benevolence. Consideration for the ant means consideration for the tiniest of all creations. Thus housewives in the south and east of India start their day by making beautiful designs out of rice flour on the ground outside their houses. These designs are called kolam in Tamil Nadu and alpana in Bengal. The rice flour may be used in powder form or mixed with water, but the message is clear: even the smallest forms of creation must be fed.

*Sacred anthill*

The fact that the ants are a part of the karmic cycle is stressed by the tale of Indra and the ants. Indra wanted Vishvakarma to build him the most magnificent of palaces. When Brahma heard of it, he sent Vishnu in the form of a young boy who pointed out a parade of ants to Indra and said that they were all Indras who had risen from the lowest forms of existence to the highest.

When consumed by pride, they went down again. Thus the onus of responsibility falls on higher life forms to appreciate and honour their status and live life accordingly. Most importantly, no life form should be killed, as they are all interrelated.

The anthill is especially sacred in rural India and dismantling one is said to bring bad luck. People leave leftover food outside anthills for ants, and decorate it with red kumkum powder to establish its sanctity. Snakes also make their homes in anthills, making the formation doubly sacred. The anthill is symbolic of how two species live together in peace and is an example to be emulated. Poojas for the worship of snakes generally take place outside anthills and the food left for snakes is not eaten by the snakes (who are carnivores). This becomes food for the ants.

The anthill is called valmikah. The author of the *Ramayana* was Valmiki, so-called because he reappeared, after years of meditation, from an anthill. Today the Valmikis are a Scheduled Caste in India.

The black ant is called Pillaiyaar erumbu—or Ganesha ant—in Tamil. Killing it is a heinous sin.

Jainas are so wary of killing ants even by accident as they walk that monks and nuns sweep the ground before them before stepping forward.

In Karnataka, ants are considered to be so sacred that people leave rice and sugar near anthills. It is believed that when children distribute rice and jaggery at an ant colony, they stop bed-wetting (Ardhya, 2005).

In the sacred groves of Ratnagiri district of coastal Maharashtra, anthills abound. In some groves, the anthills are regarded as the abode of Lord Shiva and worshipped with reverence (Godbole and Sarnaik, 2006).

The ant is revered in other cultures also. The Book of Proverbs in the Bible holds up ants, for human beings, as examples of hard work and cooperation. In parts of Africa, they are messengers of the gods. While the bite of some ant species is believed to have curative properties, the bite of other species is used in male initiation ceremonies as a test of endurance.

### Ecological Role and Current Status

There are more than 12,000 species of ants, with greater diversity in the tropics. They are known for their highly organized colonies and nests, which sometimes consist of millions of individuals. Ants are divided into sterile females ('workers', 'soldiers', and others), fertile males (drones), and fertile females ('queens'). Ant colonies can cover a wide area of land and operate as a unified entity. Ants are found in almost every landmass on earth, and probably constitute 15 to 25 per cent of the total terrestrial animal biomass.

Ants are the ultimate 'cleaners', removing dead insects, food and other biodegradable bodies. They play an invaluable role in the ecology, by keeping down several pest populations and aerating the soil. Weaver ants are used for biological control in citrus plantations in China.

~

# Antelope

There are several species of antelope in India. Of these, only two are considered to be sacred: the blackbuck and the blue bull.

Antelopes are distinct from deer because of their horns, which grow out of their skull and are found on both males and females. The horns are very strong and stay attached to the skull all the time, unlike deer that shed and regrow their horns, making them vulnerable to predators. Adult antelopes are feared by predators because of their strong horns which can tear the predators' skin and flesh and cause considerable harm.

## Blackbuck

| | | |
|---|---|---|
| Scientific name | : | *Antilope cervicapra* Linn |
| Common names | : | Kadiyal, Kala hiran (Hindi) |
| | | Krishna jinka (Telugu) |
| | | Iralai maan (Tamil) |
| | | Ena/Mriga (Sanskrit) |
| Distribution | : | Plains of India |

The antelope first appears as the vehicle of Vayu, the Wind, and the steed of the Maruts, the storm deities and the sons of Rudra and Diti (Rig Veda, VIII.96.8). The association with Vayu is derived from the animal's ability to run swiftly, like the wind.

The antelope is also the vehicle of Soma, the divine drink whose effects were probably as swift as the wind, and the Moon god Chandra, also known as Soma in later literature.

*Vayu, the Wind on antelope*

Shiva holds a horned stag in his hand, to represent his control over the restlessness of the mind and thoughts, for thoughts are like the antelope that fly swiftly as the wind.

The antelope mentioned in Sanskrit texts is the blackbuck, a fast-moving antelope found in north India. It has been associated with speed and dexterity, and kings of ancient and medieval India hunted them in large numbers.

The slaughter of antelopes in the medieval period became so alarming that a movement came up for its protection. This can be traced back to the fifteenth century, with the birth of Guru Jamboji in 1485 CE, and his establishment of the Bishnoi cult. The blackbuck is held sacred by the Bishnoi tribe of Rajasthan, probably the most ecologically conscious community in the world, whose religion prohibits them from cutting a tree or killing an animal. The Bishnois, a sub-sect of Hindus, give primacy to animals and trees. Bishnois worship blackbucks as 'Jamboji' and revere them as their ancestors. They are, therefore, objects of veneration. Before his death, Guru Jamboji had said that in his absence, his followers should revere the blackbuck as his manifestation. That belief continues and hunting the blackbuck is akin to killing the guru.

The blackbuck is the object of the Bishnoi prayers and killing it is an unpardonable sin. The Bishnois have chased poachers at the cost of their own lives. Many Bishnoi men have died protecting the blackbuck, while Bishnoi women have even breastfed the animal. The protection afforded to the animal, thanks to the Bishnois, has been so good that the animal has multiplied into hundreds of thousands. Bishnois have played a major role in conserving blackbucks. Their crops are shared with wild animals and orphaned blackbuck fawns are adopted and brought up by Bishnoi women.

Unfortunately, no information is available on the sacrifices made by the Bishnois to protect the blackbuck, although there are records of people sacrificing their lives to protect the khejri tree, the staple food of the blackbuck and a plant essential to the desert economy. In 1661 CE, Karma and Goura, two women from Ramasari village in Jodhpur district, sacrificed their lives to protect the khejri trees by clinging on to them. In 1730 CE, 363 persons, including sixty-nine women and 294 men, laid down their lives to save the khejri trees from the solders

*Maruts*

of Maharaja Abhay Singh of Jodhpur. The Chipko movement of the Garhwal Himalayas, probably the world's first environmental movement, was inspired by these incidents. This would make the blackbuck a part of India's environmental history.

The blackbuck, known as Krishna jinka in Telugu, is the state animal of Andhra Pradesh. However, there is no explanation from the state government as to why it was chosen, except that it was found in vast numbers in the state. At Ranibennuru and Mydanahalli of Madugiri taluk in Tumkur district of Karnataka, the blackbuck or Krishna jinka is regarded as a sacred animal and protected by local people.

*Ecological Role and Current Status*

The blackbuck is a species of antelope, a very fast runner who can outrun most predators over long distances. The maximum life span recorded is sixteen years and the average is twelve years. The horns of the blackbuck are ringed with three to four turns and can be as long as 28 inches. In the male, the upper body is black or dark brown, and the belly and eye rings are white. The light-brown female is usually hornless. Blackbucks roam the plains in herds of fifteen to twenty animals with one dominant male.

*Shiva holding an antelope*

The blackbuck's diet consists of grasses, pods, flowers and fruits. By feeding on the khejri tree [*Prosopis cineraria*], which is almost the only tree that rises to some height and yields shade, fodder and ultimately some timber, the blackbuck ensures its speedy regeneration, thereby making the harsh arid desert livable. The khejri is a hardy tree, known as the lifeline of the desert because of its multiple uses.

Although blackbucks are protected by law, there are incidents of poaching, while the remaining populations are under threat from inbreeding. The natural habitat of the blackbuck has been encroached upon by man's growing need for arable land and grazing ground for domesticated cattle. Exposure to domesticated cattle also exposes the blackbuck to bovine diseases. Once large herds freely roamed in the plains of north India, where they thrive best, but they no longer do.

During the eighteenth and nineteenth centuries and the first half of the twentieth century, the blackbuck was the most hunted wild animal all over India. Until India's independence, many rulers hunted this antelope and the other local Indian gazelle, the chinkara, with specially trained Asiatic cheetahs. Cheetahs

*Soma, the Moon*

would be taken to hunting fields in low-sided bullock carts or on horseback, hooded and blindfolded, and kept on leash, while dogs flushed out their prey. When the prey was near enough, the cheetahs would be released and their blindfolds removed. This strange method of hunting was carried out to conserve the cheetah's energy and watch the fastest predator chase and kill the fastest species of antelope. This tradition of hunting with the cheetah was introduced into India by the Persian invaders, and continued well into the twentieth century by Indian princes who enjoyed watching this macabre hunt.

The blackbuck is protected under Schedule I of the Wildlife Protection Act of 1972. Its protected status gained considerable publicity through a widely reported court case in which Salman Khan, a leading Hindi film star, allegedly killed two blackbucks and several endangered chinkaras. The determined protests of the Bishnois, who claimed to have caught the actor red-handed and on whose land the hunting had taken place, resulted in his arrest and trial.

~

## Blue Bull

| | | |
|---|---|---|
| Scientific name | : | *Boselaphus tragocamelus* Pall. |
| Common names | : | Nilgai (Hindi) |
| | | Neela maan (Tamil) |
| | | Nila gauh (Sanskrit) |
| Distribution | : | North Indian plains |

The nilgai or blue bull is actually a species of antelope, commonly seen all over north India. It looks like a cow, hence its name (nil means blue, gai means cow).

The blue bull is regarded as a bovine animal, leading to the local belief that the nilgai is a cow and hence sacred. This has protected it from hunters (see cow).

### Ecological Role and Current Status

Blue bulls live in herds of thirty to 100 animals over northern India. They avoid dense forests and prefer the plains and low hills with shrubs. Blue bulls are usually found in scrub jungle (acacia forests), grazing upon kader grass. Their main predators are tigers and lions. Leopards cannot kill full-grown nilgai but may hunt calves. As a result of the reduction of the tiger population, the population of the nilgai has multiplied considerably.

Blue bulls can survive for days without water, but they live close to waterholes. Deserts earlier limited their range, but the extension of irrigation canals and proliferation of tube-wells in the Thar Desert have helped them colonize the desert districts of Jodhpur, Barmer, Jaisalmer, Bikaner and Ganganagar.

～

# Bear

| | | |
|---|---|---|
| Scientific name | : | *Melursus ursinus* Shaw |
| Common names | : | Sloth Bear |
| | | Bhaloo (Hindi) |
| | | Karadi (Tamil) |
| | | Rikshah (Sanskrit) |
| Distribution | : | Throughout India |

*Ramayana*

Jambavan the bear appears in the *Ramayana*, where he is addressed as a Riksha and as a Vanara. The second appellation, particularly for a bear that has no resemblance to nor has any relation with the monkey, suggests that the word Vanara implies vana (forest) nara (person) or forest dweller.

Jambavan was the oldest member of Rama's army, who is believed to have seen the churning of the ocean and Vishnu's incarnation as Vamana, and is described as 'more dead than alive'. He is described as the incarnation of an apsara sent by Brahma to protect Rama and help him defeat Ravana. Jambavan, with his army of bears, aided Rama in his war against Ravana. As the oldest member of Rama's army, he was the wise old man, sage and counsellor, who advised Rama, Lakshmana and the Vanaras through the war.

*Jambavan*

During the war, Lakshmana was seriously injured by a magical weapon fired by Ravana's son Indrajit. Jambavan sent Hanuman to the Himalayas where the Sanjivani herb, which could bring the dead back to life, grew on the Drona and Chandra mountains between the Rishabha and Kailasa peaks. Unable to identify the herb, Hanuman lifted and brought the whole mountain to Lakshmana. The herb was then identified by Jambavan and Lakshmana survived to kill Indrajit himself.

Jambavan, as the wisest person, told Hanuman that he was the son of Vayu and Anjana, and gave the information that Hanuman was blessed by Brahma and Indra with invincibility, but also by svechchha marana (death by desire), by which Hanuman had amnesia unless he was reminded of his power.

Jambavan contributed to the popular belief that sloth bears are wise, a motif that resonates even in Rudyard Kipling's *Jungle Book*.

## Mahabharata

Jambavan was born in each of Vishnu's incarnations.

In his Krishna incarnation, Jambavan came to possess the shyamantaka jewel, which protected the good and harmed the evil. The jewel had been given by Surya (the Sun god) to King Satrajit, whose evil brother Prasena wore it and went hunting. Prasena was killed by a lion, who was killed by the bear Jambavan. However, Krishna was suspected of having killed Prasena for the jewel.

Krishna went in search of Jambavan and, after fighting him for twenty-one days, received the jewel from Jambavan. Jambavan then became Krishna's ally and gave his beautiful daughter Jambavati (a human) in marriage to Krishna.

In view of Krishna's marriage to Jambavati, it is obvious that Jambavan represented a tribe whose symbol or totem was the bear, rather than actually being a bear.

Jambavati, the daughter of a bear, was also the mother of Shamba who was one of the five who formed the panchavyuhas (five cosmic emanations) that characterize the Pancharatra sub-sect of Vaishnavism. This would have been possible only if she were human, for Shamba was human.

## Jainism

The emblem of the fourteenth Tirthankara Anantanatha is the bear.

## Ecological Role and Current Status

Jambavan is generally recognized to have been a sloth bear. The bear's sanctity appears to have totemic origins, for the animal does not have a known ecological role in the areas where it is sanctified.

Sloth bears have shaggy black coats, long snouts, large tongues and broad, flat molars. Their bodies, with huge feet and enormous claws, are awkward. They can voluntarily open and close their nostrils, giving them a good sense of smell, but their sight and hearing are poor. They are excellent climbers. Sloth bears are insectivores, with termites as their staple diet, but they also eat leaves, honey, flowers and fruits. This species was fairly common in India and Sri Lanka until as recently as twenty years ago, but now they are harder to find.

The bear is a nocturnal animal that comes out at night in search of food, although it does move around in the daytime in forests that are far away from human habitation. It climbs trees in search of honeycombs and raids sugar cane fields. In central India, it likes to eat the mahua fruit and flower, which have an intoxicating effect.

Rama, hero of the *Ramayana*, is believed to have met Jambavan the bear at Kishkindha, near Hampi, in Karnataka. The Goravas of Karnataka claim that Jambavan belonged to their tribe, and wear the bear's hide as a crown.

However, sloth bears are nonetheless captured and trained to dance by the Goravas of Karnataka and the Kalandars, a north Indian community, and killed for their bile which is used in traditional medicine. They are used as bait for bear-baiting (by dogs), once a common pastime in north India, which still continues in Pakistan, and live lives of torture and fear.

# Bee

*Bumblebee*

| | | |
|---|---|---|
| Scientific Name | : | *Bombus* sp. |
| Common Names | : | Bhramara (Hindi) |
| | | Tumbi (Tamil) |
| | | Bhramarah (Sanskrit) |
| Distribution | : | Throughout India |

The bumblebee is revered at the Shaktipeetham at Srisailam (one of the twelve jyotirlingas) where Parvati is believed to have taken birth as the humble insect, giving her the name bhramarambika, in order to be near her Lord Shiva who resides in the Srigiri Hill in the form of mallika or jasmine. Thus the temple is known as Bhramarambika Mallikarjuna Devalaya (Srinivasulu and Srinivasulu 2005).

*Ecological Role and Current Status*

There is not much differentiation between honeybees and bumblebees. Bumble bees feed on nectar and gather pollen. While bumblebees do not stockpile honey, they are extremely useful in agriculture as pollinators because they can pollinate plant species. Like most insects, bees are endangered in India due to habitat destruction and pesticide damage.

*Honeybee*

| | | |
|---|---|---|
| Scientific Name | : | *Apis cerena* Fabricius |
| Common Names | : | Madhumakhi (Hindi) |
| | | Then-ee (Tamil) |
| | | Bhramarah (Sanskrit) |
| Distribution | : | Throughout India |

Krishna is called Madhava or 'born of honey (madhu)', while the bow Kama, the Indian Cupid, consisted of a string of bees.

Several tribes revere the honeybee, from which they obtain honey and wax. Honey is a major food for several tribes.

The Jenu Kurubas of Karnataka depend on harvesting honey and wax, which is their sole livelihood (Ardhya 2005).

The Kurumbas of the Nilgiris climb up sheer rock faces to collect honey from the beehives hanging from rock edges. As this is their chief source of livelihood, they paint beautiful pictures of hanging rocks and climbing up to the honeycombs to celebrate their occupation.

### Ecological Role and Current Status

Honeybees represent a small fraction of bee diversity. These bees are the only living members of the tribe *Apinae*, producing and storing liquefied sugar ('honey') and constructing colonies of nests out of wax secreted by the workers in the colony.

Indigenous people gather the honey of all species of *Apis* for consumption, although only *Apis mellifera* and *Apis cerena* have been exploited for commercial purposes. Thanks to the large market for honey, the insect is well protected.

~

# Boar

| | | |
|---|---|---|
| Scientific Name | : | *Sus scrofa cristatus* Linn |
| Common Names | : | Indian wild boar |
| | | Suar (Hindi) |
| | | Panri (Tamil) |
| | | Varaha (Sanskrit) |
| Distribution | : | Throughout India |

In Indian tradition, the boar is associated with rain and is believed to dig the earth before the onset of the monsoon. His ability to dig up the earth with his tusks is linked with agriculture and food production. As the boar ploughs the earth, he teaches mankind to plough, till and fertilize the land. Thus Lord Vishnu chose to incarnate himself as a boar to teach human beings agriculture, to plough the earth and produce food. The boar is thus a symbol of food production and fertility as he is compared to the regenerative qualities of human beings.

*Varaha*

*Glory to you, O Lord of the universe, who took the form of a boar;*
   *When the earth fell into the ocean, below the universe,*
   *You caught her on your tusk, where she looked beautiful,*
   *Like a dot on the moon.*

*Gita Govinda* by Jayadeva

Varaha is the third of the ten incarnations of Vishnu. However, the earliest Varaha story appears in the *Taittiriya Aranyaka* and *Shatapatha Brahmana*, according to which the universe was originally water and the earth as small as the span of a human hand. Becoming the boar Emusha—black with a hundred arms—Brahma lifted the earth, his spouse, out of the water.

The epics tell a different tale. Kashyapa, a Vedic progenitor, married Aditi and Diti, besides the other daughters of Daksha. Aditi was the mother of the Adityas or celestial beings, while Diti was the mother of the Daityas or demons. One of her sons was the demon Hiranyaksha. He desired to own the earth, rolled up Mother Earth in a mat, and threw her into the ocean. Mother Earth let out a cry that was heard in Vaikuntha (heaven) by Vishnu who took

*Varaha, boar incarnation of Vishnu, rescuing Mother Earth*

the form of a gigantic boar and dived into the waters. A terrible battle took place which shook the universe. Finally, Hiranyaksha was killed. Varaha dug out the earth with his massive tusks and placed her on the ocean, where she continues to float.

The age we are living in is called the Shweta Varaha Kalpa, the Age of the White Boar. According to popular legend, after his work was finished, Varaha went to live on Tirumala Hill in Andhra Pradesh. Thus the first prayer in this important temple town is offered to Varaha.

Whereas in the first two incarnations the human visage was above and the animal body below, Varaha is depicted as an enormous boar-headed figure, with a large trunk on which sits Mother Earth. Below his neck he is human, a mighty man, holding the attributes of Vishnu: the conch (shankha), discus (chakra) and mace (gada), with the fourth hand in the abhaya mudra (gesture of fearlessness). In later art, he is depicted seated, with Lakshmi on his lap. This form is known as Lakshmi Varaha.

The tradition continues that Varaha and Earth together produced a son Naraka, the lord of the underworld, the product of the Earth and proof of her fertility. Naraka became the king of the Hindu equivalent of hell.

In a Shaivite variation, Varaha became so proud of his strength and prowess that he terrorized the universe. To stop him, Shiva stood in his path in his linga form. Varaha tripped and fell, and realized his folly, after which he calmed down and was worshipped as an incarnation of Vishnu. The Varahishwara Temple in Damal village in the Kanchipuram district of Tamil Nadu contains a linga with natural whorls, representing a discus and a conch, Vishnu's attributes, believed to have been made when Varaha tripped and held on to the linga.

Varaha is represented in art as a man with a boar's head, and two enormous tusks. He always appears with Bhudevi, his spouse who is Mother Earth. Sometimes she sits on his tusks, indicating that she has been dug out of the earth, and at other times on his lap.

The boar incarnation of Vishnu appears early in Indian sculpture. At the Gupta temple at Udayagiri, there is an enormous figure of the boar carrying Mother Earth on his tusks, while she sits elegantly on his lap in the Varaha Cave at Mahabalipuram in Tamil Nadu. Recently, a four-legged boar image from the second century CE was excavated at Mamallapuram.

Another famous Varaha temple is situated at Shrimushnam near Chidambaram, where both Hindus and Muslims equally revered Varaha. Even Muslims take the name Varaha Sahib.

The boar was the symbol of the Chalukya, Kakatiya and Vijayanagara dynasties.

However, boar hunting was also a favourite pastime of ancient rulers, as evidenced in the friezes of the Chalukyan temples of Pattadakkal, at Orissa and Khajuraho and in the Vijayanagara paintings of the Lepakshi temple.

In coastal Maharashtra, the boar is worshipped on the first four days of the Ganesha festival, when no boars are to be killed or driven away from the fields. Farmers worship the boar during the sowing and planting of rice, requesting them to stay away from the fields and not to damage the crops. They believe that their prayers keep the animal away.

### Varahi

The goddess Varahi is one of the Sapta Matrikas, the Seven Mothers of Tantric religion. She is generally propitiated by the sacrifice of fowl. She is depicted with the body of a woman and the face of a boar.

The Varahis are also considered to be animal-headed dakinis in Nepal. Four aspects of Varahi preside over Kathmandu Valley in Nepal. They are

*Varahi*

- Vajra Varahi, red in colour, who presides over the west and protects livestock.

- Nila Varahi, blue in colour, who guards the east.
- Shweta Varahi, white in colour, who guards the south.
- Dhoomra Varahi, grey in colour, who protects the north and the valley against cholera..

Although Varaha is an incarnation of Vishnu, Varahi is an aspect of Durga, whose war against the asuras went on for nine days—the Navaratri festival that is celebrated in October–November. On the eighth day Durga assumed the form of each of the consorts of the incarnations of Lord Vishnu, one of which is Varahi.

### Buddhism
The goddess Marichi drives a chariot drawn by seven boars.

### Jainism
The emblem of the thirteenth Tirthankara Vimalanatha is a boar.

*Jaina Tirthankara*
*Vimalanatha*

### Ecological Role and Current Status
Fully grown wild boars are huge animals weighing over 100 kg. The canine teeth are protruding tusks which serve as weapons and grow continuously. The tusks of an adult male could measure over 20 cm, of which only 10 cm protrude out of the mouth. The upper tusks of males are bent upwards, and are regularly ground against each other to produce sharp edges. In females they are much smaller and only slightly bent upwards. This pair of elongated canines is the most distinctive feature

*Vijayanagara emblem*

of the wild boar. The animal has grey-black skin that is scantily covered with thick bristle-like hairs starting at the nape.

The boar digs deep into the earth in search of roots to eat. In doing so, he turns over the earth. Early food gatherers must have seen the regenerative qualities of the earth after it had been turned over by the boar. From this, it is believed, man learned the science of agriculture. By digging deep into the earth, the boar also enables the growth of fresh shoots, thus associating the animal with fertility.

The boar has an incredible sense of smell, but very average eyesight and hearing. It has a well-built body. It is brave and courageous, determined to live and win, challenging even the tiger. Its thick coat has a layer of fat that helps it recover from serious injuries. It is very aggressive when attacked or even threatened. Boars generally graze silently in the forest, but at night they may raid and damage crops adjoining national parks and sanctuaries.

With poaching and the loss of habitat, the number of the wild boars is fast decreasing. Once there were six to seven species in the subcontinent, but today only a single species has survived

～

# Buffalo

| Scientific Name | : | *Bubalus bubalis* Linn |
| Common Names | : | Water buffalo, |
| | | Bhains (Hindi) |
| | | Yerumai (Tamil) |
| | | Mahisha (Sanskrit) |
| Distribution | : | Throughout India |

The buffalo is associated with Yama, the Hindu god of death, synonymous with Dharma, who is usually depicted riding a fierce-looking black male water buffalo. Later, as Yama—Death—

became sinister and feared, the buffalo, as his vehicle, was equally feared.

But there have been several reasons to hate this animal, once worshipped by the indigenous people of India.

Yama

## Mahisha

Kashyapa and his wife Danu, mother of the Danavas or demons, had two sons Rambha and Karambha—who wanted to be greater than the gods. They practised severe austerities with the aid of Brahma's boon. Karambha challenged Indra, god of the heavens, but was killed. Rambha chose not to fight the gods and, instead, used his boon to have a son who could not be defeated by the gods or demons. He married Mahishi, a water buffalo, and Mahisha was born out of this union. Rambha was killed by a male buffalo and his wife chose to die on his funeral pyre.

Mahisha was born as a buffalo-headed man with the special ability to change between human and buffalo forms at will. He became the king of the demon hordes. The demons became more powerful than the gods. They controlled the priests and consumed the offerings made to the gods. Mahisha even forced the gods to worship him.

The devas went to war against Mahisha but were unable to defeat him. Realizing they could not defeat Mahisha and faced with dwindling powers, the

Mahisha

gods created Durga, a powerful goddess, an eighteen-armed beauty riding a lion, to whom each god gave his weapon. Durga announced that she would marry anyone who could defeat her in battle. Mahisha fell in love with and desired her but she rejected him. He sent his generals and his demon armies, but they were all defeated and killed by Durga. Then Mahisha took on his terrible buffalo-demon form. The fight between Mahisha and Durga took a long time and went on for several years. Finally, Durga cut off Mahisha's head with Vishnu's chakra. Mahisha and all the other demons were killed and peace was restored to the heavens.

In the *Mahabharata*, Mahisha is a monster killed by Skanda.

The modern form of Mahisha is Bhainsasura who lives in the fields and tramples the corn, unless he is appeased by an offering of a pig or worshipped when the rice is ripening.

The festival of Navaratri is celebrated to mark the nine days and nights of war between Durga and Mahisha and the eventual victory of the goddess Durga over the buffalo-demon.

Mahisha was the god-king of the pastoral indigenous people who were grazers, and came into conflict with those who had changed to food production and who worshipped the Mother Goddess. The conflict between Durga and Mahisha represents the conflict between grazers and food producers. Mahisha was the demonized buffalo god-king of the indigenous tribes of India who were supplanted by food-producers who worshipped the Mother Goddess.

When the early food producers settled down to grow food, they praised the earth as a Mother Goddess of fertility. As people built settlements, they needed protection from evil spirits, disease and pestilence. They worshipped goddesses, later identified with Durga, whose name means fortress and who protected them from disease and pestilence. They had to keep off the pastoral grazers, stigmatized as 'demons'. The defeat of the food-gathering herders by food-producing farmers is symbolized in the Durga–Mahisha war.

Unfortunately, the conflict between the buffalo god of the pastoral milk producers and the Mother Goddess of the settled food producers took an ugly turn, with gory and violent buffalo sacrifices performed to appease the goddess in various parts of India. It is particularly bad in West Bengal, the North-East and Nepal, where thousands of buffaloes are sacrificed during Navaratri, the nine-day festival celebrating the defeat of Mahisha by the goddess. Many rural rice-producing communities also sacrifice the buffalo to the goddess, particularly in the name of this festival.

Yet the cult of Mahisha lives on in several forms among many pastoral tribes of India, including the Gonds and Maria Gonds of central India, the Katkaris of western India and the Todas of southern India (Krishna 2009).

Mysore is named after Mahisha (Mahisha-ur), and an enormous statue of Mahisha, beside the hill of Chamunda, the mother goddess who killed him, celebrates the former ruler of the state. There is still a community called Mahishi, named after Mahisha's mother, in Karnataka. However, village goddesses, especially Mariamma, in Karnataka and elsewhere, are offered the blood of the buffalo. In some villages of Karnataka, male buffaloes are offered to the local Mariamma temple and allowed to roam freely for a year, with free access to the fodder of all the villagers, before they are sacrificed to Mariamma.

It is likely that the Toda tribes of the Nilgiri Hills, who graze and worship the buffalo, were the indigenous people of Karnataka who were chased away to the Nilgiri Hills, which tower over Mahisha's former capital of Mysore, by food-producing devotees of the Mother Goddess.

## Toda Buffaloes

The buffalo is sacred by the Todas, an ancient tribe of the Nilgiri Hills in Tamil Nadu in south India. The Todas

*Toda temple*

are a pastoral people and their sole mode of subsistence was the raising of buffaloes and milk production. The production of milk has a ritual significance for them, and they construct a separate temple to house the sacred buffalo and the priest. The milk of the sacred buffalo is taboo to women. The buffaloes of the dairy temples and those used for domestic use are housed and maintained separately. Central to the religion of the Todas are the sacred places associated with the dairy temples, the buffalo herds and priesthood. These are divine places taboo to outsiders who are strictly prohibited from entering the Toda dairy-temple, which is located within the Toda mund. Toda dairies, buffaloes and dairymen are graded within a complex hierarchy according to their relative sanctity, with different rites and rituals for each grade. The more sacred the dairy, the more elaborate are the rituals that accompany the milking, churning and other activities of the dairyman–priest, and the greater the ritual purity.

Unlike most indigenous tribes, Todas are traditionally strict vegetarians who lived on and traded in buffalo milk. They have separate burial areas for the sacred buffalo.

## Marias and Gonds

The buffalo is the totemic symbol of the Marias and the Maria Gonds of central India, who live along the Indravati river that flows through Bastar district. The Maria Gonds wear the buffalo (bison) horn on festive occasions. Wearing buffalo horns and performing mock fights, the men dance the virarasa dance of valour to the rhythm of the dhol, their percussion instrument, while the women dance around them, holding sticks—the pastoralist's weapon—in their hands. They worship their ancient buffalo deity as well as Danteshwari Devi. Like other ancient people, they absorbed her into their fold and do not regard her as the conqueror of the buffalo god.

There seems to be some association between the Marias and the Todas of the south, whose cairns are called moriaru manay or the house of the Marias.

### Mahishmati

The town of Mahishmati, south of the river Godavari, was founded by King Mahishmat, whose name implies that he was rich in buffaloes. The people of this region were called Mahishakas.

### Mhasoba

Mahisha is called Mhasoba (Mahisha Baba or Father/Lord Mahisha) and worshipped by pastoral tribes in western and central India. Mhasoba is worshipped by the Katkari tribe of Maharashtra and the Bhosles

*Mhasoba*

(Shivaji's clan). Mhasoba shrines surround the buffalo-breeding settlements of Pune district (Krishna, Amrithalingam and Godbole 2006).

### Jainism

The buffalo is the emblem of the twelfth Jaina Tirthankara, Vasupujya.

### Ecological Role and Current Status

Providing milk, meat and leather, the buffalo was one of the earliest animals to be domesticated on the Indian subcontinent .

Descended from the wild Asian buffalo, the buffalo has been domesticated for thousands of years. It has been bred

*Jaina Tirthankara Vasupujya*

into various smaller breeds. It weighs about 500 kg and lives in most tropical and subtropical regions. The wild Asian buffalo, which weighs 800 to 1,200 kg, is a large and powerful animal with a wide horn span. The Asian buffalo is a grazer, eating grass and leafy aquatic vegetation, feeding in the morning and evenings. During the midday heat, the buffalo wallows in water or in muddy pools which, besides keeping it cool, removes parasites, flies, and other pests.

The buffalo, however, is also the most maligned of all Indian animals, probably a consequence of the Durga–Mahisha war, and suffers the worst forms of cruelty. It is beaten, sacrificed, transported long distances and slaughtered to death in very painful ways. The defeat of pastoral food grazers by food producers is re-enacted by the ritual sacrifice, sometimes even live impalement, of the buffalo, the sacred animal of Indian pastoralists, by food-growing rural communities who revere the Mother Goddess.

There are more than 80 million buffaloes in India. Male calves are sold off for their leather or sacrificed, while the mother's milk production is increased through injections of oxytocin.

~

## Bull

| Scientific name | : | *Bos indicus* Linn |
| Common names | : | Humped bull |
| | | Saand (Hindi) |
| | | Kaalai (Tamil) |
| | | Vrishabha (Sanskrit) |
| Distribution | : | Throughout India |

The humped bull is depicted on the seals and among the terracotta figurines of the Harappan civilization. On one seal of a horned male figure, identified with Shiva as Pashupati, surrounded by several animals, one of the animals is the bull. There are several cows and bulls on the seals, suggesting that its importance in Indian civilization goes far back in time (see INTRODUCTION).

In the Rig Veda, the bull was the symbol of strength, power and male virility. The gods of the Veda were called bulls for their superior power and abilities. Indra is addressed as the bull, a macho image. In fact the bull appears throughout the Rig Veda, more often than the cow which attains greater sanctity in the post-Vedic period.

The Vedic people were conscious of the importance of the bull and the Vedas exhort the ruler 'O king. You should never kill animals like bullocks that are useful for agriculture

*Shiva, Parvati and Nandi*

or like cows which give us milk and all other helpful animals, and must punish those who kill or do harm to such animals' (*Yajur Veda*, 13.49).

The bull is also one of the animals used to proclaim Ashoka's royal power. Like the lion capital, the bull capital was equally popular and important in the Ashokan period.

### Nandi

The Vedic status of the bull was inherited by Nandi, the companion and vehicle of Shiva in later literature.

The white bull—Nandi—is the divine vehicle of Lord Shiva, the Destroyer. He is the chief of

*Nandi*

the ganas, Shiva's attendants. Nandi means 'happy'.

Nandikeshvara, lord of happiness, was one of Shiva's ganas. He was also fond of music and dance. He was born to the divine progenitor Kashyapa and divine cow Surabhi. He married Suyasha, the daughter of the Maruts. As his life was coming to an end, he prayed to Shiva to lengthen his life. Shiva granted him both immortality and the chief position over his ganas. He was given the title 'Adhikara Nandi' (or 'authoritative Nandi'), for it is only with Nandi's grace and permission that one can enter the temple of Shiva. Adhikara Nandi took on a human form as a bull-headed human standing on two legs, or even a bull standing erect on his rear legs.

Nandi's attributes were taken over by Shiva as Nataraja, the Lord of dance. Nandi ceased, thereafter, to be a deity and became the companion and, later, the vehicle of Shiva. When Shiva danced the tandava, Nandi accompanied him on the mridangam (a percussion instrument).

There are several other stories about Nandi's origin. According to one, Nandi was a rishi (sage) who performed such severe austerities that Shiva granted him the wish of becoming the head of his ganas.

According to another legend, Nandi was born from Vishnu's right side as a gift to the Brahmin Salankayana. This was Nandi's forty-ninth rebirth.

Nandi is more than Shiva's vahana or vehicle. As the chief of Shiva's attendants, he is also the guardian of all four-legged animals. Nandi is essential to every Shiva temple—the sanctum sanctorum of each temple, where the deity may be in human or linga form, has an image of Nandi facing the shrine. The devotee will first touch the Nandi image and ask for his blessings before entering. Sometimes, Nandi may be as big as or even bigger than the image within.

In the Chola temple of Brihadishvara at Tanjore, Nandi has his own shrine. An enormous sculpture of Nandi is sculpted out of a single block of granite and is beautifully embellished. Nandi has his own shrine in several south Indian temples and worshippers enter the sanctum only after first praying to Nandi.

There is a story that Vrishabha Deva or Nandi was very proud of his role as the vehicle of the Supreme Lord Shiva himself. To teach him a lesson, Shiva placed a lock of his hair on the bull, who was unable to bear the weight. Realizing that he had been arrogant, Nandi begged Shiva's pardon. Shiva forgave him and initiated him into divine knowledge. Vrishabhavahana murti (the image of Shiva leaning against his bull vehicle), a bronze of the Chola period in south India, is one of the most beautiful works of art.

In paintings and sculptures, Nandi is invariably a part of Shiva's family. Shiva and Parvati, with either one or two or even neither of their sons, sit on Nandi's back in the family scene of Uma Maheshwara. In recent paintings and calendar art, inspired by Raja Ravi Varma's paintings, Nandi faces Shiva and Parvati in adoration, even as their two sons Ganesha and Kartikeya sit or play nearby.

Nandi completes the image of the happy family. In days gone by, people depended on the bull for transportation. The bull was thus the vehicle both of Shiva and of people. He is also a symbol of how a powerful animal, imbued with divine authority, is also a gentle and humble worker, of help to the gods and man.

## Basava

In Karnataka, Nandi is known as Basava, and the famous Bull Temple of Bangalore is situated at Basavangudi, which means the temple of Basava, or Nandi the bull. The bull in this temple is the object of worship in its own right, not merely as the vehicle of Shiva. In fact, the temple is an important pilgrimage and tourist site of Bangalore.

According to a local legend, the peanut fields in the villages surrounding present-day Bengaluru were ransacked every full-moon night. Believing this to be the work of thieves, the villagers armed themselves with crowbars, axes and rods and waited one full moon night to catch the thief. When they heard the rustling sounds, the farmers rushed in that direction and hacked to death what felt like a large body. Thereafter, the farmers learned to their horror that they had killed a huge golden bull, which had come to guard their fields. The next morning, the bull had mysteriosly disappeared. Soon after, a stone bull was found on top of the hill, overlooking the fields. They connected the image with the incident and begged Nandi's forgiveness. When Kempe Gowda, the founder of Bengaluru (Bangalore), visited the site soon after the incident, the villagers told him the story of what had happened. He went up the hill and offered worship to the bull, and later built a temple for the image.

It is believed that the image of Basava the bull has been growing every year from its original height of 4.57 m to 6.2 m, and from a length of 5.1 m to 6 m. In fact iron rods have been planted in the bull's head to prevent further growth.

Every year, the first peanut crop is offered to the bull in a thanksgiving ceremony called kadalekayi parishe. It is believed that good rains and a bountiful crop depend on the offerings made at this temple. Huge crowds visit the temple on Shivaratri.

Basavanna, the great religious and social reformer of Karnataka and founder of the Virashaiva or Lingayat cult, is considered an incarnation of Nandi, particularly the bull of Basavangudi—bulls are thus held very sacred in Karnataka.

### Biroba

Biroba or Viroba the bull is worshipped by the Dhangar, a nomadic shepherd community of Satara, Sangli, Pune and Kolhapur districts of Maharashtra. A major pilgrimage of Biroba is celebrated in the month of Ashvin (September–October).

*Biroba*

Biroba represents the Shiva linga. There are two stone sculptures of bulls accompanied by a stone image of a Vir (Bir), a servant of Shiva, in the forest of Biroba.

### Durga's Vehicle

Two of the Sapta Matrikas (Seven Mothers), aspects of Durga or Shakti, have bulls as their vehicles: Maheshvari and Varahi.

Initially the bull was sacrificed, but as its sanctity increased, the sacrifices stopped and a bull or bull calf was released to honour ancestors in shraddha ceremonies.

*Maheshwari*

### Festivals

Bailpola is a festival celebrated throughout Maharashtra in the month of Shravan (July-August) by farmers to pay respect to the bullocks who help them in their fields. On this day bulls are decorated and taken out in a procession. They are fed with special sweet items made of wheat and jaggery.

Bulls and cows are also worshipped during Dev Divali celebrated in the month of Margashirsha (December–January).

Mattu Pongal is celebrated in Tamil Nadu on the day after Pongal (14 January), a harvest festival. The cows and bullocks that have been the farmers' friends through the year are worshipped on that day.

Unfortunately, about three hundred years ago, some people in the district of Madurai decided to organize bullfights on the day after Mattu Pongal. Initially, the idea was to catch and garland the strongest bull with one's bare hands to proclaim the strongest man. Greed, however, resulted in heavy betting and large rewards. Today the bulls are tortured, with chilli powder rubbed into the anus, force-fed country liquor, beaten and poked with sharp objects until it is crazed with pain, turns violent and runs fast and angrily, harming and even killing many stupid young men along its path. A petition to ban the cruel sport of jallikattu is awaiting the decision of the Hon'ble Supreme Court of India.

*Jainism*

The bull is the emblem of Adinatha or Rishabhanatha, the first Jaina Tirthankara. The bull is also one of the fourteen auspicious signs that both Brahmani Devananda and Queen Trishala, mother of Mahavira, saw. In Jaina Kalpasutra paintings, two bulls are depicted on the left and right corners, with water flowing out of their horns. This is a reference to the bull's symbolism of fertility.

*Jaina Tirthankara Rishabhanatha*

*Zoroastrianism*

According to the Zend-Avesta, the bull is an incarnation of Verethraghna, the Iranian version of Vritrahan, another name for Indra the killer of Vritra, demon of drought. This is a parallel to the Rig Vedic view of Indra's designation as a bull.

*Ecological Role and Current Status*

Humped cattle appear in the earliest images of India—on the Indus Valley seals and terracotta figurines and on rock paintings found all over the country. They are well-adapted to the tropical environment.

The wild zebu was probably the first species to vanish from the Indian wilderness during the time of the Indus Valley civilization when it roamed the region between the Indus Basin and western India. Its disappearance was possibly due to interbreeding with domestic cattle and the resulting fragmentation of wild populations due to loss of habitat.

Indian cattle are distinguished by the hump on their backs. They have more sweat glands than taurine cattle, and have pest resistances not seen in other domestic cattle.

The bull occupies several important positions. As the castrated bullock (ox) which ploughs the field and pulls the cart, he is an essential part of the economy, providing India's maximum draught power. As the father, spouse and son of the cow, he becomes as important as the Gaumata. And as Nandi, the vehicle of Shiva, he occupies a position of authority.

There is, in fact, a shortage of draught animals in India: for the estimated seventy million farms in India, requiring 140 million draught animals, only eighty-three million oxen are available. If a bullock dies, it spells disaster, for the farmer has to borrow money to hire a bullock to pull his plough. The dung is used as antiseptic, fuel and manure. Dung used as cooking fuel is estimated to replace forty-three million tonnes of coal and fuel worth 1.5 billion dollars of foreign exchange (Harris 1978).

Yet, like the buffalo, few animals are treated as cruelly as the bull. He is castrated without pain killers, in the cruellest possible way. He is then made to pull overloaded carts and work round the clock with little sustenance. He is whipped, beaten, poked with sharp pointed metals and his tail is broken to make him work harder, move faster. He is made to fight in the cruel sport of jallikattu in Tamil Nadu or run in bullock-cart races, for which the animal is ill equipped. Finally, when all the cruelties can no longer make him function, he is loaded in a truck, with thirty to sixty others, all with broken legs and backs, transported, without food or water, over several hundred kilometres for days until he reaches an abattoir in Kerala or West Bengal, or smuggled to Bangladesh, where he undergoes a slow agonizing death. For all the sanctity accorded to the bull, it probably lives the worst life in India.

～

# Butterfly

| | | |
|---|---|---|
| Scientific Name | : | Lepidoptera (order) |
| Common Names | : | Titli (Hindi) |
| | | Vannaathipoochi (Tamil) |
| | | Chitrapatangah (Sanskrit) |
| Distribution | : | Throughout India |

In Indian philosophies, the life cycle of the butterfly is held up to explain the importance of meditation. Just as the egg becomes a caterpillar that metamorphoses into a beautiful butterfly after spending time in the cocoon, human beings must practise meditation to metamorphose from mere mortals into enlightened souls.

*Ecological Role and Current Status*

Butterflies are notable for their unusual life cycle, with a larval caterpillar stage, an inactive pupal stage, and a spectacular metamorphosis into a familiar and colourful winged adult form. Most species fly by daylight, so they attract attention. The diversity of their colourful, beautiful wings and their graceful flight have made butterfly watching a fairly popular hobby. Butterflies feed primarily on nectar from flowers. Some also derive nourishment from pollen, tree sap, fruit, dung, and dissolved minerals in wet sand or dirt. Butterflies play an important ecological role as pollinators. Like many other insects, wild butterflies are endangered in India due to habitat destruction and collateral pesticide damage.

~

# Cat

| Scientific name | : | *Felis silvestris* Linn |
|---|---|---|
| Common names | : | Domestic cat |
| | | Billi (Hindi) |
| | | Poonai (Tamil) |
| | | Marjarah (Sanskrit) |
| Distribution | : | Throughout India |

The domestic cat is the vehicle of goddess Shashthi, a goddess of fertility who is popular in West Bengal and Maharashtra. Shashthi means sixth and generally stands for the sixth day of a fifteen-day phase of the moon. Shashthi is also worshipped on the sixth day after the birth of a baby. The goddess, depicted carrying a baby, is also called Skandamata or mother of Skanda, who is worshipped on Skanda Shashti in the Tamil month of Kartigai (November–December) in south India, for defeating the demon Taraka with the spear given to him by his mother. In fact every shashthi, which comes every fifteen days, is a sacred day for Skanda worshippers. The cat is sacred to Shashthi.

*Shashthi*

However, a cat crossing one's path is considered to be inauspicious, and a superstitious person would go back and restart his mission.

The cat is beautifully depicted on the rock-cut relief of Arjuna's penance at Mamallapuram, where he stands on two legs in meditation.

### Ecological Role and Current Status

Cats are carnivorous mammals. The highly predatory instincts of all species of the cat family appear equally in domestic cats, who aggressively hunt small mammals and birds. Most cats have thirty teeth, including large canine and carnassial teeth, but few in their cheek, enabling them to crush bones and tear, cut, and grip the flesh of their prey.

*Meditating cat at Mamallapuram*

Members of the cat family live all over the world, except in Antarctica, Australia, and New Zealand, although domestic cats have been introduced and now live in the wild in the latter two countries.

India has several cat species. Apart from the five large species—tiger, lion, leopard, clouded leopard and cheetah (now extinct)—there are several wild small species, such as the marbled cat, leopard cat, golden cat, jungle cat, desert cat, caracal, lynx and Pallas' cat. Many domestic species are derived from these. Besides, in recent years, several exotic species, such as Persian and Siamese cats, have been imported into the country.

Unlike dogs, which are common companions in India, cats are not often kept as pets. They are, however, encouraged to live in the compounds of homes and buildings as they hunt and kill rats and mice. It is this role that makes the carnivore very acceptable.

~

# Cow

| | | |
|---|---|---|
| Scientific name | : | *Bos indicus* Linn |
| Common names | : | Gaai (Hindi) |
| | | Pasu (Tamil) |
| | | Pashu, Gau (Sanskrit) |
| Distribution | : | Throughout India |

The domestic cow, descended from the zebu and better known as humped cattle, is found all over India and has lived here since the earliest known occupation of the subcontinent. It appears on Indus Valley seals, among the earliest terracotta figurines found in the subcontinent, and on rock paintings. In the Indus Valley civilization, there was very early domestication of cattle, as indicated on the seals, potsherds and terracotta figurines.

The cow occupies a special place in Hindu culture. She symbolizes dharma, the Law of Righteousness. The reverence for the animal has been one of the central themes of Hinduism since ancient times. The animal is equated to one's mother, because she gives milk, hence the expression 'Gaumata' (cow mother). In the Hindu tradition, the cow represents both the mother and the earth—the mother, because cow's milk is the first replacement for mother's milk, and the earth because the cow is a symbol of fertility. In times of distress, the earth is believed to take on the form of a cow to pray for divine aid.

## Pashu and Pashupati

Pashu means cow and but also represents the world of animals, for Shiva as Pashupati is the lord of all animals, of which the cow is the foremost. Pashu is cognate with the Latin *pecu*, from which are derived words pertaining to money, such as *pecunia* (Latin) and impecunious (English).

In the Indus Valley seal of the three-headed horned male figure surrounded by many animals, the humped cow is present. Thus the concept may be of very ancient origin.

## The Cow in Vedic Literature

Cattle were very important to the Vedic people. The Rig Veda VI.28.1) says, 'The cattle have come and brought good fortune: let them rest in the cow pen and be happy near us. Here let them stay prolific, many coloured, and yield through many mornings their milk for Indra.'

In the *Yajur Veda* (13.49), the ruler is entreated not to kill and to punish those who kill: 'O king. You should never kill animals like bullocks, useful for agriculture, or like cows, which give us milk, and all other helpful animals, and must punish those who kill or do harm to such animals.'

The *Shatapatha Brahmana* (IX.3.3.15–17) says that the 'shower of wealth, the (cow's) body is the sky, the udder the cloud, the teat is the lightning, the shower (of milk) is the rain from the sky, and it comes to the cow.'

The references to the sanctity of the cow are endless. Her home is the firmament or heaven (*Rig Veda*, III.55.1); she is synonymous with Ushas or Dawn in several hymns; similarly, she is often synonymous with the earth, plenty, clouds, speech, waters and light. Her greatness and importance are apparent in Rig Vedic literature itself.

The belief in the sacred cow was shared by the Indo-Iranians. In the Zend-Avesta, the sacred book of the Zoroastrians, the *geuvarsan* or *goshuran* is the Soul of the Cow, a divine being.

Cattle were essential to the economy. Wealth was estimated by the number of heads of cattle owned either by an individual or the community. A cowherd (gopalaka) who took the cattle out to graze and brought them back home to the village in the evening, where they were housed in covered stalls, cared for the cattle. He was generally paid in kind, and was entitled to the milk of one cow out of every ten. The cows were milked twice a day except in spring, when the milk was reserved for the calves. Often quarrels broke out between villages over cattle.

There were strict punishments in ancient India for killing a cow. The Vedic people were largely pastoral and depended on their cattle for much of their livelihood. A man's wealth was counted by the number of cattle he possessed. Milk, fuel, fertilizer, medicines, disinfectants and anti-pollutants were all supplied by the humped cattle. Even the dowry and bride price were paid in cattle. Killing a cow was punishable by death in ancient India. In fact one of the causes for untouchability was the killing of a cow. Killing a cow was a heinous crime, on par with the killing of a Brahmin. The killer's head was shaved and he was fined ten cows and a bull (*Mahabharata*, III.240).

According to later (Puranic) mythology, Brahma created the Brahmins and the cow at the same time, the Brahmins to recite the Vedas and the cow to provide ghee for the sacrifices. She is even addressed as the mother of the gods and Brahma declares that she should be worshipped.

The importance of the cow in Indian culture may be seen from the number of words derived from gau/go. One's ancestral family name is the gotra (or cow pen), within which the family lived with its cattle. So sacred is the gotra, or the male lineage, that two people from the same gotra cannot intermarry, even if one belongs to Kashmir and the other to Kanyakumari.

The gateway to a temple is called gopuram, which means the village/town of the cow.

Gorocha was the worship of the cow as the god of one's choice. This was done by devoting oneself to many cows.

Gauri, the consort of Shiva, is named after the Rig Vedic buffalo-cow (Rig Veda, I.164.41).

During the shraddha ceremony (death rites), a cow must be gifted to a Brahmin. It is believed that the dead person will receive the cow in heaven, and the cow will liberate the dead soul from all its sins.

The cow is so sacred in Indian culture that the term 'sacred cow' signifies an idea or institution unreasonably held to be above criticism.

The cow is the national animal of Nepal and is held is special reverence by Hindus, Buddhists and Jains.

The life-giving rivers are compared to cows, for they are equally sacred.

The sanctity of the cow was so great that Babur, the first Mughal emperor, in his will to his son Humayun, advised him to respect the cow and avoid cow slaughter. The Mughal king Akbar chose to ban cow slaughter and thus endeared himself to his Hindu subjects.

The Indian Revolt of 1857 was prompted by the British colonizers asking the Hindu sepoys to bite a bullet that was, it was believed, greased with fat from cows (and pigs too, prompting Muslims to refuse, similarly, to bite the bullet).

*Was the Cow Eaten in the Vedic Period?*

The eating or not eating of beef in the Vedic period has become a subject of great controversy, with historians of the left and right taking opposing points of view depending on their political beliefs and not on what was said in the early Vedas. There is no doubt a stratum of society killed cows and ate beef, which eventually made them 'untouchable'. There is also the archaeological evidence of knife marks on cattle bones, but this means nothing—the people killing cows probably used its leather too. The question that needs to be asked is whether beef-eating or killing the cow was sanctioned by any or all of the four Vedas.

The case for beef eating rests on one word—goghna—which appears in the *Shatapatha Brahmana* and *Vashishtha Dharmasutra*, and was translated by one Taranath, in the early twentieth century, as 'killer of the cow' or serving beef to the guests. However, this is at total variance with Panini, the ancient grammarian, who translates the word as 'receiver of the cow' or one who receives a cow as a gift.

On the other hand, the Rig, *Sama*, *Yajur* and *Atharva Veda* say that the cow is

> Aghnya, one that ought not to be killed;
> Ahi, one that must not be slaughtered;
> Aditi, one that ought not to be cut into pieces.
> (*Nighantu* 11.4 by Yaska, commentator on the Vedas)

The terms aghnya, ahi and aditi are synonyms for gau, meaning cow.

The *Yajur Veda* is replete with instructions to protect the cow:

> Do not kill the cow which is the splendour of life and inviolable. (13.43).
> You men and women, both of you together protect your cattle. (6.11).

The *Atharva Veda* (VIII.3.25) adds: 'A man who nourishes himself on the flesh of man, horse or other animals or birds or who, having killed untorturable cows, debars them from their milk, O Agni, the King, award him the highest punishment or give him the sentence of death.'

There are many more references where killing the cow is specifically banned.

By the epic period, all followers of Sanatana Dharma, had given up beef eating. In the later and post-Vedic periods, there is enough literary evidence to prove that the Vedic religion did not permit the killing of cows or the consumption of its flesh. With the vast amount of literature giving a special status to the cow, it is impossible to believe that the Vedic people ate beef.

One of the defining features of medieval Hinduism was the ban on cow slaughter and the refusal to eat beef. Considering the diversity of Hinduism, the refusal to slaughter cows was a common criterion which rallied Hindus. There are many instances when Hindus were forced to eat beef. They were then excommunicated by their caste and forced to convert to Islam. Kashmir was one such place where, in the fourteenth century, during the rule of Sikandar, masses of people were forcibly converted to Islam by being made to eat beef. When they wanted to reconvert to Hinduism, they were not accepted by the local Brahmins. The failure of the Hindu clergy to relax the criteria for defining a Hindu—and refusing to accept eaters of beef back into the religion—forced many people who were converted to continue as Muslims. The most important criterion, in most cases, was abstinence from eating beef.

In fact many of the castes that became 'untouchable' were those who slaughtered the cow or ate beef. Some of them converted to Islam in the medieval period and to Christianity in modern India, while most remain Scheduled Castes.

The ban on non-Hindus from entering temples, seen everywhere in India, was actually a ban on beef eaters from entering the temple. Given that many present-day Hindus, especially those who travel abroad extensively, eat beef, the current ban on 'non-Hindus' from entering temples is hypocritical. Further, even while many Hindus may not actually kill the cow, they have no compunction in selling them to Muslims when they can no longer give milk or produce calves, thereby turning a blind eye to the fact that the animal will be killed.

The origin of vegetarianism in India has often been linked to the protection and veneration of the cow in Hindu culture. This probably originated from the pastoral Aryans, whose sacred books, the Vedas, call for non-violence towards all bipeds and quadrupeds and prescribe punishment for meat eating. Often, the killing of a cow is equated with the killing of a human being, especially a Brahmin. There is no doubt that the influence of Vedantic religion, Jainism and Buddhism, all of which condemned animal sacrifice, ultimately contributed to the ban on cow slaughter in all three religions. Having developed as a reaction to the excessive use of animals for sacrifice, they contributed to the total ban on cow slaughter and beef eating.

### The Cow as Vehicle

In Vedic literature, Ushas or dawn, a female deity, rides a chariot driven by seven cows. This was the equivalent of Surya, the sun, who rode a chariot driven by seven horses.

### Kamadhenu

Kamadhenu is the wish-fulfilling cow, born of the divine progenitor Kashyapa and his wife Krodhavasa, a daughter of Daksha. Kamadhenu's other names are Nandini (delight) and Surabhi (fragrant). She was the mother (Aditi) of all cattle. Kamadhenu, the wish-fulfilling celestial cow, is said to be the mother of all gods, and can grant any wish to the true seeker.

The *Mahabharata* says that Surabhi worshipped Brahma for a thousand years, after which she was blessed with divinity. She became

*Kamadhenu*

the goddess Kamadhenu and presided over Goloka, the heaven of cows.

In another epic story, Kamadhenu came out of the ocean during the samudra manthana or churning of the ocean. She was taken out by the seven rishis who make up the Great Bear. When the devas (gods) and asuras (demons) churned the celestial ocean of milk for amrita, the nectar of immortality, the navaratnas (nine gems) surfaced. One of these gems was the divine cow Kapila, identified as Kamadhenu in Puranic literature.

According to a later myth, Kamadhenu belonged to the sage Vashishtha. She was stolen by Satyavrata, his student, who killed and ate a part of Kamadhenu, giving the remaining flesh to Vishwamitra's family. Satyavrata was cursed by Vashishtha for three of the worst sins: killing a Brahmin, stealing from one's teacher and killing a cow.

### Surabhi

Surabhi, the cow, belonged to sage Vashishtha and was coveted by King Kaushika. The former refused to part with her and the cow too refused to leave the sage. This led to a terrible feud till the king realized the spiritual power of the sage, renounced his kingdom and became the sage Vishwamitra.

'The cow of plenty', Surabhi, sometimes came out of the ocean of milk during the churning of the ocean (samudra manthana), and was then identified with Kamadhenu. She is revered as a fountain of milk and curds and one who grants every desire. She is the mother of all cows, all of whom are descended from Surabhi.

However, Surabhi is also described as the calf of Kamadhenu.

### Nandini

The word means one who gives happiness. She was another cow of plenty, daughter of Surabhi, and belonged to sage Vashishtha.

*Sabala*

Parashurama was the sixth incarnation of Lord Vishnu on earth. His human father, the sage Jamadagni, had an extraordinary cow named Sabala, that was coveted by King Kartavirya. When the sage refused to part with her, he was killed by the king. When Parashurama saw his dead father and learned the cause of his death, he avenged himself by wiping out twenty-one generations of Kshatriyas, till he was halted in his terrible mission by Rama, the seventh incarnation of Vishnu.

*Krishna the Cowherd*

The cow is most commonly associated with Lord Krishna, who is usually depicted as a cowherd. The Yadavas and Ahirs, the tribes to which he belonged, were cowherds. Lord Krishna is known as Gopala, 'protector of cows' and Govinda, or 'cow keeper'. Krishna lived in Gokul (the family of cows), and his heaven is Goloka. The famous hill of Brindavan, where Krishna lived, is Govardhana.

*Krishna, the cowherd*

Krishna is usually portrayed holding a flute and standing beside a cow. It is believed that Krishna persuaded the cowherds (gopalas) and cowherdesses (gopis) of Brindavan to stop their worship of Indra and to worship Govardhana instead, for the mountain provided pasture for their cattle. To protect them from Indra's anger, which manifested itself as a terrible storm, Krishna raised the mountain Govardhana to protect the cowherds, cowherdesses and the cows. This image appears throughout in Indian art, from the Govardhana Giridhari cave temple at Mamallapuram to the exquisite Rajasthani and Pahadi miniature paintings, as does the scene of a calf suckling its mother. Such scenes kindled the religiosity of the devotee.

The worship of the cow gained impetus with the growth of the Krishna cult, for Krishna is acclaimed as the divine protector of cows. He rejected the worship of the Vedic Indra and regenerated the traditional beliefs of worshipping Mount Govardhana and cattle.

It is believed that there is no salvation or liberation for one who kills the cow and that he will rot in hell. Eating beef is the most heinous sin for a Hindu, Buddhist and Jain. However, the cow is eaten in most Buddhist countries and by Indian Buddhists, in spite of the Buddha's specified reverence for the cow.

## Festivals of the Cow

The cow is worshipped on the first day of Vaishakha when, it is believed, Brahma created the cow. The horns are painted yellow or saffron and the cow is bathed by milkmen.

In Tamil Nadu, the day after Pongal (or Sankranti, 14 January) is Mattu (cow) Pongal, when the cow is washed, her horns painted and she is worshipped in gratitude and reverence.

Godana or gifting a cow is an act of great religious merit. It is an essential part of the death ceremonies and may be performed whenever possible and affordable.

## Panchagavya

Panchagavya—the five products of the cow, including cow's milk, curds, ghee (clarified butter), urine and dung—is purificatory and medicinal. Every produce of the cow is used beneficially in Indian culture. Panchagavya is used in religious rites, as a medicine and in every aspect of life. Milk is lauded for its sattvik qualities. Butter is churned from the milk and then clarified into ghee, which is used in all rituals involving the sacred fire and for preparing the sacred food offered to the gods, including the ritual prasad and sweets at temples and during festivals. Cow dung has several uses: as a fertilizer for the field, as a disinfectant in homes where it is spread over the floor, and as fuel for the kitchen and the sacred fire. Modern science has confirmed that cow dung smoke is an excellent disinfectant and anti-pollutant. The cow's urine is used in rituals, as a medicine and insecticide.

### The Cow in Ancient Europe and Egypt

Ancient Egypt had several cow deities: Nut, the sky goddess; Mehueret, the flood; Hesat whose milk was called the 'beer of Hesat'; Bata, the goddess of fertility, who was a deity of Upper Egypt or Sudan, which had a special relationship with cows; and Hathor, the daughter of Ra, who had the horns of a cow and carried the sun's disc between them.

There was a European parallel in the economic importance of cows. The Greeks named Europe after Europa, once a Phoenician maiden desired by Zeus whom Hera turned into a cow and chased westwards.

### Contemporary Status

The cow is a symbol of health and abundance, and its image is used everywhere—from temples to images in advertisements.

The cow holds a special place in the Indian Constitution which recommends the banning of cow slaughter. However, this has to be implemented by the states, some of which have not done so. Further, only milch cows are protected in many states. Once it stops giving milk, its killing is permitted. Cow slaughter is banned in Nepal, once a Hindu kingdom.

In many cities cows roam free, causing traffic jams. When cows stop giving milk, some owners abandon them, letting them go on the streets. This way, they avoid both the expense of feeding them as well as the sin of killing a cow, which would be her fate if sold.

Cow worship often carries into politics, with the Hindutva parties supporting the ban on cow slaughter and other objecting, pandering to the minority vote.

Cows are maintained by several temples to enable the worshippers to earn merit by feeding the cows. The cow is worshipped on specific days, such as the Pongal or harvest festival in Tamil Nadu, during gau-poojas and wedding and death ceremonies, when one may even gift a cow and calf.

Today the reverence for the cow is expressed, unfortunately, by intensive milk farming by the dairy industry, with cattle grazing a major occupation. India is the world's largest producer of milk and an exporter of milk. However, this has worked to the detriment of the cow which is injected with oxytocin to make her produce more milk while her calf, especially if it is male, is taken away from her.

There are more than 200 million cattle in India, more than any other country in the world. In order to increase milk production, male calves are often either abandoned or suffocated or just allowed to starve to death while the mother's milk production is increased through injections of oxytocin.

Cows produce less that 50 per cent of India's milk. The buffalo produces more milk with a higher fat content, is valued by Indians for the thicker and larger quantity of yoghurt, butter and ghee, all essential parts of the Indian cuisine, it produces. However, cow's milk is considered to be healthier and more easily digested.

The cow is also protected for producing male calves, which, as adult bullocks, become tractor, thresher and transport vehicles for most Indians. Actually the prohibition against beef includes the flesh of bulls and bullocks also, but only the cow is regarded as sacred, because she can produce the other two.

Old cows that can no longer give milk are required to be cared for till their death in pinjrapoles, retirement homes for cattle, maintained by Hindu and Jain religious trusts, temples and individuals. Where there are no pinjrapoles, cows are abandoned and left to fend for themselves—they generally survive by rummaging through dustbins—till they die.

The Constitution of India says that cow slaughter should be banned, yet very few states have banned the slaughter of cows. Cows are killed for their skin, which is exported in large quantities. As a result of the limited market for its flesh, beef is the cheapest meat in India. As the best market for beef is in the state of Kerala, where non-Hindus comprise 44 per cent of the population, cattle are trucked for several days, without food or water, heaped and crowded into trucks meant for six animals but carrying between thirty and sixty cattle till they reach their destination in this state. Many are smuggled over the border to Bangladesh. Many are badly hurt and maimed, while the lucky ones die before they reach the slaughter house. There are an estimated 30,000 illegal slaughter houses all over India which operate in filthy surroundings, using the cruel halal system of slaughter carried out by Muslims who are not banned from killing cows.

The leather industry is also a big consumer of cattle skin, with India exporting cattle skin worth nearly Rs 100 billion ($ 2 billion) annually.

Thus, in spite of the Constitutional protection promised to the cow, it is still butchered for its skin and meat, and over-milked in its lifetime.

〜

# Crane

| | | |
|---|---|---|
| Scientific Name | : | *Grus antigone* Linn |
| Common Names | : | Sarus crane |
| | | Saarus, Sras (Hindi) |
| | | Saarus kokku (Tamil) |
| | | Sarasah (Sanskrit) |
| Distribution | : | North and central India |
| | | (especially the Gangetic plains) |

With its long black neck and black head contrasting a white body, and the scarlet mop atop its head, like a divine blessing, the crane is a symbol of love, fidelity, long life and marital bliss. Its long life span, averaging eighty years, together with the fact that the same pair mates every year, and that it follows the same long path to and from the subcontinent, has contributed to create its mystique.

*A crane in a Kangra painting*

The birds fly into India every winter and are considered to be reincarnated beings who return to help other souls achieve enlightenment. They are regarded as a good omen for crops in north India and farmers encourage them to nest in their fields.

## Ramayana

When Valmiki, the author of the *Ramayana*, saw a hunter kill a pair of mating cranes, he cursed the hunter with disquiet and unease for the rest of his life and was then inspired to write the epic *Ramayana*, celebrating the true love of Rama and Sita. Unlike other kings of yore, Rama had only one wife and remained faithful to her all his life, resulting in his image as the perfect man. The fidelity of the sarus crane is held up as an image to be replicated.

The sarus crane is depicted beautifully in Kangra paintings. The birds fly in long rows and love the rain—this is lovingly reproduced by Kangra artists.

## Buddhism

According to Buddhist tradition, sarus cranes arrive at exactly the same day every year, fly three times in a clockwise direction, around the monastery that stands on a hill above their marsh, before they settle in Bhutan to roost for the winter. Their arrival is awaited and celebrated by the monks

Bagalamukhi is a crane-headed Buddhist goddess of black magic and poison who, when invoked, eradicates the troubles of her devotees.

*Bagalamukhi*

## Ecological Role and Current Status

The sarus crane is found in freshwater marshes and plains. It is very large in size, about 156 cm in length. The male is larger than the female, attaining a maximum height of approximately 200 cm with a wingspan of 250 cm, making the crane the world's tallest flying bird.

Adult birds are grey, with red heads and long dark pointed bills. They fly with their long necks kept straight and the black wing tips visible. Their long red or pink legs trail behind them. Young birds are brown. They usually live in small groups. Sarus cranes forage while walking in shallow water or in fields, probing the ground for insects with their long bills. They are omnivorous, and eat insects, aquatic plants and animals, crustaceans, seeds and berries, small vertebrates and invertebrates.

The birds breed throughout the year, nesting on the ground, each female laying two to three eggs. Both the male and female take turns sitting on the nest, but the male is the main protector. Sarus cranes mate for life.

The Indian population of sarus cranes is less than 10,000 birds, and their survival is under threat, caused by habitat destruction, hunting and environmental pollution. Diseases from other species are also life-threatening for the cranes.

~

# Crocodile

| Scientific Name | : | *Crocodylus palustris* |
|---|---|---|
| Common Names | : | Indian crocodile |
| | | Mugger (Hindi) |
| | | Mudalai (Tamil) |
| | | Makarah (Sanskrit) |
| Distribution | : | Throughout India |

The makara or crocodile is one of the ashtanidhi—the eight symbols of prosperity—and its head, with garlands emerging on either side, is called the kirtimukha (face of glory). It is a symbol that keeps away the evil eye and evil vibrations, hence its use as a decorative element in temples and homes, especially above doorways and on pillars.

*Makara*

In literature, makara refers to a crocodile, but is often depicted as mythical sea-monster that somewhat resembles a crocodile, probably representing man's fear of the sea.

### Gajendra Moksha

The crocodile features in the famous legend of Gajendra moksha in the *Srimad Bhagavatam*.

A gandharva named Hoohoo had been cursed by sage Devala, for playing with apsaras in the water in the presence of the sage, to become a crocodile. He caught hold of the foot of Gajendra, the elephant king, till lord Vishnu killed the crocodile and released the elephant. Released from Devala's curse, the crocodile-gandharva fell at Lord Vishnu's feet and returned to heaven.

## Zodiac Sign

Makara also represents the sign of Capricorn in the Hindu zodiac.

Makara Sankranti is a very important Hindu festival, celebrating the sun's entrance into the northern hemisphere and the tenth house of the zodiac (Capricorn or Makara) on 14 January. The passing of winter is celebrated in various ways in different parts of the country, the most important being in Tamil Nadu where it is celebrated as Pongal. Rice, lentils and jaggery are cooked in a clay stove outside the house and offered to the sun before it is eaten by the members of the family. The next day is Mattu Pongal, when the cows and bullocks are worshipped as a thanksgiving for helping the farmer. In Assam it is called Bhogali Bihu when prayers are offered to the god of fire to mark the end of harvest. Kites are flown in Gujarat.

## Bengal

In many parts of the two districts of North and South Twenty-four Parganas of West Bengal, the Gajan festival commences with the worship of the crocodile of Shiva. A huge crocodile is made out of clay, finished and plastered, with scales made out of tamarind seeds and its mouth smeared with vermillion. A clay model of a child is placed before the crocodile. It is made when the festival commences and is believed to protect children and confer merit on women.

## Goa

The crocodile has been worshipped for centuries in Goa, a practice that is believed to owe its origin to the flooding of the paddy fields by sea water which would destroy the crops. The villagers decided to pacify the sea by worshipping the crocodiles that lived in the sea at that time. Early Portuguese documents mention that at the time of Muslim occupation, forty years before the Portuguese conquest, the entire island was infested with enormous animals that they called 'Lizards of Water'. The mugger crocodile is found in the Cumbarjua canal of Goa. In Bhoma and Durbate Wadi in Ponda taluka, along the canal, the local people perform mange thapnee, worship of the crocodile.

The new-moon day in the month of Pausha (according to the Hindu calendar) coincides with the commencement of the threshing of the harvested paddy crop. Farmhands assemble on the bunds separating the paddy fields, step into the waterlogged paddy fields and scoop out the silt, which they fashion into crocodiles on the bunds. The eyes are marked with clam shells, teeth with small and straight sticks. A little hole is scooped out on the back of the mud crocodile and a live chick placed within and closed with a coconut shell. The crocodile is decorated with flowers and vermillion and a garhane, or community prayer, takes place. Puffed rice and jaggery are offered to the crocodile deity and then shared by his worshippers. In Bhoma, the crocodile is worshipped with a goat sacrifice. The goat is taken along the bunds in a ceremonial procession and then sacrificed. Its meat is shared by the worshippers. The crocodile, which still in habits the Cumbarjua canal, continues to be worshipped by the local people, especially the youth (Alvares 2002).

*Vehicle*

The animal is sometimes associated with Kamadeva, the god of love. Hence his wife Rati carries it wherever she goes.

The crocodile is depicted as the vehicle or vahana of goddess Ganga, the river Ganga. The entrances to the Kushana temples of Mathura are flanked by Ganga on the crocodile and Yamuna on the tortoise. Later,

*Ganga*

the crocodile also became the vehicle of the river goddess Narmada.

Varuna, an ancient Rig Vedic deity, who was both asura and deva and the king of the sky, becomes, in later literature, the god of the ocean. He rides the makara or crocodile. Sometimes the makara may be depicted as a dolphin, but it commonly refers to the crocodile.

*Varuna, the Ocean*

Shukra or Venus also rides a crocodile.

## Jainism

The symbol of Suvidhinatha (Pushpadanta), the ninth Jaina Tirthankara, is a crocodile.

## Ecological Role and Current Status

The Indian saltwater crocodile or mugger is among the largest of the world's crocodilians. Another Indian species is the gharial, which has a long, slim nose which curves upwards, making the makara of Indian art a cross between the two species— a mugger with a gharial's nose (resembling an elephant's trunk)—and thus a monster.

A crocodile is any species belonging to the family Crocodylidae, which

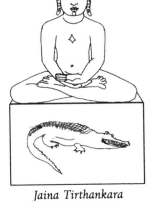

*Jaina Tirthankara Pushpadanta or Suvidhinatha*

includes both muggers and gharials. Crocodiles are large aquatic reptiles that live in the tropics. They prefer freshwater habitats like rivers, lakes, wetlands, but are also found in brackish water. They feed on vertebrates like fish, reptiles, and mammals, and sometimes on invertebrates like molluscs and crustaceans. They are ambush hunters, waiting for fish or land animals to come close, and then rushing out to attack. As cold-blooded predators, they are lethargic, surviving long periods without food, and rarely need to go hunting. Crocodiles are top predators in their environment and have been observed attacking and killing sharks.

Crocodiles are of ancient lineage, and are believed to have changed little since the time of the dinosaurs. Size greatly varies between species, from the dwarf crocodile to the enormous saltwater crocodile. Large species can be over 5 m long and weigh 1,200 kg.

~

# Crow

| Scientific Name | : | *Corvus splendens* Viellot |
|---|---|---|
| Common Names | : | House crow |
| | | Kowwa (Hindi) |
| | | Kakam (Tamil) |
| | | Kakah (Sanskrit) |
| Distribution | : | Throughout India |

The house crow occupies a special place in Hindu religious rituals. It is usually identified with departed souls or ancestors.

Throughout the country, several communities observe the ritual of pinda pradana (offering of cooked rice balls) to the crow during ancestral worship.

The crow is supposed to be a connection between the living world and the world of the dead. It is believed that dead souls will take food and offerings through a variety of crows called bali kakah. Every year, people whose parents or relatives have died will offer food to crows as well as to cows on the shraddha day. This is called pindadana.

In traditional Hindu homes, crows are offered a handful of rice before any meal. This is regarded as akin to feeding one's ancestors.

The bird's black colour and unattractive appearance has also associated it with Alakshmi, goddess of ill luck.

The first day of Dipavali in Nepal is celebrated as Kag Tihar or Puja. Good mimics caw like crows till the birds gather around and are fed by the local people.

### Vehicle

The crow is the vehicle of Shani (Saturn), one of the navagrahas or nine planets of Hindu astrology. Shani protects the home against thefts, a quality for which the crow is known. By sitting on the bird, Shani controls possible thefts.

### Buddhism

*Shani*

The Dharmapala (protector of dharma) Mahakala is represented by a crow in one of his earthly forms. Avalokiteshvara, who is believed to be reincarnated on earth as the Dalai Lama, is often closely associated with the crow because it is said that when the first Dalai Lama was born, robbers attacked the family home. The parents fled and were unable to get to the infant Lama in time. When they returned the next morning, expecting the worst, they found their home untouched, and a pair of crows caring for the child.

It is believed that crows heralded the birth of the First, Seventh, Eighth, Twelfth and Fourteenth Lamas, the last being the current Dalai Lama, Tenzin Gyatso. Crows are mentioned often in Buddhism, especially Tibetan disciplines.

### Ecological Role and Current Status

The crow is a remarkably intelligent creature, and the hero of children's stories from the *Panchatantra* to *Aesop's Fables*. The story of the Crow and the Water Jug—wherein the thirsty bird fills the jug with stones to raise the water level—is just one of the many stories that indicate human appreciation of the crow's intelligence.

Some species of crows are able to manufacture and use their own tools in their day-to-day search for food, including dropping seeds into a heavy trafficked street and waiting for a car to crush them open. They use a large variety of tools, plucking, smoothing and bending twigs and grass stems to procure a variety of food. Research has shown that crows are able to outsmart apes when it comes to finding a way to access food.

Their natural enemies are raptors, who soar high above the trees and hunt on bright, sunny days when there is a sharp contrast between light and shade. Crows manoeuvere themselves through the dappled shades of the trees, where their black colour makes them invisible to their enemies flying above.

~

## Cuckoo

| | | |
|---|---|---|
| Scientific Name | : | *Eudynamys scolopaceus* Linn |
| Common Names | : | Koel (Hindi) |
| | | Kuyil (Tamil) |
| | | Kokila (Sanskrit) |
| Distribution | : | Throughout India. |

The cuckoo is a symbol of fertility, fun and good times.

The bird is the vehicle of Jayakara, the companion of Kamadeva, god of love, an Indian Cupid. Jayakara rides a chariot drawn by cuckoos, is white and carries a garland of flowers, an arrow, a wine glass and bow.

*Jayakara*

The cuckoo is sacred to the Lepchas of Sikkim, whose agricultural calendar is decided by the cuckoo. The arrival of the bird is celebrated with song and dance, for they are the messengers of the mother goddess.

*Ecological Role and Current Status*

The cuckoo family includes the koels. Most cuckoos are insectivorous, eating caterpillars and other hairy insects. Several koels feed on fruit, but they are not exclusively frugivores. The parasitic koels and channel-billed cuckoos consume mainly fruit.

The bird is commonly seen all over India, especially during the rains. It is an important pest controller for the farmer. Unfortunately, the use of pesticides to control insects has driven away the cuckoo from several places.

~

# Deer

| | | |
|---|---|---|
| Scientific name | : | *Axis axis* ErxLeben |
| Common names | : | Chital/hiran (Hindi) |
| | | Pulli maan (Tamil) |
| | | Harin (Sanskrit) |
| Distribution | : | Throughout India |

Deer are distinct from antelopes because of their horns, which do not have a born core. Males shed their horns every autumn and regrow them in spring, while females have no horns, making the animal vulnerable to predators.

There are several species of deer in India. Of these, only the spotted deer is regarded as sacred. The spotted deer is the most common member of the deer family and appears in innumerable stories in Indian mythology. It is often referred to as the golden deer in literature. Being a gentle and friendly animal, it appears in several stories.

## Ramayana

The spotted deer plays an important role in the *Ramayana*. Ravana, king of demons, decides to abduct the beautiful Sita, wife of Rama, prince of Ayodhya, in revenge for Rama's treatment of his sister. Ravana makes Maricha, his demon minister, transform himself into a golden spotted deer. Attracted by the beautiful animal, Sita desires the deer and sends her husband Rama after the animal. As Rama follows it, he realizes that its disappearance and reappearance indicates that it is a demon and shoots an arrow at the deer. As Maricha is dying, he calls out for Lakshmana, Rama's younger brother, in Rama's voice. Sita forces

*Rama and the deer Maricha*

Lakshmana to leave in search of his brother, thus leaving the way open for her abduction by Ravana, king of Lanka.

## Mahabharata

In the *Mahabharata*, Pandu, king of the Kurus, kills a stag mounting a doe. As it is a great sin to kill any creature during copulation, the stag curses the king with instant death if he touches any of his wives. Pandu's wives agree to remain celibate, but the king could not contain himself and embraced his wife Madri, leading to his death and subsequently Madri's by sati. This paves the way for the coronation of his blind brother Dhritharashtra, whose 100 sons, the Kauravas, are determined to prevent the legitimate heirs, their cousins, the sons of Pandu, from regaining their patrimony. This leads to the Kurukshetra war and the annihilation of the Kurus.

## Shaivism

Lord Shiva took the form of a spotted deer while in the Shleshmantak forest in Nepal. There is a shrine dedicated to his consort Parvati, as Vatsyaleshvari, who encountered and married the divine deer.

Shiva is also depicted as wearing the skin of a spotted deer, indicating the yogi's mastery over the mind, which is as fast-moving as the deer.

Sanyasis and ascetics sit on a deer skin mat during meditation. The idea is that the deer skin will calm the mind. However, it is emphasized that the deer should have died a natural death, otherwise the stress and sorrow of its death will be transferred to the ascetic.

## Buddhism

The spotted deer is sacred to Buddhists too, for the Buddha's first sermon took place in the deer park at Sarnath. Thus the Buddhist Wheel of Righteousness (dharma chakra) is flanked by a male and female deer. In the tankha paintings made by Mahayana Buddhist monks, the four entrances to the Buddhist wheel are guarded by deer, making the whole represent the deer park at Sarnath, where the Buddha preached his first sermon. In fact, the deer has a very special place in Buddhism, for its gentleness and kindness represent those qualities that the Buddha was trying to emphasize.

There is a Jataka story about one of the Buddha's former lives in which he was born as a golden deer, with eyes like jewels, silver antlers, a red mouth and diamond-like hooves. He was the ruler of the Banyan Deer, while another herd nearby was known as the Branch Deer. The kingdom was ruled by a king who loved hunting deer and eating venison. Since he wanted all his countrymen to hunt with him, they built an enclosure and drove the two herds of deer within. Every few days either he or his cook would go and kill two or three deer for meat. The deer were terrified whenever they saw the men arrive, but were helpless. Finally, the chief of the Banyan Deer suggested to the chief of the Branch Deer that each herd would send one animal every day, which would lie down before the hunter and place its head on a stone. The king or cook would get their deer that way and fewer animals would suffer. The king agreed and granted the two chief stags their lives.

One day it was the turn of a Branch Doe who had just given birth to a fawn. She begged her chief to let her live till her fawn could survive without her, but her ruler refused to change the rules. If it was her turn, she had to die. In despair, she turned to the ruler of the Banyan Deer, who offered to take her place.

The next day the cook was surprised to see the royal stag and informed the king who went down to investigate the phenomenon. The king asked the stag why he had come when he had been granted his life. The stag explained that he

*Shleshmantak deer dance*

had come to prevent a double tragedy in the death of the doe and her fawn. As he could not ask any other deer to go in the doe's place, he decided to offer his life instead. Thereupon, the king granted both the stag and the doe their lives and promised to never again hunt deer either in the park or in the forest or anywhere else in his kingdom.

Avalokiteshvara, the Bodhisattva of Compassion, wears a deer skin over his shoulder. Buddhist monks, like Hindu ascetics, may sit on a mat made of the skin of a deer which died a natural death.

## Jainism

The emblem of the eleventh Tirthankara Shantinatha is the deer.

### Ecological Role and Current Status

*Shantinatha*

The spotted deer is the most common deer species in India. It has a reddish-fawn coat, marked with white spots, and a white underbelly. Its antlers are three-pronged and curved, extending to 75 cm, and are shed annually. It lives for twenty to thirty years.

Deer eat grass and vegetation, as well as their shed antlers, which are an added source of nutrients. By grazing on the grass and eating green leaves, the deer ensure their regeneration.

An interesting relationship has been observed between the spotted deer and the grey langur (*Presbytis entellus*), a leaf-eating monkey of South Asia. Spotted deer benefit from the langurs' good eyesight and ability to watch from a height, from treetops. Langurs raise an alarm when predators approach, thereby giving deer time to escape. For the langurs, the deer's superior sense of smell warns them of possible predators. Thus it is common to see langurs and spotted deer foraging together. The deer also eat fruit, such as the *Terminalia bellerica*, dropped by the langurs from trees. Alarm calls of either species indicate the presence of a predator, such as a tiger or leopard.

Deer are the basic food for the carnivores, a sad role assigned to them by nature.

# Dog

| | | |
|---|---|---|
| Scientific Name | : | *Canis lupus familiaris* Linn |
| Common Names | : | Kutta (Hindi) |
| | | Naay (Tamil) |
| | | Kukkurah (Sanskrit) |
| Distribution | : | Throughout India |

At Bhimbetka, in the Raisen district of Madhya Pradesh, prehistoric paintings (7000 BCE) of the Upper Paleolithic, Mesolithic and Chalcolithic periods reveal several figures of dogs, including one on a leash, led by a man. The domestication of the dog and the companionship between the animal and man obviously go back very early on the Indian subcontinent.

Terracotta figurines of the Harappan period (circa 3000 BCE) include dogs wearing collars and a collared dog begging on its haunches, obviously a result of training.

The earliest mention of the dog is in the Rig Veda (X.108.1–11), where Indra's divine dog Sarama pursued and recovered the cows either belonging to or stolen by the Panis, enemies of the Aryans, who had hidden the cows in the netherworld of Patala. The conversation between Sarama and the Panis brings out several interesting facts: that the dog was a herder, as kept by pastoral tribes; that the dog was deeply loyal, and refused to be bribed into changing camps. The Rig Veda (VII.55.1–5) refers to the dog as Vastospati, the presiding deity of the house, the guard of the home.

The Rig Veda (X.14.10–12) goes on to identify Sarama's children, the Sarameyas, with Yama, the god of death, an association reflected in the later *Mahabharata* story of Yudhishthira's ascent to heaven. The Sarameyas were ferocious, with four eyes each, who looked on men and guarded the path to Yamaloka. The *Atharva Veda* (VIII.1.9) calls the Sarameyas Shyama (the dark one) and Shabala (spotted), the latter term also used in the

Rig Veda. In fact many of the later associations of the dog can be traced back to the Vedas, for the *Atharva Veda* ((XI.2.30) describes Rudra, a form of Shiva, as surrounded by dogs with large mouths, who make a terrible noise and are saluted. This association is carried over to Bhairava, a later aspect of Shiva belonging to the post-Vedic period.

Sarama also symbolized Ushas, the dawn, while the cows were the rays of the sun that had been carried away by the night. Much later, in the *Bhagavata Purana*, Sarama is described as one of the thirteen daughters of Daksha. She married sage Kashyapa and became the mother of all carnivores.

Indian dogs were used in wars and for hunting. Herodotus (1.192) mentions a Persian satrap, Tritantaechmus of Babylon, who assigned the revenue of four large villages for the care of his Indian hounds. Herodotus also mentions that Xerxes I (486–465 BCE) used Indian dogs in his army when he went to war against the Greeks. Aelian (8.1) says that Alexander of Macedonia received a gift of four fighting dogs from India (Debroy 2008).

## Ramayana

The breeding of dogs in the north-west of the subcontinent since Vedic times continued in the epic period. In Valmiki's *Ramayana* (I.70.20), the maternal grandfather of Bharata, Rama's brother, was the king of Kekeya, now western Punjab. His daughter Kaikeyi was responsible for Rama's banishment into the forest. When Bharata returns to his father's kingdom at Ayodhya (in present-day Uttar Pradesh) on the urgent summons of the minister, his maternal grandfather sends rich gifts of gold coins, horses and dogs that were 'gigantic, with sharp teeth, as powerful as tigers, who were bred in the palace'.

The *Ramayana* prohibits the eating of dog meat and a Brahmin who beats a dog is punished.

*The Manu Samhita*

The *Manu Samhita* (3.164), which belongs to about 200–400 CE, mentions the breeding of sporting dogs. Obviously this was a very old and continuing tradition, although such breeders are also called Chandalas (outcastes) by the *Manu Samhita*. Kings accompanied by hunting dogs became a common feature of later literature. Apparently, north-west India (present-day Pakistan) bred and exported dogs that were known for their fighting skills and courage. Thus canines in India were companions, herders, watchdogs, hunters and fighters from very early times.

Since this was obviously a common profession in the modern regions of West Punjab and the North-West Frontier Province, one wonders whether their stigmatization as outcastes prompted the conversion to Islam of the dog breeders. The breeding of dogs for fighting and bear-baiting continues in contemporary Pakistan.

*Mahabharata*

The *Mahabharata* begins and ends with a dog. The epic begins with the story of Janmejaya and his three brothers who were going to perform a sacrifice to destroy all snakes, when a dog appeared. The brothers beat up the dog who went crying to its mother. The mother dog came and asked Janmejaya why her son had been beaten up, when he had committed no crime. As Janmejaya and his brothers had no explanation and were forced to keep silent, the mother dog cursed Janmejaya that a great tragedy would strike him.

The dog is also the important figure on which the *Mahabharata* ends. According to the 'Mahaprasthanika parva', after installing Parikshit as the king of Hastinapura and Vajra as king of Indraprastha, the Pandavas decided to leave the world. First they went east where Arjuna abandoned his weapons, then south and then west to Dwarka, which was now under water. Finally, they turned northwards, where they crossed the Himalayas, the desert and Mount Meru. As they walked, a dog accompanied them. Along the way, Draupadi and four Pandava brothers died one after another, leaving Yudhishthira and the dog. Indra appeared and offered to take Yudhishthira to heaven in his chariot. First Yudhishthira asked that his brothers and Draupadi should be taken too, and Indra promised that he would meet them in heaven. Yudhishthira alone would be permited to enter with his physical body. Yudhishthira wanted the faithful dog to accompany him to heaven, but Indra demurred, exhorting the king to give up the dog. Yudhishthira refused to leave behind one who had sought refuge with him, as such behaviour was un-Aryan and equivalent to the sin of killing a Brahmin. He preferred the animal's company to the pleasures of heaven. Seeing his adherence to righteousness, Indra was pleased and praised Yudhishthira. Then Dharma, the god of death Yama who was also Yudhishthira's father, emerged from the dog, whose form he had taken, echoing the Vedic Yama and his dogs. The dog had been used to test Yudhishthira, who could now proceed to heaven to be united with his brothers and spouse.

Before the commencement of the Kurukshetra War and, more importantly, the Bhagavat Gita, Arjuna prays to Durga, who is addressed as Kokamukha, or dog-faced. This is a rare instance of a goddess with a canine association, although the *Matsya Purana* (179.17) mentions the creation by Shiva of the Sapta Matrikas or seven mothers, one of whom is Kukkuti, named after a dog.

The *Mahabharata* and all later literature also prohibit the eating of dog meat, the consumption of which makes a person into a Chandala (outcaste).

### Bhairava

Bhairava, the wandering sanyasi, a form of Lord Shiva, is usually accompanied by a dog or rides a dog who is his vahana. Just as many bairagis (sanyasis) keep dogs as their companions,

Bhairava is a bairagi, a sanyasi and wanderer, whose companion is the dog. Feeding and taking care of dogs is believed to be a way of showing one's devotion to Lord Bhairava. In the Tantric tradition, there are sixty-four Bhairavas or Kshetrapalas, each with a dog companion in a different position. Of these, the dog is the vehicle of Vatuka Bhairava and Kala Bhairava (of Nepal).

*Bhairava*

In Nepal, the second day of Dipavali is reserved for Kukkur Tihar, when all dogs—even street dogs—are decorated with big red tikas (vermillion) on their foreheads, garlanded, fed lavishly and worshipped with arati. The dogs are worshipped as the vehicle of Bhairava, in which role they also guard homes from theft and destruction.

In the Varahishvara Temple at Damal in Kanchipuram district of Tamil Nadu, the outer mandapam, built in the Vijayanagara period, is supported by pillars depicting the sixty-four Bhairavas, each accompanied by a dog.

Bhairava is also regarded as the god of veterinarians.

### Dattatreya

Dattatreya, son of sage Atri and Anasuya, is looked upon as the incarnation of the holy Trinity of Brahma, Vishnu and Shiva. According to the *Bhagavata Purana* (1.3.6–13), Dattatreya was the sixth (out of twenty-four) incarnations of Vishnu. He is usually accompanied by four dogs, which symbolize the four Vedas and his complete mastery over them. Dattatreya lived as an outcaste and is popularly worshipped in Maharashtra and Karnataka.

According to the *Brahmanda Purana*, a hermit named Ani Mandavya was meditating under a vow of silence when some robbers, pursued by the king's guards, dropped their loot beside him and ran away. The guards, finding the looted items beside the yogi, dragged him off to prison, where the king ordered his death by impalement. Meanwhile Silavati, a devoted housewife, was carrying her husband Ugratapas, who was a leper, to a brothel, as per his wish. They passed the impaled Ani Mandavya, who was still

*Dattatreya*

alive, though impaled. Seeing the devotion of a good woman, Ani Mandavya cursed Ugratapas to die before sunrise. However, Silavati was a siddhi and used her power to prevent the sun from rising. Then Brahma, Vishnu and Shiva asked Anasuya to help them solve the problem with Silavati, who was preventing the sun from rising. They succeeded by promising her that Ugratapas would not die, and that, as per Silavati's request, the three gods would be born as her sons: Vishnu as Dattatreya, Shiva as Durvasa and Brahma as Chandra. Dattatreya grew up as a hermit with wonderful siddha powers.

The association of the four dogs with the Vedas goes back to the story of Adi Shankara who, one day, was going with his disciples to bathe in the sacred river Ganga at Varanasi, when a Chandala appeared before him, holding four dogs on chains. Shankara asked the Chandala to move aside. Thereupon, the Chandala asked the great philosopher, 'Who are you asking to step aside? The soul, which is all-pervading, pure and inactive? Or the body, which has no will of its own? How is my body different from yours? Is there any difference between a Brahmin and a Chandala? And you call yourself a learned man!' Adi Shankara fell at the Chandala's feet and hailed him as his master. The Chandala and the dogs disappeared, and Shankara realized that it was Lord Shiva himself, accompanied by the four Vedas, who had come to teach him a lesson.

## Khandoba

Khandoba is another incarnation of Lord Shiva and the patron deity of the Marathas, especially the warrior, farming and herding castes, including the Bhonsle clan to which Shivaji belonged. He rides a bull or a horse and is accompanied by a dog. He has several names: Khanderao, Khandariya Mahadev, Malhari Martand and Martanda Bhairava, which explain his canine connection. He kills the demons Mani and Malla with the help of his spouse Mhalsa and his canine companion. Mani and Malla received the boon of invincibility from Brahma and were harassing the rishis. Approached by the sapta rishis (seven sages), Shiva assumed the form of Martanda Bhairava, or Khandoba, and fought the demons alongside his wives Mhalsa or Parvati and Banai or Ganga. However, even as they killed the demon and his blood flowed, each drop created a new demon. Eventually, his dog swallowed all the blood and the demons were put to rest.

Khandoba was originally a folk deity, worshipped in Jejuri, Maharashtra, in the ninth–tenth centuries. Later, his story was incorporated as the 'Malhari Mahatmya' in the *Brahmanda Purana* around the fifteenth–sixteenth centuries, along with

*Khandoba*

the Sanskritization of the deity. He is also worshipped by Muslims as a Pathan called Malluka Pathan or Mallu or Ajmat Khan, with a Muslim wife and Muslim horse-keeper. Even the 'Malhari Mahatmaya' mentions that Muslims are his devotees.

*Buddhism*

Several Bodhisattvas were believed to have been born as dogs. In the *Kukkura Jataka* No. 2, the Bodhisattva lived as a dog in a cremation ground and prevented the mass slaughter of stray dogs by King Brahmadatta of Varanasi. According to the *Abhinha Jataka* No. 27, the friendship between King Brahmadatta's elephant and a stray dog was destroyed by the mahout who sold the dog to a villager. When the elephant stopped eating and bathing, the king's minister, who was a Bodhisattva, deduced the problem and a proclamation was issued for the dog. The villager released the dog, who ran back to the elephant who wept with joy and ate only after his canine friend had eaten. In the *Sunakha Jataka* No. 242, a dog who had been bought and taken away by a visitor was helped to freedom by the Boddhisattva who advised the dog to gnaw through his leash and escape to his old master. The *Maha Kanha Jataka* No. 469, *Mahabodhi Jataka* No. 528 and *Maha Ummaga Jataka* No. 546 see the dog playing major roles, while they appear in several other Jataka stories.

The Buddha himself is believed to have traversed the country accompanied by a little dog, who took on the form of a lion to scare away robbers who tried to attack the Buddha. In Tibet the dog's superiority depends on its resemblance to the Buddha's lion-dogs, while the Buddhist temples of China are guarded by statues of dogs with leonine faces.

Asanga was a Buddhist who saw a sick dog covered with maggots. Instead of removing the maggots with his hands, which would kill them, he licked the maggots off the dog's body with his tongue. Immediately, Maitreya, the future Buddha, appeared before him and carried Asanga on his shoulder. Similarly, Kukuraja was a Buddhist sage who lived in a cave in Pullahari in western Magadha, surrounded by dogs (Debroy 2008).

The cults of Shaivism, Vaishnavism and Buddhism recognized the importance of the dog, especially its loyalty, and gave the animal a superior position in life and literature.

### Zoroastrianism

Ahura Mazda declared, 'No house would stand firmly founded for me on the Ahura-created earth were there not my herd dog or house dog' (*Vendidad*, 13.49). Responsibility towards dogs is repeatedly linked with responsibility towards humans. A sick dog is to be looked after as carefully as a sick person (*Vendidad*, 13.35); a bitch in whelp as solicitously as a woman with child (*Vendidad*, 15.19); puppies are to be cared for six months, children for seven years (*Vendidad*, 15.45).

Dogs were used by the ancient Persians to dispose of the dead. The dead body was placed on a stone slab out in the open. Then a dog was brought near in order to inspect the face of the dead person, for it was believed that it had an ability to see and chase away any evil spirits that may have been associated with the corpse.

Dogs were sacred to the Roman god Mithras, of Persian origin, who was the ruling deity of the Roman emperor Julian in the fourth century CE, called the Apostate by the Christians for his Mithraism. In fact Mithraism, derived from Zoroastrianism and Buddhism, was the popular religion of the Romans till the conversion of Constantine to Christianity.

### Islam

It is incorrectly believed that dogs are shunned as dirty animals by Islam. Prophet Mohammed's injuction to wash one's hand seven times after contact with a dog's saliva had a very good reason. Rabies was rampant in medieval Arabia and, in the absence of running water and soap in the desert (the recommended first-aid for dog-bites today), washing the hands several times was the best alternative.

*Saluki*

The Koran calls the saluki, a Yemenese dog, a 'gift of Allah', 'al-hor' (the noble one) and 'al-baraha' (the blessed one). Obviously, much rereading of the Koran is required.

*Ecological Role and Current Status*

The dog is a domesticated subspecies of the wolf. The term encompasses both feral and pet varieties. The domestic dog has been (and continues to be) one of the most widely kept working and companion animals in human history. The dog has developed into hundreds of varied breeds.

Based on DNA evidence, the wolf ancestors of modern dogs diverged from other wolves about 1,00,000 years ago, and dogs were domesticated about 15,000 years ago. This date would make dogs the first species to be domesticated by humans. As humans migrated from place to place, a variety of dog forms migrated with them. Agriculture and urbanization led to an increase in the dog population and specialization of breeds, creating specialized working dogs and pets. The relationship between human beings and dogs has deep roots, with archaeological and genetic evidence indicating a time of domestication in the late Upper Paleolithic Age, between 17,000 and 14,000 years ago.

India has among the largest dog populations in the world. During the British period they were killed by shooting and, later, by the use of very cruel methods such as electrocution. The passing of the Dog Control (ABC) Rules, 2001, by the Government of India has stopped the killing of dogs by municipalities, to be replaced by spaying/neutering and vaccination. This has brought down the dog population and eliminated rabies wherever it has been carried out properly and consistently.

~

# Donkey

| | | |
|---|---|---|
| Scientific Name | : | *Equus asinus* Linn |
| Common Names | : | Gadha (Hindi) |
| | | Kaludai (Tamil) |
| | | Khara (Sanskrit) |
| Distribution | : | Throughout India |

The ass, donkey and mule have rarely been differentiated in India, although they are known to be different animals.

The donkey is the vehicle of Shitala Devi, the goddess who is invoked to ward off smallpox, even as her anger can bring it on. Shitala's Buddhist equivalent is Hariti, whose vehicle is also the donkey. Both Shitala and Hariti are propitiated with animal flesh, although animals are sacrificed in temples of Shitala while the meat alone is offered in temples of Hariti.

This is a case when the identification with a goddess has only served to hurt an animal. The hatred for Shitala, the goddess of smallpox, has been transposed onto the poor donkey.

*Shitala Devi*

*Ecological Role and Current Status*

The term 'ass' usually refers to a larger, horse-sized animal, and 'donkey' to a smaller, pony-sized one. Asses were first domesticated around 4000 BCE, at about the same time as the horse, and are found all around the world. There are several domesticated species. As 'beasts of burden', asses and donkeys have worked for humans for centuries. Donkeys have a reputation for stubbornness, but this is due to mishandling. Although they are not credited with much intelligence, donkeys are actually intelligent, cautious, friendly, playful, and eager to learn. They are often pastured or stabled with horses and ponies, and are believed to have a calming effect on nervous horses. If a donkey is introduced to a mare and foal, the foal will often turn to the donkey for support after it has been weaned from its mother.

The donkey is a much maligned animal. It is used as a beast of burden everywhere in India, especially by dhobis (washermen). It is overworked, underfed and mocked: when a man is publicly mocked by his village society, he is generally made to sit backwards on a donkey, which is then whipped to run away. Often, it is made to carry heavy bundles with its forelegs tied together to prevent it from running away.

The wild ass of the Rann of Kutch in Gujarat is a protected animal, much respected unlike its unfortunate domestic counterpart.

~

# Dove

| Scientific Name | : | *Columba livia* Gmelin |
|---|---|---|
| Common Names | : | Dove/pigeon |
| | | Kabutar (Hindi) |
| | | Puraa (Tamil) |
| | | Kapota (Sanskrit) |
| Distribution | : | Throughout India |

In the *Agni Purana* the dove is associated with Yama, the god of death.

It is believed that Shiva and Parvati live in the form of a male and a female dove, called Kapoteshvara and Kapoteshvari respectively, in the Amarnath Cave in Kashmir, where they survive even through the bitter winter cold. The Amarnath Cave, home to the ice Shivalinga is open to visitors for about two months in the year, during summer. For the rest of the year the place is uninhabitable.

Doves (or white pigeons) are released on special occasions by Hindus and Muslims. The joy of the freed birds is a blessing for the releaser.

The dove has always been a symbol of love. The loyalty of the couple to each other has made them a symbol of togetherness.

*Amarnath linga*

*Ecological Role and Current Status*

In religious parlance, the terms 'dove' and 'pigeon' are often interchanged. They are stout-bodied birds with short necks and slim bills. The species commonly referred to is the feral rock pigeon, commonly seen in many cities, while the dove is generally white in colour. The young ones are called squabs.

Pigeons and doves survive well in urban areas with human constructions where they build their nests and breed in large numbers.

~

# Eagle

| | | |
|---|---|---|
| Scientific Name | : | *Spilornis cheela* Latham |
| Common Name | : | Crested serpent eagle |
| | | Dogra cheel (Hindi) |
| | | Kalugu (Tamil) |
| | | Garuda (Sanskrit) |
| Distribution | : | Throughout India |

The eagle first appears on the obverse of a unique rhomboid seal from Mohenjo Daro, which contains a flying eagle with its head turned to a side, its wings and tail relieved with rows of deeply incised lines. Above its outstretched wings are two snakes.

The eagle is a bird of prey or 'raptor', a meat-eating bird that uses its strong feet, talons and hooked beaks to catch and kill its prey.

The eagle fascinated the ancient world. The visual appeal of a huge bird flying towards the sun, the golden reflection of the solar orb, the formations of the flock, and the total fearlessness of the big birds as they catch their prey—poisonous snakes or small mammals—added to their mystique. The ability of the birds to spot their prey from great heights and their flight directly towards their goal in one swoop has made them objects of admiration.

In Sanskrit literature, there is much confusion about the birds of prey, particularly the Brahmani kite, eagle and vulture. Each is identified with one or another of the great mythological birds such as Garuda, Jatayu, Sampati and others. To identify the correct bird with his mythological character, it is important to see what literature had to say about each.

The eagle, called Garutman ('the winged one') and Suparna ('beautiful wings'), first appears as an associate of Indra (Rig Veda, I.164.46) and the sun (Rig Veda, X.149.3) and is associated with Vishnu later, in the *Atharva Veda* (XIII.2.31). He is called Garuda only in the *Taittiriya Aranyaka* (X.16). Garuda could visit the heavens, the realm of the gods, carrying them on his wide outstretched wings. It is this ability that was later transferred to Garuda when he became the vehicle of Vishnu. He is suvarnakaya (golden-bodied), gaganeshvara (lord of the sky), khageshvara (lord of the birds) and uragashana (devourer of snakes). Indian literature is full of the conflict between the eagle and the snake. The antagonism between the two is derived from nature and immortalized in literature.

## Garuda

Garuda is the greatest of the eagles and the visual impact of the bird soaring in the sky has impacted several civilizations. The bald eagle is the crest of the American government, while Garuda himself is the symbol of the Indonesian government.

One of the most important aspects of the eagle is his enmity towards the snake. This antagonism is the basis of the stories of Garuda, the vehicle of Lord Vishnu the Preserver.

Garuda

In the *Ramayana*, when Rama and Lakshmana were rendered unconscious by Indrajit's snake arrows, Garuda, the king of birds, approached them. Immediately, the arrows that had become snakes and bound the brothers uncoiled and fled. Garuda was so powerful that his mere touch of the princes healed all their wounds, while their intelligence, energy, vigour, memory, good looks and virtues doubled. Garuda warns them against trusting a rakshasa on the battlefield, for the latter fight with duplicitous means.

The 'Adiparva' of the *Mahabharata* (I.20–34) gives a long story to account for this enmity. Kadru and Vinata were two of the daughters of Daksha and wives of the divine progenitor Kashyapa. Vinata laid two eggs, neither of which hatched. In haste, she broke it open and out came a half-developed being Aruna, who later became the charioteer of the sun god Surya. Aruna cursed his mother for his misfortune, saying that she would have to serve as a slave to her co-wife Kadru.

Kadru was the mother of a thousand snakes or Nagas. Kadru and Vinata had a wager regarding the colour of the tail of the divine horse Uchchaishravas. Kadru cheated by making her snake sons cover the horse's tail so that it looked black. Vinata lost the bet and had to become Kadru's slave.

Vinata allowed the second egg to hatch in its own time, and Garuda was born in due course. When Garuda entered the world, he was fully grown, possessed of extraordinary power and illumined all directions by his brilliance. His body expanded and touched the sky and the mountains trembled as he spread his wings. His lustre was so brilliant that the gods mistook him for Agni and worshipped him. He was named Garuda, meaning one who soars in the sky.

Garuda wanted to free his mother, the price of whose freedom was the nectar of immortality, amrita, for his half-brothers, the snakes. He procured the amrita, fighting the gods, without drinking any himself, and his mother was set free, but Indra, king of the heavens, took it away before the snakes could drink it. Since he did not drink the amrita, in spite of having it in his possession, Garuda was granted a boon by Indra, by which the snakes became his food.

Vishnu was very pleased with Garuda's unselfish motive in freeing his mother and giving up the nectar of immortality. He asked the bird to choose two boons, to which Garuda replied that he wanted to 'stay above' Vishnu and to be immortal, even without the amrita. Granting Garuda's wishes, Vishnu asked the bird to become his vehicle and to sit above him, on his flag staff.

There is a clear hint of the assimilation of Garuda on fairly equal terms although later, the worship of Vishnu became more popular than the cult of Garuda. There is always an undercurrent of conflict between Garuda and Vishnu over snakes and an open one between Garuda and the Nagas. When Vishnu gives the snake Sumukha shelter, Garuda challenges Vishnu, who eventually throws the snake over Garuda's neck. His antagonism towards and control of snakes has given him the title Vinayaka (which he shares with Ganesha) as the remover of obstacles, snakes being the obstacles in this case. There is a continuous enmity between him and the snakes, with Garuda constantly on the lookout to devour them. He is credited with the power to cure those bitten by snakes. Thus the bird is invariably represented with a snake over his neck.

Garuda has the head, wings and claws of the eagle, and the body and limbs of a man. His wife was Unnati or Vinayakaa, with whom he had a son called Sampati. But there is no attempt to identify his son with Sampati who appears in the *Ramayana*.

However, in spite of Garuda's antagonism for snakes, he does no harm to Vishnu's other vehicle, the snake Ananta, who forms a couch for Vishnu (as Narayana) to rest on, since Ananta refused to accede to his mother's order to cover Uchchaishravas's tail.

Was Garuda an eagle or a Brahmani kite? Both birds have been identified with Garuda. While the earlier descriptions call him golden-bodied—the colour of the eagle—later descriptions give him a white head, the colour of the Brahmani kite.

But there is one unique description of Garuda that identifies him with the eagle. It is said that the gods gave him the snakes as his food, and he is called Nagantaka, Pannaganashana (destroyer of snakes) and Sarparati (the enemy of snakes). The unique characteristic of the eagle and Garuda is as a predator of snakes, which he searches out and devours.

While the snake has been worshipped, it has been equally feared: in fact it is probably the most feared animal in India, for people were subject to sudden death by snake bites. Except snake-catching tribes, the common people were unable to distinguish between venomous and non-venomous snakes and presumed that all snakes were poisonous. Many deaths were probably caused by fear, but the fear of poisonous snakes remained. The eagle's ability to search out and consume

*Harappan seal*

snakes made him a hero and thus it is most likely that Garuda was the eagle.

This is further confirmed by the fact that snake charmers are called Gaarudis and the cure for snake bites is known as Garuda vidya (knowledge of Garuda). The eagle is the tormentor of snakes, so Garuda must have originally been an eagle.

The *Garuda Purana*, named after the eagle, is a philosophical treatise discussing the passage of the afterlife and rituals for the dead. Vishnu originally recited the story of Garuda's birth from Vinata in the *Garuda Kalpa*, and the *Garuda Purana* originally had 19,000 stanzas, many of which are now missing.

### Zoroastrianism

Ahura Mazda is represented as an eagle with wings, not unlike the Rig Vedic Suparna. Sometimes he is enclosed within a circle.

*Ahura Mazda*

### Ecological Role and Status

There are several eagle species, but of the lot the crested serpent eagle was probably the original Garuda, for it is a hunter and eater of snakes, which is a recurring theme in Sanskrit literature. The story of Vishnu throwing the snake over Garuda was probably invented to explain the serpent crest.

The crested serpent eagle is a medium to large raptor, about 55–75 cm in length. The bird has a dark brown upper body and head, with a hooded appearance at rest. Underneath its body and wings it is a pale brown. In flight, the broad wings are V-shaped. The tail and underside of the flight feathers are black, with broad white bars.

The crested serpent eagle, as its name suggests, is a reptile eater which hunts for snakes and lizards. The sexes look similar, but young birds have a whitish head, underparts and underwing. This also fits in with the later descriptions of Garuda as having a white head, something he shares with the Brahmani kite.

Eagles are protected in India under Schedule I of the Wildlife Protection Act of 1972.

# Elephant

| Scientific name | : | *Elephas maximus indicus* Cuvier |
|---|---|---|
| Common names | : | Hathi (Hindi) |
| | | Yaanai (Tamil) |
| | | Gajah (Sanskrit) |
| Distribution | : | Western Ghats and the |
| | | trans-Himalayan zones of India |

Elephants are found on the Indus Valley seals and among early terracottas. They were probably domesticated by this period.

The Rig Veda praises the strength and virility of the elephant. The term *hastipa* (elephant keeper) indicates that the elephant had been tamed. One verse in the Veda (X.106.6) likens the Ashvins (twins) to two elephants rushing together against the enemy. However, there is no other reference to the use of elephants in war. As the Vedas and the Indus Valley civilization overlap in time, this is yet another proof of the animal's domestication in the Indus region.

Neither the *Ramayana* nor the *Mahabharata* mention the use of elephants in war, although the animal is one of the navaratnas (nine gems) that come out of the ocean during the Samudra Manthana. According to the Puranas and Buddhist texts, a chakravartin or universal ruler must possess seven gems: chakra (wheel or discus), chariot, jewels, queen, treasure, horses and elephants.

In 326 BCE, Alexander faced an army of elephants when he fought King Purushottama (Porus) of the Punjab. According to the Greeks, the elephants prevented the horses from landing on the opposite bank.

In 305 BCE Seleucus I Nicator, the Greek governor of Babylon, went to India and waged war against Emperor Chandragupta Maurya. Seleucus fared poorly and did not achieve his aims. The two leaders ultimately reached an agreement whereby Seleucus ceded a considerable amount of territory to Chandragupta in exchange for 500 war elephants, which were to play a key role in the battles that were to come.

In the *Arthashastra*, Kautilya, Chandragupta's mentor, mentions the Gajasena or elephant division as one of the four main divisions of the king's army.

Hannibal of Carthage, Tunisia, employed Indian mahouts to drive the elephants over the Alps when he attacked Europe.

Much later, the royal emblem of the Gangas of Kannada desha was the elephant.

The Mughul period saw war elephants turned out with heavy armour, then a recent innovation.

However, elephants were not very reliable in war as they tended to panic, especially at the sight of fire, and would turn around and stampede, killing their own soldiers. There are many stories of panic-stricken elephants that crushed their armies to death. They would also trample prisoners to death.

The elephant is a very patient animal. However, temple elephants in Kerala often run amuck when they see big crowds or are subjected to excess cruelty. During the Republic Day celebrations in New Delhi in 2008, an elephant that carried child winners of bravery awards wandered off the main path, necessitating the mahout to use a lot of cruelty to bring it back. In response to the objections of animal activists and the possible erratic behaviour of the animal, it was removed from the Republic Day parade of 2009.

According to the *Gaja Shastra*, the science of catching and training elephants, the sage Varana settled beneath a vata (*Ficus krishnae*) tree in the Himalayas where he undertook a great sacrifice that gave him the name Dirghatapas. Elephants, believed to be winged at the time, were playing in the tree and thus disturbed the sage's meditation. The sage cursed them with the loss of their wings, and brought them down to earth. The *Hastyayurveda* is a medical encyclopedia for elephant management. Thus the science of taming elephants has a long history in India.

### Ganesha

> *vakratunda mahakaya*
> *koti surya samaprabha*
> *nirvighnam kurume deva*
> *sarva karyeshu sarvada*

> (You of the twisted trunk and massive body,
> With the dazzle and light of a million suns;
> Lead me on a path that has no obstacles or hindrances,
> Clearing the way in all that I do, ever, always.)

There are several myths regarding the birth of the elephant-headed Ganesha. The most popular story is of the creation of Ganesha by Parvati, wife of Shiva. As the goddess was going for her bath, she rubbed oil and dust from her body and created a young boy, into whom she infused life. Parvati told him that he was her son and asked him to keep watch while she went to bathe. Soon after, Shiva came to see his wife, but the boy would not let him in. He cut off the boy's head in anger. Parvati, when she saw her headless son, was furious and threatened to destroy the heavens and earth, for she was also

Ganesha

Shakti, the Ultimate Power. To pacify her, Shiva and the gods sent out Shiva's army of ganas (dwarfs) to bring the head of the first living being with his head to the north, which is the auspicious direction associated with wisdom. The first living being they met was an elephant sleeping with its head to the north. They brought back the animal's head, which Shiva placed on the severed body. Parvati was overjoyed and named her son Ganesha or Ganapati, Lord of the Ganas.

Ganesha is the bachelor god of the Hindu pantheon. He was only willing to marry a spouse as beautiful and as perfect in character as his mother Parvati. The gods are believed to still be looking and Ganesha waits.

However, in Maharashtra, Ganesha is believed to have two wives—Siddhi and Buddhi— representing the mind's twin qualities of success and wisdom.

Ganesha is the anthropomorphic form of the Asian (or Indian) elephant, the remover of all obstacles in one's path. If the elephant—an animal that needs vast spaces—continues to exist in Indian forests, it is only because of the people's reverence for the elephant as Lord Ganesha.

No Hindu prayer or ritual may commence without a prayer to Ganesha. He is Vighneshvara, the dispeller of obstacles, and Ganapati, the lord of Shiva's army of ganas. Every Hindu ritual commences with an invocation to Ganesha: although he is a bachelor, he gives progeny to the childless, he gives knowledge to the seeker, and prosperity to those who desire material gains. The sheer size and power of the elephant, who can remove any obstacle on his path, makes Ganesha the god who removes all obstacles from the paths of his devotees.

Ganesha is the most beloved of all the Hindu deities, for he combines in himself the elephant, a sacred and much-loved animal that is gentle and kind even as he is large and strong. Ganesha has the ability to modify himself to his devotee's desire. There are any number of stories associated with the birth of Ganesha and his various feats, but we will restrict ourselves to the best-known and most relevant.

The earliest elephant-headed human figure holding a quill appears on a plaque dated to between 1200 and 1000 BCE from Luristan in western Iran. This figure is reminiscent of Ganesha as he wrote the *Mahabharata*, at Rishi Vyasa's dictation. The *Taittiriya Aranyaka* (X.1.5) refers to Dantin (the tusked one), with a twisted trunk (vakratunda) and he who holds a sheaf of corn, a sugar cane and a club. Many early Ganesha figures were found in Afghanistan, giving rise to the belief that the god was revered in the north-west before the region became Islamic. Later, Ganesha became very popular in the Deccan.

In later literature, ganas are malevolent spirit hosts and, as their leader (ganapati), Ganesha is believed to have kept them in check, a quality that he inherited as Vighneshvara, the remover of obstacles. He is also known as a Naga, which may refer to his origin among the snake worshippers of yore, among whom the Gajas (elephant) were a sub-caste.

Ganesha is generally a stone figure placed under a pipal tree, surrounded by snake stones, with two, four or many arms. Ironically, he holds a pasha (noose) and an ankusha (elephant goad) in his rear hands and a modaka sweet in his front left hand—all three are associated with the elephant. The reason for the irony is that the goad and the rope or noose are used to torture the elephant into submission—they are certainly not trophies. Ganesha's right hand is in the abhaya mudra, indicating 'do not fear'. He wears a snake around his waist and sits on a mouse. The short, plump figure with the large elephant-head would be ludicrous if it were not so sweet, like a lovable teddy bear. He is depicted both seated and standing, and is often shown dancing, for he is believed to enjoy music and dance.

A distinguishing feature is the single broken tusk. According to a legend, Ganesha, after eating a huge meal of modakas, his favourite sweet, was riding home one day on his mouse which tripped on a snake and dropped him. Ganesha's stomach burst open and the modakas tumbled out. Seeing the comic sight, the moon laughed. Ganesha got up angrily, tied the snake around his waist, broke off a piece of his tusk and threw it at the moon, condemning him to stop shining. So there was no more night and the sun shone incessantly night and day. The gods pleaded with Ganesha to take back his curse. Ganesha relented, but limited the moon's shining to alternate fortnights, which is why the moon waxes and wanes.

Ganesha is also believed to have been a scribe who used his broken tusk to write the epic *Mahabharata*. According to legend, Sage Vyasa meditated on Brahma to ask who would write the *Mahabharata* even as he dictated it in verse. Brahma suggested Ganesha, who agreed on condition that Vyasa should dictate continuously, without pausing. Vyasa agreed, but with the stipulation that Ganesha understand every word and its implication before writing. So, whenever Vyasa found that Ganesha had completed writing a verse, he would dictate one with very complicated meanings, which required Ganesha to stop and think. Thus the epic was written with a very definite message: the *Mahabharata* should not be read in a hurry.

Ganesha is famed for his wisdom. One day, Shiva and Parvati were playing with their two sons Ganesha and Kartikeya. They had been given a divine fruit containing Supreme Knowledge and immortality, and both the sons wanted it.The parents said that whoever circled the earth three times and returned first would get it. Kartikeya got on to his peacock vehicle and set off. Ganesha circumambulated his parents thrice, for they were his entire world. Naturally, he won the fruit.

By sitting on the mouse, Ganesha also keeps under control the farmer's enemy, a pest of the agricultural fields.

There are thirty-two forms of Ganesha ordained by the canons (*shastra*). Some, like Heramba, have five heads, while Shakti is one of the many forms of Ganesha in which the bachelor becomes a married man, with his wife seated on his lap.

Maharashtra is famous for the ashta (eight) Vinayak. They are Mayureshvar (Moreshvar) at Morgaon, Chintamani at Theur, Mahaganapati at Ranjangaon, Siddhivinayak at Siddhatek, Vighneshvar (Vighnahara) at Ojhar, Girijatmak at Lenyadri, Ballaleshvar at Pali and Varad Vinayak at Mahad. These images are svayambhu (self-manifested) and made out of single rocks where the head, trunk and body of the elephant can be discerned. Besides these, the temple of Siddhi Vinayak of Mumbai is very famous.

According to the *Mudgala Purana*, Ganesha takes on eight incarnations to conquer the vices that afflict man. They are:

- Vikata, who defeated Kamasura or lust;
- Lambodara, the vanquisher of Krodhasura or anger;
- Gajanana, who conquered avarice or greed, Lobhasura;
- Mahodara, who defeated Mohasura, the demon of delusion;
- Ekadanta, the conqueror of Madasura, the demon of vanity;
- Vakratunda, riding a lion, who subdued Matsura, the demon of envy;
- Vighnaraja, riding the divine serpent Sesha, who vanquished Mamasura, the demon of desire; and
- Dhumravarna, who destroyed Abhimanasura, the demon of egotism;

But the Ganesha image may be even simpler. At the beginning of every Hindu ritual, turmeric is mixed with water and made to stand as a cone less than two centimetres high. This represents Ganesha. Sometimes a natural wood formation on a tree, resembling a twisted elephant's trunk, may be revered as Ganesha. He is among the simplest of gods, yet the most powerful. He can be created as his devotee conceives him, which is why there are endless forms of Ganesha when his annual festival—Ganesh Chaturthi—takes place.

*Symbolism*

Every aspect of Ganesha has a meaning:

- His corpulent body reminds us that outward appearance has nothing to do with inner beauty.
- His trunk is the pranava, or the sound Om, the symbol of creation, the Brahman.
- The head of the elephant is symbolic of his superior intelligence.

- The snake around his waist symbolizes cosmic energy.
- The noose represents worldly attachments, which are like a noose around ones neck.
- The goad goads people on to the path of righteousness.
- The modaka is reminiscent of the sweetness of one's inner self.
- Sometimes he holds rosary beads, a reminder of the importance of prayer.
- The broken tusk in his hand symbolizes knowledge, for he used it to write the *Mahabharata* as it was dictated by the poet Vyasa.
- The elephant represents wisdom and the strength of the mind, and the ability to remove obstacles.
- As the elephant is large yet gentle, Ganesha represents the importance of right over might.
- His large ears sift out the bad, so that only the truth of the Vedas can be heard.
- His trunk is curved to make up the symbol of Om in Devanagari and other Indian scripts.
- Just as the elephant's trunk can break open a coconut and scoop out the soft kernel within, Ganesha represents viveka or discrimination, an essential quality for a person.
- His ability to uproot trees, leaving the tiny shoots, pushing massive logs down a river and distinguishing good from the useless, represents wisdom.
- His huge belly represents his ability to swallow the sorrows of the universe.
- Ganesha's vehicle is the mouse or mushika, although it often appears as a rat in his images. The tiny animal represents the equal importance of big and small people to God.

However, it is ironic that the elephant, revered as the great Lord Ganesha, is subject to the utmost cruelty from its mahouts and owners.

*Airavata*

The elephant is ridden by gods and kings. The Creator, Brihaspati, rides an elephant.

The word Airavata means a fine elephant and comes from the word Iravat or 'produced from water'. Iravati is the name of the famous river of Burma where, even today, the 'white elephant', a symbol of both divinity and royalty is found. To celebrate the royal divine, the white elephant was made the mount of the king of the heavens, Indra. The divine elephant was the progenitor of all elephants and is symbolized by the huge rain clouds that bring prosperity.

Airavata carries Indra, king of the heavens, in a stone relief from Bhaja

*Indra on Airavata*

belonging to 200 BCE. Airavata was the greatest of elephants, the vehicle of Indra, king of the heavens. According to tradition, he was one of the gems that came out of the ocean during the Samudra Manthana (churning of the ocean) along with the amrita, or nectar of immortality, and Lakshmi, the goddess of prosperity (see INTRODUCTION). The *Vishnu Purana* describes Airavata as a four-tusked white elephant that appeared out of the Samudra Manthana. This was Airavata, one of the navaratnas or nine gems, which later became the mount of Lord Indra. Just as the gods have specific colours (white for Shiva, blue for Krishna, green for Rama), and are depicted as four-armed super beings, Airavata, who is white and has four-tusks, is a super elephant.

According to another story, Airavata was a celestial elephant-king who had wings and could fly. He was descended from sage Kashyapa and Krodhavasa's daughter Bhadramata. Iravati was Bhadramata's daughter. Iravati's son was Airavata, the flying elephant.

Yet another version says that Airavata came out of the hiranyagarbha, or cosmic golden egg. Brahma took the two halves in his hands and breathed life into them. Out of one half came Airavata and seven other males: Pundarika, Kumuda, Vamana, Anjana, Pushpadanta, Sarvabhauma and Supratika, while eight females came out of the other half to be their consorts. These eight pairs became the ashta dik-gajas, the guardians of the eight cardinal points of the sky. Airavata guards the east, where the sun rises.

*Brihaspati (Jupiter)*

Other names for Airavata include Ardhamatanga (elephant of the clouds), Arkasodara (brother of the sun) and Nagamalla (fighting elephant).

Airavata appears in the cave temples of western India by the second century BCE. The wings are a later addition, not known to early art. He sports wings on a medallion from Bharhut.

### Protectors of the Directions—Dikpalas

The eight cardinal directions are protected by eight elephants (and their wives) who bear eight deities. They are:

- Airavata who carries Indra (Rain), lord of the east, and his wife Abhramu.
- Pundarika who carries Agni (Fire), lord of the south-east, and his wife Kapila.
- Vamana who carries Yama (Death), lord of the south, and his wife Pingala.
- Kumuda who carries Surya (Sun), lord of the south-west, and his wife Anupama.
- Anjana who carries Varuna (Ocean), lord of the west, and his wife Anjanavati.

- Pushpadanta who carries Vayu (Wind), lord of the north-west, and his wife Shubhadanti.
- Sarvabhauma who carries Kubera (Wealth), lord of the north, and his wife Tamrakarna.
- Supratika who carries Soma (Moon), lord of the north-east, and his wife Anjanavati.

The *Ramayana* gives a slightly different list:

- Virupaksha is the elephant of Indra, lord of the east.
- Saumanasa is the elephant of Varuna, lord of the west.
- Mahapadma is the elephant of Yama, lord of the south.
- Himapandara is the elephant of Kubera, lord of the north.

The elephant is symbolic of strength and stability and represents the unchanging nature of the directions. He protects the universe from the vagaries of change.

In later architecture, stone elephants often form the base of temples, from the eighth century jagati at Ellora to the twentieth century Akshardham Temple at Delhi, suggesting that the temple— and therefore the world—is carried on the backs of super elephants, the dikpalas.

*Companions of Prosperity—Gajalakshmi*

The elephant is associated with the goddess Lakshmi, the Hindu deity of wealth and prosperity. One of her eight manifestations, known as the ashtha (eight) Lakshmi, is Gajalakshmi, in which she is flanked by two elephants, on either side, showering water over her.

In Hindu homes there is invariably a picture of Lakshmi at the entrance or in the prayer room. The most popular form of Lakshmi is Gajalakshmi. The elephants are a symbol of good luck, fertility, strength and stability; water is the source of all existence, besides representing the sacred elephant, and hence the combination of elephants and Lakshmi.

This image became very popular in the late nineteenth and early twentieth centuries, when Raja Ravi Varma, the first

'modern' artist of contemporary India, painted Gajalakshmi and made several oleograph prints of the goddess, which were bought by people all over India to hang in their homes. Later, many artists copied his paintings and printed them.

*Gajalakshmi*

Today, Gajalakshmi is the most popular form of the goddess of good luck and prosperity.

### Gajendra Moksha

Indradyumna, ruler of the Tamil country, was a great devotee of Vishnu. He relinquished his kingdom in order to become a sanyasi, taking the vow of silence in order to meditate upon Vishnu. One day, sage Agastya came by and halted at the ashram. Indradyumna did not move or offer any reception, resulting in Agastya's

*Gajendra Moksha*

curse that Indradyumna would be reborn as an elephant ignorant of self-knowledge. Indradyumna accepted the curse calmly as a decision of Lord Vishnu and was reborn as an elephant.

Gajendra, the king of elephants, with his females and all other animals, lived in peace and harmony on a mountain in the milky ocean. One day, he went to a lake on the mountain to assuage his thirst. All the elephants also stepped into the pool, causing a rush and confusion. A crocodile, who was earlier a gandharva who had been cursed by the sage Devala, caught hold of the foot of Gajendra. The other elephants pulled and so did Gajendra, but they were unable to release his foot from the tight grip of the crocodile. This went on for years till Gajendra prayed to Lord Vishnu who immediately mounted his vehicle Garuda and reached Gajendra, whom he rescued by cutting off the crocodile's neck with the Sudarshana chakra. The crocodile let go and Indradyumna was released from Agastya's curse, reaching the Supreme Abode of Lord Vishnu. Gajendra moksha is a very popular theme in art, the earliest instance being the Dashavtara Cave at Deogarh.

The story of Gajendra moksha may have been derived from the Rig Vedic story of Indra's war with Vritra, demon of drought. In the Puranic age, Vishnu took over many of Indra's functions and characteristics. The elephant, as a symbol of water and fertility, stands for the rain-filled clouds that are released when Vishnu kills the crocodile, who takes on the role of Vritra.

### Buddhism

Elephants are also sacred to the Buddhists. Since they are among the seven royal gems, the animal is the first to be carried in a procession before the Buddha. In the Buddhist

*Maya's dream signifying the birth of the Buddha*

art of Amaravati and Nagarjunakonda, the chakravartin or king is accompanied by the seven gems, including the white elephant.

In the Buddhist kingdom of Thailand, the white elephant is an assurance of good luck and prosperity. In the sixteenth and seventeenth centuries, the rulers of Thailand, Cambodia and Laos battled each other for the possession of white elephants. The death of a white elephant due to mishandling resulted in certain death. The cult of the sacred white elephant is still practised in Thailand and Burma.

Like Ganesha, the elephant represents wisdom and strength of mind in Buddhism. It is believed that the Buddha, in the incarnation preceding his birth as Siddhartha who became the Buddha, was Chaddanta, the legendary white elephant with six tusks. There is an entire Jataka named after Chaddanta, and a white elephant is the most sought-after animal in Buddhist temples. There is a legend associated with the birth of the Buddha. Mayadevi, wife of King Shuddhodana of Kapilavastu, dreamed of a white elephant before she conceived Siddhartha. Mayadevi saw an elephant enter her womb. That was the Bodhisattva Chaddanta, who was to be born as Siddhartha and become the Buddha. According to Buddhist mythology, as Chaddanta had already resolved to be born as a Buddha, he was waiting as a Bodhisattva in the Tushita heaven for the propitious moment. He entered the golden palace, circled Mayadevi thrice and entered her womb from the right side. When the king consulted the Brahmanas, he was told that he would be the father of a male child who would become a chakravartin or universal monarch if he lived in the palace, or a Buddha who would remove ignorance if he left the palace.

Later, Gautama's jealous cousin Devadatta tried to make a mad elephant Nilagiri charge at the Buddha and kill him. But the Buddha stopped the charging animal in its tracks and pacified it. The animal prostrated before the Buddha and became his devotee.

The elephant is so closely associated with the Buddha that the birth of Gautama is invariably represented by the elephant entering Mayadevi's womb in the sculptured friezes of Bharhut, Sanchi, Gandhara and Nagarjunakonda.

In another Jataka tale, the Bodhisattva was born as a white elephant who ruled over eighty thousand elephants, at a time when Brahmadatta ruled Benares. He was captured and given to the king, but refused to eat without feeding his blind mother, for which he was freed by the king.

There is a variant of the Gajendra moksha story in Jataka literature, where a giant crab catches the Bodhisattva elephant's leg but is crushed to death. This story is sculpted on an architrave at Bharhut.

The world rests on the head of Mahapadma, a great elephant, and earthquakes are attributed to the moving of Mahapadma's head. The elephant represents the powers of a Buddha: miraculous aspiration, analysis, intention and effort.

According to the Theravada tradition, when Gautama was practising austerities alone in the wilderness, an elephant gave him food and shelter. In the annual Dantadhatu (tooth relic) festival of Sri Lanka, the elephant alone could carry the sacred tooth of the Buddha in procession. The vehicle of Akshobhya, the primordial Buddha associated with consciousness (vijnana) is the elephant, as is the vehicle of Balabhadra, brother of Krishna, who presides over agriculture and holds the halayudha (plough) as his weapon.

## Jainism

The second Tirthankara Ajitanatha is represented by the elephant which is carved on the base of his statues. Beside him stands his attendant Mahayaksha, whose vehicle is also the elephant.

Matanga, a Jaina Yaksha, sits on a seat with the elephant beneath his leg, or rides an elephant. Yaksheshvara is accompanied by the elephant.

*Jaina Tirthankara
Ajitanatha*

## Elephant as Demon

An elephant demon named Gajasura harassed gods and men and even tried to conquer Kashi (Benares). As Shiva's ganas were weakened by the constant battles, Shiva was forced to intervene. Destroyed by the god, the demon asked that his skin be stripped and used to shade Shiva's head and the elephant head be strung on Shiva's garland of skulls. Thus the image of Shiva dancing with an elephant's skin held over his head and the elephant's head either beneath his feet or strung on his garland of skulls is described as Gajasamharamurti.

Gajamukha (elephant-faced) was yet another demon who performed severe austerities and obtained a boon of invincibility from Shiva. He then harassed the gods who were unable to destroy him. They approached Ganesha, who broke his right tusk and threw it at the demon, cursing him to turn into a mouse. He then quickly got onto the back of the mouse and keeps it under control permanently.

The Pandava prince Ghatotkacha's son drove a chariot driven by Gajanibha, elephant-like demonic creatures.

*Elephant Festival*

In ancient India, the elephant was also a folk deity called Airavata gaja, according to the Bhagavat Gita. The *Matiposhaka Jataka* refers to the worship of a stone elephant and several Jatakas refer to the elephant festival of Hastimangala, when the king gifted elephants to Brahmins well-versed in the Vedas and the *Hastisutra*. The *Hastyayurveda* says that during the annual festival of Lakshmi, an elephant was painted with sandal paste, decorated with flowers and paraded through the town. It was worshipped by the ruler, his ministers and generals. The Veda goes on to say that if the ritual is not performed, fortune and prosperity, associated with the elephant, will disappear. When it is invoked, it is believed to conjure the winged elephants—or the rain clouds—to bring forth rain.

It is likely that the folk worship of the elephant led to the festival of Ganesh Chaturthi. As the auspicious symbol of the festival, Ganesha is also called Mangalamurti. Ganesh Chaturthi, or the birthday of Ganesha, is celebrated on the fourth day of the waxing moon in the month of Bhadrapada (August–September). It is a holiday in most parts of India.

Traditionally, summer is the time when the lakes and ponds are desilted to prepare for the monsoons which arrive in June–July in western and central India. The desilted clay was used, by local terracotta craftsmen, to make unbaked clay images of Ganesha. Prayers, sweets, coconut and milk are offered to the images. On the third day, after Chaturthi, the image would be immersed into a well, a local pond or the sea. It was a very eco-friendly festival during which the excess clay thrown away during the desilting process was used and good rainfall was prayed for, to fill the lakes and provide water for drinking and irrigation.

In the early twentieth century, Lokamanya Tilak, a great freedom fighter from Maharashtra, used the occasion to rally people for the freedom movement. Huge Ganeshas, baked and painted, were installed in common arenas and people came out to worship and celebrate together for eleven days. The festival of Ganesha became an occasion for people to come together, and a clarion cry for the freedom movement.

Unfortunately, today the Ganesha images are covered with toxic paint and are non-biodegradable, a far cry from the small images made out of clay and silt.

## Temple Elephants

Elephants are a common but sad sight in Hindu temples in south India. Their condition is pitiable, for one leg is chained and develops wounds and arthritis, while the animal has to stand for hours on hot granite or concrete floors. Further, they are generally kept singly, which is a tragedy, for the animal lives in large social communities in the wild.

Temple elephants are used to carry the utsava murti or the festival images made of bronze. Kerala has the largest number of temple elephants. At Trichur, during the Pooram festival, the elephants of several temples are brought for a grand celebration where each drummer tries to be louder than the next. At Mysore, during the Navaratri festival, the elephant carries the image of

Chamundi to celebrate the defeat of the demon Mahisha at the hands of the goddess. Elephants are also commonly used in temples in Tamil Nadu, Andhra Pradesh and Pondicherry .

*Ecological Role and Current Status*

Elephants are the most majestic of the animals of the Indian subcontinent. They once roamed the entire subcontinent and are celebrated in the literature of every Indian language. Kings vied to maintain elephants. Belying its huge size, the elephant is a gentle giant that does not cause hurt or damage. While the African elephant is large, large-eared and both males and females bear tusks, the Asian elephant is a mild, gentle animal. Only the males bear tusks, which have led to their relentless killing, leaving mostly tuskless animals today.

The elephant is a 'keystone species' and plays a very important role in the forest ecosystem. Today elephants are primarily found in the Western Ghats, the North-East and the trans-Himalayan zones of India, in big family groups headed by a grand matriarch. They clear the forest of old plants, rejuvenating and allowing new shoots to appear. As they walk through the forests, they create gaps which allow sunlight to penetrate, resulting in the growth of several plant species and the survival of other fauna. During the hot dry summers, elephants use their tusks to deepen waterbodies, and this becomes the sole water source for other animals. Elephants pull down trees and break branches to eat leaves. They pull out roots and create open areas where new trees can grow. As they push down trees through the forests, they make pathways through which other animals can access otherwise inaccessible areas.

Several other species depend on the elephant for their survival. For example, termites eat the faeces of elephants and build their homes (mounds) under the faecal matter dropped by elephants. Elephant dung is believed to have medicinal qualities and has many uses for indigenous tribes.

The conversion to Christianity of the Mizo and Naga tribes of the North-East has resulted in their killing the elephant for food in recent times. As the North-East also has the largest number of wild and working elephants, this has changed their population and profile for the first time. Today their numbers are decreasing rapidly, making them an endangered species under Schedule I of the Indian Wildlife Act.

While the threat to the African elephant is the ivory trade, the Asian elephant, which lives in the jungles of South and South-East Asia is threatened by the loss of habitat and the decreasing vegetation, for the elephant requires about 140 kg of food a day, which is eaten up by the growing numbers of cattle and other herbivores whose numbers are multiplying rapidly as the carnivores are disappearing. The recent incidents of elephants raiding cultivated land in eastern India is a result of human encroachment into forest land. At this rate it is doubtful whether elephants can survive in the wild. Their very survival is threatened as man and animal battle for the shrinking land resources, as human populations grow.

The sanctity conferred on elephants has also resulted in great suffering and torture. The capture of the elephant (in the kheda) and its training have involved unbelievable cruelties, while its use in battle, temple festivals, circuses and timber logging has been traumatic for this gentle animal. The elephant is threatened with fire and made to learn tricks such as standing on its head and riding bicycles to amuse crowds who throng circuses. The mahout controls it by poking a sharp goad behind its ear, causing it great pain and thereby forcing it to submit to the mahout.

Elephants are social animals who live in big family groups presided over by a benign matriarch. They are miserable and unhappy when in solitary confinement. Tragically, in spite of all talk of the sacred elephant in India, the animal is still forced to perform stupid antics in circuses, and undergoes terrible cruelties as it is put to work.

The gentle elephant has endured capture and mistreatment at human hands. He has been trained to fight in wars, made to fight other elephants and wildlife, like tigers and lions, for human amusement, and trained with fire and pain to entertain audiences in circuses. He is made to carry heavy logs to clear forests for commercial use. His power is so great that he can destroy the mahouts who torture him. Yet he allows himself to be led.

The reverence in which the elephant is held is probably the reason why it still survives, in spite of the pressures of shrinking habitats and the ivory trade which, though banned, continues underground.

~

# Fish

| | | |
|---|---|---|
| Scientific Name | : | *Teleostii* (Sub-class); genera not known |
| Common Names | : | Machhli (Hindi) |
| | | Meen(Tamil) |
| | | Matsya (Sanskrit) |
| Distribution | : | Salt and fresh water |

*Vishnu's Incarnation—Matsya*

*Glory to you, O Lord of the universe, who took the form of a fish;*
*When the sacred hymns of the Vedas were lost in the great flood,*
*You swam like a boat in the vast ocean to rescue them.*

Gita Govinda by *Jayadeva*

The story of the fish that saved the world first appears in the *Mahabharata*. One day, when Manu, the primeval man, was carrying out his rituals on the riverbank, a little fish swam up to him and said that if Manu were to take care of him, the fish would protect Manu from the forthcoming deluge (pralaya). On receiving Manu's consent, the fish instructed him to keep him in a jar and protect him from other fish. After a while, the fish outgrew the jar and told Manu to put him into a tank. When he outgrew the tank, the fish wanted to be taken to the river Ganga, and when the river was no longer large enough, to be taken to the sea. There, the fish instructed Manu to build a ship and protect himself from the deluge. When the deluge began, Manu tied the ship to the fish, who took him away from the floods and towards the Himalayas. When Manu stepped out of the boat he found himself all alone in a lost and lonely world, for every other creature had been wiped out by the flood. The fish then identified himself as Brahma and gave Manu the power to create and repopulate the world.

The *Matsya Purana*, named after this incarnation of Vishnu, has a variation on this story. The Vedas were stolen by the demon Hayagriva. When Vishnu came to know of this, he took the form of a small fish, which came into the

*Matsya, the fish incarnation of Vishnu*

hands of Satyavrata who was performing a religious ceremony. The fish begged to be saved from the larger fish, so the king put the fish in a small pot. As in the earlier story, the fish outgrew the pot, the tank, the river and even the sea. Then Satyavrata asked the fish to identify himself. The fish said he was Vishnu and that a great deluge would flood the earth for a hundred years. Satyavrata was instructed to build a boat and fill it with one of every species—animals, plants and seeds—with the Vedas above them. Then the fish attached the boat to his fins with a rope that was a long snake. When the deluge arrived, the fish kept aloft Satyavrata's boat with all its contents. Finally, when the waters receded, the creatures of the boat came out and created new life on earth.

The story of the great flood first appears in the Babylonian tablets and in the creation story of every ancient civilization on every continent. It is obviously a memory of an event that actually happened long ago.

There are only two temples to Matsya, one of which is the Shankhodara temple at Bet Dwarka in Gujarat. The original Dwarka, which adjoined Bet Dwarka, as described in the *Mahabharata* and confirmed by underwater archaeology, was destroyed by a great flood that wiped out the entire race of Yadavas, to which Krishna belonged. This was obviously a great environmental event that has remained etched in human memory.

What is important in all the flood stories is the protection of all species by a tiny fish. The message is that each species is equally important in the divine scheme of the world, which is why this incarnation of Vishnu protected every animal, plant and seed.

The image of Matsya is depicted on sculptures and paintings on Vishnu temples. Matsya is generally represented as a half-man half-fish, the lower half sporting a fish's fin, the upper half human and generally four-armed, holding the attributes of Vishnu: conch (shankha), discus (chakra) and mace (gada), the fourth hand in the abhaya (meaning do not fear) mudra (position).

It is said that whoever hears this story is delivered from the ocean of sin. The insignificant fish, killed by the million, is the origin of all life on earth, the saviour of the human race.

*Matsya Purana*

This Purana is so-called because it was narrated by Vishnu, in the form of a fish, to Manu. It consists of between 14,000 and 15,000 stanzas.

*A Country*

Matsya is the name of a country once situated in north India. Manu places it in Brahmarshi, while the *Mahabharata* says that the capital of King Virata was Matsya, his people were called Matsyas and he himself was styled Matsya. It has been identified in the neighbourhood of Jaipur, with the town of Virat or Bairat, 168 km south of Delhi, as its capital (Dowson 1982).

## Meenakshi

She is the fish-eyed goddess of Madurai in south India. However, the epics also describe her as the daughter of Kubera. She was married to King Soundarapandiyan. Later, Meenakshi and her consort were identified with Parvati and Shiva, while the imagery of Vishnu giving away his sister Meenakshi in marriage to Shiva is very popular in south Indian art.

Many dynasties chose the fish as the emblem, including the Pandya and Vijayanagara dynasties.

## Buddhism

The Mahayana goddess Varahi holds a Rohita fish in her right hand. This is probably influenced by Tantricism where the fish is one of the five essentials.

One of the eight auspicious signs (ashtamangala) of Mahayana Buddhism is a pair of golden fish called suvarna matsya. They symbolize happiness, although they may also represent the rivers Ganga and Yamuna. Fish also represent transcendental wisdom as they can cross and swim the seas all over the world (Majupuria 2000).

## Jainism

The emblem of the eighteenth Tirthankara Aranatha is the fish .

*Jaina Titthankara Aranatha*

*Mahasheer*

This is a species of fish considered to be sacred and therefore protected in several rivers, particularly the Kaveri and the Tunga, besides many waterbodies of Karnataka, especially at the pilgrimage towns of Shishila, Subrahmanya, Sringeri and Ramanathapura (Ardhya 2005).

~

# Flying Fox

| | | |
|---|---|---|
| Scientific Name | : | *Pteropus giganteus* Brunnich |
| Common Names | : | Indian flying fox / fruit bat |
| | | Badur, bada chamkathad, gadal (Hindi) |
| | | Vavval (Tamil) |
| | | Vrikshabhaksha (Sanskrit) |
| Distribution | : | Throughout India |

The Indian flying fox, better known as the fruit bat, is the only species of bat that is regarded as sacred.

About 64 km east of Madurai in Tamil Nadu, there is a small village called Puliangulam. There, a single huge banyan tree with its branches spread wide and aerial roots falling to the ground stands in the middle of agricultural fields. It is home to an enormous colony of fruit bats—over 500 strong—that are considered to be sacred and are given special care and treatment by the villagers. The bats, they believe, are protected by Muniyandi, a spirit who lives in the tree. Failure to protect even one bat may result in punishment, which may be atoned by an offering of prayer, followed by the distribution of sweet rice, coconuts and bananas. Other places where this flying fox is protected include Keelarajakularaman, 90 km south-west of Madurai, and Sri Vaikundam, 300 km south of Madurai, all in Tamil Nadu (Marimuthu 1988).

At Enadhikottai, near Paramakudi in Ramanathapuram district, an enormous banyan tree stands tall, home to thousands of bats that hang from its branches. The tree itself is the object of worship and the bats are regarded as angels and messengers of the gods. Bird hunters are not allowed to enter the village, while weddings and other festive occasions are celebrated in silence, without loudspeakers or crackers, which may disturb the bats. Seeing a bat before setting

*Flying foxes on a sacred tree*

out to work is a good omen and nothing is done to disturb the animals (Sivarajah 2007).

In Karnataka, fruit bats are protected at the Bavali Vana sacred grove at Koli village, Belthangadi Taluk; at the Lakshmi Temple at Puttur, Dakshin Kannada; and at Belur in Hassan district (Ardhya 2005).

## Ecological Role and Current Status

The Indian flying fox is one of the largest of all bats and has a wingspan of about a metre. The animal was named for the shape of its head and its reddish brown fur, which resemble those of a fox. It favours the same roosting sites, often reused for many years. Bat colonies have a typical musky odour and may contain several thousand flying foxes. They roost in large trees such as the banyan and the tamarind. During the day, the bats are noisy and active, resting, mating and communicating loudly.

After the sun sets, they leave the tree to feed on a rich meal of fruits—mangoes, guavas, figs and neem—giving them the name fruit bat. The flying fox feeds almost exclusively on a variety of fruits. While it once fed mainly on wild fruit, dispersing the seeds and manuring the crops which made it the farmer's favourite, the bat now increasingly raids fruit orchards, bringing it into direct conflict with man. In some areas it it is even being poisoned as it is considered to be a threat to fruit farmers.

In Pakistan, flying foxes are hunted for their fat, which is used for medicinal purposes.

The animals are important dispersers of seeds; hence they are declared sacred and to be protected. Large commercial tree species such as the mango depend on these rodents, which eat the fruit and excrete the seed.

~

# Frog

| Scientific Name | : | *Rana tigrina* |
| Common Names | : | Indian bullfrog/tiger frog |
| | | Manduk (Hindi) |
| | | Thavalai (Tamil) |
| | | Mandukah, Mandukiparni (Sanskrit) |
| Distribution | : | Throughout India |

Till avarice obtained the better of faith, frogs were never killed. It was believed that killing a frog would result in the killer's skin drying up—like a frog's.

The tiger frog wears the sign of the namam, the Vaishnavite symbol of three vertical lines on the forehead, and is therefore considered blessed.

The frog is also a symbol of reincarnation, for it goes through several forms—from egg to tadpole, breathing through its gills, to the air-breathing reptile. This is likened to the many forms a soul may take.

There is an entire philosophic treatise, the *Mandukya Upanishad*, which explains the meaning of the sound om or aum as three stages of consciousness: 'a' is the state of wakefulness, 'o' of dreams and 'm' of deep sleep.

The 'singing' of the frogs indicates that the rains have come and is a time for celebration, while the silence of the frogs means that nature and the gods have forsaken man. This, of course, is attributed to human evil. If frogs are killed, the rains, it is believed, will forsake man.

## Buddhism

The vehicle of Brihaspati (Jupiter), the fifth of the nine planets, who carries a rosary and a kamandalu (water pot) is a frog (Majupuria 2000).

## Ecological Role and Current Status

The Indian bullfrog is quite large, with a snout-vent length up to 110 mm in males and 160 mm in females. These frogs are green, with strong hind limbs with large webbed feet. They live around ponds and in paddy fields. Males have vocal sacs on both sides of the throat, forming longitudinal folds.

At the beginning of the monsoon, breeding males, which are bright yellow in colour, gather around standing waters and loudly call the females, in what is called the song of the bullfrog.

Overexploitation for the consumption of frogs' legs in Europe resulted in a steep decline in their population, especially in northern India, accompanied by a striking increase in pest populations and pesticide use in paddy fields. Recent legal protection of this species has limited this decline, although it has not suppressed it entirely. Till the ban on the export of frogs' legs, the animal was caught and killed in large numbers. The indiscriminate use of pesticides and rapid urbanization has resulted in the disappearance of several frog species.

$\sim$

# Goat

| Scientific Name | : | *Capra aegagrus hircus* Linn |
|---|---|---|
| Common Names | : | Bakri (Hindi) |
| | | Aadu (Tamil) |
| | | Khhagah (Sanskrit) |
| Distribution | : | Throughout India |

The vehicle or vahana of Agni, the
Hindu fire god, is a ram or mesha.
Sometimes it is the vehicle of Pushan,
identified with Surya in the Rig Veda
and as Surya's son in later literature.

In Hindu mythology, Daksha is
depicted with the head of a goat.

Daksha was the father of Sati and,
following a disagreement with his
son-in-law Shiva, did not invite his
daughter and son-in-law for a sacrifice
he was performing. In spite of Shiva's
warnings, Sati went to her father's

*Agni*

sacrifice, where Daksha insulted Shiva. Unable to bear the
humiliation, Sati committed suicide in the sacrificial fire. Furious,
Shiva sent his attendant Virabhadra, who killed Daksha. The gods
then prayed to Shiva for forgiveness for Daksha. Pacified, Shiva
said Daksha could live again with the head of the first living
being he met. Since that being was a goat, Daksha was given

a goat's head. His killing by Shiva is
used to justify the use of the goat in
sacrifices although the goat's head
came after he was killed.

Daksha is also the grandfather of
all creation, for his thirteen daughters
were married to Kashyapa, the divine
progenitor, and each gave birth to a
different species.

Occasionally Kubera, the god of
wealth, is also depicted as a ram.

*Daksha*

Prakriti (Nature) is depicted as a goat whose colours of red,
black and white represent the three gunas (qualities).

Goats are commonly sacrificed to the Mother Goddess—in
the Kalighat Temple at Kolkata, they are sacrificed everyday to

Kali. Sometimes Kali, in a more benign aspect, is seated on a black goat.

## Jainism

The emblem of the seventeenth Tirthankara Kunthunatha is the goat.

## Sacrificial Goats of Islam

Id-ul-Zuha is one of the most celebrated festivals among the Muslim community. Muslims around the world sacrifice an animal on the occasion of the festival to replicate the sacrifice of Ibrahim (Abraham, a Semetic *pater*).

*Jaina Tirthankara*
*Kunthunatha*

In India, the animal most commonly used for the sacrifice is a goat, which is why the festival is also known as Bakr-Id (although the festival originally had no association with the goat). Unfortunately, the symbolism of the festival has been forgotten in the large-scale slaughter of goats. The idea was that Ibrahim was willing to sacrifice that which he held dearest to himself, his son, on the instructions of his God. Seeing his total obedience, God permitted him to sacrifice a goat instead. The idea of sacrificing that which is precious to oneself and sharing it with the poor has been replaced by the mass sacrifice of goats.

## Ecological Role and Current Status

The goat is a domesticated subspecies and is closely related to the sheep. Goats are one of the oldest domesticated animals, having been used for their milk, meat, hair and skin over several millennia. Goats were probably first domesticated roughly 10,000 years ago in the Zagros Mountains of Iran. Ancient cultures and tribes kept them for easy access to their milk, hair, meat and skin. Goats were maintained in herds that wandered in grazing areas, tended by goatherds who were frequently children or adolescents, similar to the more widely known shepherd. Such methods of herding continue even today.

⁓

# Hare

| | | |
|---|---|---|
| Scientific Name | : | *Lepus nigricollis* |
| Common Names | : | Black-naped hare |
| | | Khargosh (Hindi) |
| | | Muyal/musal(Tamil) |
| | | Shashah (Sanskrit) |
| Distribution | : | Throughout India |

It is believed that the hare occupies a permanent place in the moon, which gives it the name Shashodhara.

Hares were reared by the ancient sages of India as pets. Many mathas, like the Murugarajendra Math at Chitradurga in Karnataka, rear hares (Ardhya 2005).

## Buddhism

The hare is sacred to Buddhists in many ways. In a Jataka story about the Buddha's lives, the Buddha was a hare who lived in the forest and had three friends: a monkey, a jackal and an otter. Sakra, king of the heavens, decided to test his virtue. Dressed up as a Brahmin, he went to the hare to ask for food. Immediately, the hare offered itself and jumped into the fire. But Agni could not burn the hare because it was a future Buddha. Sakra blessed the animal and proclaimed that his virtue would be celebrated forever. Thereafter, Sakra picked up the hare and drew its outline on the moon using the juice of the mountain as ink and then put the animal down on the grass. And so, it is believed, there is a hare on the moon (Coomaraswamy and Nivedita 1967).

According to the *Shasa Jataka*, the hare offered its own body as food for his guests. It gave up its body for a starving man and, as reward, was pushed to the moon. The animal is a cultural hero who teaches medicine, dance and the arts of life (Majupuria 2000).

In all Buddhist stories, the killing of the hare is made to appear as a voluntary sacrifice by the animal to justify the eating of the hare's meat.

*Ecological Role and Current Status*

The Indian hare is a mammal of open fields and plains and is generally found in areas where large tracts of bush and jungle alternate with farmland. They are also commonly sighted in coastal and hilly areas.

Hares are usually nocturnal. By day, they rest in hollows scooped out of grass. The hare differs from the rabbit which lives in a burrow, but is not found in India. The hare likes to feed on vegetables. It is herbivorous, although the types of vegetation it eats varies depending on the season. During the monsoons, short grasses are preferred, while more flowering plants are consumed during the dry season. It also eats crops and germinating seeds, making it a farmer's nightmare.

The hare is an important prey for many carnivores, such as the wolves in the Velavadar National Park in Gujarat, where hares are the second most consumed species. They are eaten by leopards and dholes, as well as by local people. The hare was introduced to the Seychelles to provide food for plantation workers. Its population has been reduced by snaring and shooting and the destruction of plant cover.

～

# Horse

| | | |
|---|---|---|
| Scientific Name | : | *Equus caballus* Linn |
| Common Names | : | Ghoda (Hindi), |
| | | Kudirai (Tamil) |
| | | Ashvah (Sanskrit) |
| Distribution | : | Throughout India |

The Rig Veda celebrates the horse to an extent that the equine Dadhikra was an object of worship (Rig Veda, IV.33). Indra's horse Uchchhaishravas was the subject of several legends.

Later, the ashvamedha became an important ritual to establish the domain and strength of a king. A horse was allowed to wander for a year, followed by the king's men, and all the lands it covered were annexed in the ruler's name. If anybody stopped the horse or challenged it, he had to fight the king and the winner kept the kingdom. At the end of the period, the horse was brought back and sacrificed. While this was a sad end for the magnificent animal, it was an acknowledgement of the animal's importance, for the horse alone could establish the extent of an empire.

In the 'Uttara Kanda' of the *Ramayana*, a later interpolation, Rama conducts an ashvamedha, when his horse is stopped by two young boys. The occasion is used to introduce Rama to his twin sons Lava and Kusha, born and brought up in the ashrama of Valmiki, who fight and defeat their father's brothers, the army of Ayodhya and even Hanuman. Rama then goes to fight them himself, when the sage comes forward to introduce Rama to his sons and heirs. When Rama returns to Ayodhya with his sons (after Sita refuses to follow him and calls on her Mother Earth to take her back), he performs the ashvamedha sacrifice, establishing himself as a chakravartin or emperor.

*Kubera*

One of the navaratnas (nine gems) that surfaced during the churning of the ocean (Samudra Manthana) was a seven-headed flying horse named Uchchhaishravas, which, along with Airavata, became the mount of Lord Indra. Uchchhaishravas is said to have been snow-white.

The incarnation of Kalki, the tenth and final avatara of Lord Vishnu (which is yet to manifest) is generally depicted riding a white horse.

Lord Kubera, the Hindu God of Wealth, sometimes uses a horse as his vehicle.

The chariot of Lord Surya is pulled by seven horses. Hence, he is sometimes referred to as Saptashva (Lord of Seven Horses).

### Hayagriva

Hayagriva is not one of the ten incarnations of Vishnu, but he is one of the additional figures who is identified as an incarnation. This incarnation is not to be confused with the other Hayagriva who appears as a demon in the story of Matsya, the fish incarnation.

There are two stories regarding the origin of the divine Hayagriva. In one, he is an incarnation of Vishnu.

*Hayagriva*

In another he is merely a Deva, or celestial being.

In the first story, Hayagriva was an asura or demon, the son of Kashyapa, the divine progenitor and his demon wife Danu. After practising austerities for a thousand years, Devi appeared before him. Hayagriva asked for the boon of immortality, but had to settle for the boon of being killed only by another Hayagriva, or one with the neck of a horse. Thereafter, he went on the rampage and tormented even the devas, till the celestial beings decided to wake up Vishnu. Brahma bribed the termites with a promise of the leftovers of the yajna (rituals) if they gnawed through Vishnu's bowstring, which was held beneath his chin and the ground, so that it would wake him. The termites obliged, but gnawed so well that the bowstring cut off Vishnu's head. The various accounts vary at this point, some saying that Vishnu found a horse's head, others that the devas found a horse's head for Vishnu. In any case, Vishnu became a Hayagriva and, in this form, he killed the demon and ended the evil that stalked the world.

In another version, Vishnu assumed this form to recover the Vedas, which had been stolen by two asuras.

According to another story, Agni (Fire), Indra (Rain), Vayu (Wind) and Yajna (Sacrifice) began a ritual

*Uchchhaishravas*

with the intention of sharing the offering equally. But Yajna took away the offering and drove the others away with Devi's gift of a divine bow. So the gods created termites which ate through the bow with such force that it cut off Yajna's head. Taking pity, the devas put a horse's head on Yajna's shoulders.

Hayagriva is very likely to have been a horse-headed deity who was absorbed into the Hindu fold as an incarnation of Vishnu. Vishnu as Hayagriva is barely recognizable as an incarnation, all of whom came specifically to save the world from evil.

### Hayashiras

The 'horse head' form of Vishnu was created when sage Aurva cast his anger into the sea. According to the *Bhagavata Purana*, Brahma says that Bhagavata was Hayashirsha, with the colour of gold, of whom the Vedas and the sacrifices are the substance

*Kalki*

and the gods the soul. When he breathed, charming words came out of his nostrils (Dowson 1982).

## Buddhism

The Buddha is also represented by the horse which represents his royal birth. In early sculptures, before he is represented in human form, the horse canopied by an umbrella represented Gautama the prince. Later, he is depicted as a young man on a horse, canopied by an umbrella.

## Jainism

The emblem of the third Tirthankara Sambhavanatha was the horse.

## Haihaya

*Jaina Tirthankara*
*Sambhavanatha*

The Haihaya dynasty traces its birth to a divine horse. Goddess Lakshmi was charmed by King Revanta's horse, when he came to visit Vishnu, and therefore did not hear her husband call her. Angry, Vishnu cursed her to be born as a mare. Contrite, Lakshmi asked him to suggest a penance to reverse the curse. Vishnu stated that the curse would be reversed when she produced a child equal to Vishnu. After praying to Shiva and Parvati for a thousand years, Shiva sent Vishnu to earth as a horse. When the child Haihaya (born of a horse) was born, Vishnu and Lakshmi returned to their heaven Vaikuntha, leaving the child alone in the forest. The child was found and adopted by King Shatajit and his wife who named him Ekavira. After he grew up, they left the kingdom to Ekavira and retired to the forest. This story was invented to give a divine origin to the Haihaya dynasty.

## Solar Symbol

Surya drives a chariot pulled by seven horses representing the seven days of the week. The image appears time and again in

Indian art and architecture, the most famous example being that of Konarak, where the temple itself is the chariot of the sun.

*Surya, the Sun*

According to the later Puranas, Vivashvat, the solar steed, married Sharanya, daughter of Tvashtra, and bore the twins Yama and Yami. Unable to bear the heat Vivashvat raidiated, Sharanya fled disguised as a mare. She left her double who bore a son Manu, the lawgiver and author of the *Manusmriti*. However, Vivashvat noticed the deception and found the mare that subsequently gave birth to the Ashwins, the celestial twins.

*Votive Offerings*

The honour of riding the horse belonged to kings and warriors. As a symbol of royalty and power, it became a votive offering in many parts of India.

The most famous are those gifted to Ayyanaar, the 'watchman' of every village of Tamil Nadu. It is believed that he lives in the sacred grove and wanders around on the horse at night. Terracotta horses from one to six metres tall are given to the deity to redeem a vow. The village potter is also the temple priest, creating the horse and giving it life. The horses are majestic works of art, decorated and painted elaborately, and belong to popular folk religion. The earliest representation of Ayyanaar and the horse is seen on a seventh-century Pallava sculpture from Alagramam in south Arcot. The terracotta horses of Bankura in Bengal, Gorakhpur in Uttar Pradesh, Pavagad in the Panchmahal region of East Gujarat and Ambaji in north Gujarat are tribal areas where this tradition still exists. The territory covered by a real horse as it roamed for a year was claimed by the tribe, possibly derived from the ashvamedha ceremony. But the votive offering could be a redemption from anything, from a simple illness to a battle for land.

*Ecological Role and Current Status*

Horses have long been among the most economically important domesticated animals. However, their importance declined with the introduction of mechanization.

The horse is a prominent figure in religion, mythology and art, besides playing an important role in transportation, agriculture, and warfare. Hundreds of distinct horse breeds were developed, allowing the specialization of horses for specific tasks: lighter horses for racing or riding, heavier horses for farming and those tasks that requiring pulling power. In some societies, horses are a source of food, both meat and milk; in others it is taboo to consume their products. In many parts of India they are used as working animals. Horses and humans have lived and worked together for several millennia in India.

There are remains of the horse in late Indus sites, although there are no representations on the seals. Some of the terracotta animals could pass off as horses, although they could equally be the ass, as the figurines are very rudimentary, though attractive like all folk art.

〰

# Jackal

| | | |
|---|---|---|
| Scientific Name | : | *Canis aureus* Linn |
| Common Names | : | Golden jackal |
| | | Gidhar (Hindi) |
| | | Nari (Tamil) |
| | | Srigalah (Sanskrit) |
| Distribution | : | Throughout India |

While there is no sanctity attached to the jackal, his cunningness is much admired, and he is the hero of common folklore. There is a David–Goliath resemblance in the folk stories that surround the animal, where he pits his brains against the lion's might and comes off as the winner. In the Panchatantra stories, the jackal is invariably the cunning hero who outwits the arrogant lion.

The prevailing myths about the jackal have led to the belief that the animal has superior powers. Therefore the sight of a jackal is considered to be a good omen.

Jambuka, the great sage of yore, was so-named because he would never sit nor sleep, traits believed to belong to the jackal. He became a follower of the Buddha and joined the sangha along with his disciples.

In ancient Egypt, the jackal-headed Anubis was the god of the afterlife. In India too jackals are depicted stealing half-dead bodies from crematoria.

### Ecological Role and Current Status

Jackals are capable of maintaining speeds of 16 km per hour for long periods. They are nocturnal animals, active at dawn and dusk. They are probably the closest to the ancient *canids*.

They are not protected under law. However, they are becoming rare in most places due to the destruction of their habitats.

∼

## Kite

| | | |
|---|---|---|
| Scientific Name | : | *Haliastur indus* Boddaert |
| Common Names | : | Brahmany kite |
| | | Brahmany cheel (Hindi) |
| | | Krishna parunthu (Tamil) |
| | | Khemankari (Sanskrit) |
| Distribution | : | Plains and forests of India |

Garuda has also been identified with the Brahminy kite, which has a beautiful white head and is very impressive. Today it is the kite that is regarded as Garuda and is revered.

Later mythology describes Garuda as having a white face, red wings and a golden body. His lustre was so brilliant that the gods mistook him for Agni. His wife was Unnati and his son Sampati.

Both the eagle and the Brahminy kite have been identified with Garuda. The earlier descriptions call him golden-bodied—the colour of the eagle—but later descriptions describe him with a white head, the colour of the Brahminy kite.

However, it is said that the gods gave Garuda snakes for food. The unique characteristic of the eagle and Garuda is as a predator of snakes, which he searches out and devours.

Brahminy kites are, on the other hand, scavengers, rather than hunters, although they do hunt for a variety of small prey.

The Rig Veda does not indicate any prevalence of snake worship. Later, in the epics, Garuda became a 'controller' of snakes, rather than their killer.

Over millennia, Garuda has been identified with both the eagle and the kite. But the eagle is the more probable bird.

*Ecological Role and Current Status*

The Brahminy kite is a familiar bird of prey and often referred to as the Singapore bald eagle. Brahminy kites are scavengers, rather than hunters, but they do hunt for small prey like fish, crabs, shellfish, frogs, rodents, reptiles and even insects. They forage both over water and land, soaring 20–50 m above the surface, and swooping down and snatching their prey with their talons. Brahminy kites do not dive into the water— they only catch prey found on the water surface. They generally scavenge from food scraps and garbage and are thus commonly found at harbours and coastal areas. They capture animals running away from fires and steal from other raptors, while their catch is eaten on the wing, to prevent theft. Often several kites quarrel noisily over a catch.

~

# Lion

| Scientific Name | : | *Panthera leo* Linn |
|---|---|---|
| Common Names | : | Asiatic Lion |
| | | Sher (Hindi) |
| | | Singam (Tamil) |
| | | Simha (Sanskrit) |
| Distribution | : | Confined to the Gir forest in Gujarat |

The lion is a symbol of power and majesty. He is regarded as the king of animals in literature and art. He represents the chakravartin or the supreme ruler, a heraldic emblem of overlordship and all-powerful emperor. The emperor's throne is called the simhasana.

The lion first appears on Harappan pottery, though not on the seals. The lion in the Rig Veda represents the strength of gods like Indra and Agni. Obviously its territory once extended over a larger area. However, it does not appear on the Indus seals, which means that it did not live in the Sindhu–Sarasvati Basin.

The lion once roamed Mesopotamia (ancient Iraq–Iran) till it was wiped out. Today the Gir forest in Gujarat is the sole home of the Asiatic lion.

## Symbol of Royalty and Royal Power

The lion appears on the capitals of the Ashokan pillars, proclaiming that ruler's universal all-encompassing vision of dharma. The four majestic lions stand back to back, in Persepolitan style, for pillars topped by majestic lions with deeply incised manes were first seen in the palaces of Persepolis in ancient Iran.

The state emblem of contemporary India is adopted from the famous lion capital of Ashoka's Pillar at Sarnath, Uttar Pradesh. The capital was erected by Emperor Ashoka to mark the site where Lord Buddha delivered his first sermon to his five disciples.

Several dynasties proclaimed their power by sculpting roaring lions. The lion appears on the Amaravati stupa. The base (adisthana) of the pillars of the Pallava rulers of south India was a seated lion.

*Ashoka's lion capital*

The yali, a mythical animal popular in the Vijayanagara period, was based on the lion.

Lion hunting was also the sport of kings, and its depictions of such scenes appear frequently on the gateway of Bharhut and Sanchi, while the lion-killing coins of Chandragupta II commemorate the conquest of Malwa and Saurashtra.

## Narasimha

> *Glory to you, O Lord of the universe,*
> *Who took the form of a Man-Lion;*
> *As easily as you would crush a wasp with your fingers,*
> *You tore apart the demon Hiranyakashipu,*
> *With the sharp nails of your bare hands,*
> *Which are as beautiful as the lotus flower.*

*Gita Govinda* of Jayadeva

Narasimha, the fourth incarnation of Lord Vishnu was half-man (Nara) and half-lion (Simha). He killed a demon named Hiranyakashipu.

After the death of Hiranyaksha, who appears in the boar incarnation of Vishnu (see BOAR), his brother Hiranyakashipu swore to avenge his death. By performing severe austerities, he obtained a powerful boon from Brahma the Creator: that neither man nor animal could kill him, not at night or in the day, not on earth, sky or water, neither inside nor outside and with neither weapon nor fire or water. This made the demon so powerful that he became arrogant, savage and cruel, ruling the earth with brutality and terror. He challenged the gods themselves and proclaimed himself to be divine.

*Narasimha*

But the demon's son Prahlada was a devout worshipper of Lord Vishnu, a devotion the demon could not accept. He tried to change his son's views by cajolement, threats and even, finally, by trying to kill him. But Prahlada was undaunted, for he knew that Vishnu would save his devotee. Finally, Hiranyakashipu asked Prahlada where his beloved Vishnu was. Prahlada answered: 'everywhere'. Then the demon kicked a pillar and asked whether Vishnu lived in the pillar. Suddenly, Narasimha, a lion-faced man—neither man nor animal—sprang out of the pillar and a terrible fight ensued. Narasimha fought the wicked demon all the way to the front door—neither inside nor outside the house. As the sun was setting—it was neither day nor night—Narasimha killed the wicked demon with his claws—not a weapon nor fire or water. Thus the wicked demon was destroyed without Brahma's boon being violated.

Narasimha is especially popular in Andhra Pradesh and Karnataka. Ahobalam is the site of the temple of Roudra (angry) Narasimha, where the pillar from which he emerged and the lake in which he washed his hands after killing Hiranyakashipu are situated. At Simhachalam (near Visakhapatnam) is the temple of Narasimha built by his devotee Prahlada, who was king of the east. The Jeers (religious leaders) of the Vaishnava sect are called Alagiya Singhar (Beautiful Lion), after Narasimha whom they worship.

The story of Narasimha serves to teach the devotee that the Lord is everywhere, and always comes to the help of believers.

Narasimha was a favourite deity of the Vijayanagara kings and an enormous figure dominates the ancient city of Vijayanagara (present-day Hampi). This image of Lakshmi-Narasimha (or Ugranarasimha, meaning the terrifying Narasimha) was carved in situ out of a single rock. According to an inscription found there, it was created in 1528 CE during the rule of Krishnadevaraya. The icon originally had a small image of Lakshmi sitting on his lap. The Narasimha image of Hampi is 6.7 m tall. It was mutilated and the figure of Lakshmi was damaged by the invading confederation of Muslim Bahmani kings in 1565 CE. The remaining figure indicates what an awesome image it must have once been, with a deeply chiselled and well-delineated mane, large bulging eyes and a broad chest. Narasimha sits on the coils of the snake Adisesha, who canopies him with seven hoods. The entire composition is set within a makara torana arch, with a yali face above the seven-hooded Adisesha.

*Narasimhi*

### Narasimhi

The goddess Narasimhi is one of the Sapta Matrikas, the Seven Mothers of Tantric religion. She is generally propitiated by the sacrifice of fowl.

### Lion as Vehicle

Goddess Durga, the fierce form of the goddess Parvati, is often depicted as a warrior goddess, who destroys demons. There are two forms of Durga—Vishnu Durga and Shiva Durga. Vishnu Durga rides the lion, which aids her in the battle against the buffalo demon Mahisha.

She is referred to as Sheravali in north India, as her vahana is a lion. Sometimes crude images of lions are given as votive offerings at Durga temples. The lion often sits on the roofs of Devi temples. In fact, the lions on the roof of the Balaji temple at Tirumala in Andhra Pradesh in southern India has given rise to the theory—believed by a considerable number of faithful followers—that the deity within is actually Durga.

*Durga on her lion mount*

The lion also is the doorkeeper in several Shiva temples.

The yali or mythical lion—a lion-faced gargoyle—is an architectural feature in several temples, sometimes decorating pillars, sometimes supporting the main structure and often serving to keep away evil.

*The Lion in the Near East*

The most famous lion figure of the ancient world was the sphinx, with the lion's body and a human face, depicting the power and majesty of Egyptian kings.

Durga was neither the first not the only goddess to ride a lion. Qadesh (meaning 'holy' in Assyrian) rides a lion. She was the goddess of love and beauty, the beloved of Ptah, consort of Min and the mother of Reshep.

The destructive aspect of the Egyptian goddess Hathor was the lion-faced Sekhmet, a solar symbol who illuminates the darkest corners and burns out all opposition. She was the goddess of war who was married to Ptah.

Osiris, the god who resurrected the dead and introduced agriculture to man, is often depicted as a lion.

Ishtar is the Babylonian and Assyrian goddess of war and fertility, not unlike Durga. She rides a lion and it is commonly believed that the association of Durga with the lion is derived from that of Ishtar.

*Yali*

The Jewish tribe of Judah had a lion emblem. As their capital was also Jerusalem, the united Israel–Judah territory was called Judea by the Romans.

When Haile Selassie became emperor of Ethiopia in 1929, he took the lion as his emblem and the title Lion of Judea, as Ethiopians are believed to be the descendants and subjects of the Queen of Sheba who married Solomon, King of Israel.

### Kumbhodara

Shiva steps on the lion Kumbhodara in order to mount his vehicle Nandi. As the lion is depicted as constantly ravenously hungry, Shiva's footstep depicts the conquest of hunger, which is at the root of desire.

### Buddhism

The Buddha was described as Sakyasimha (Lion of the Sakyas) or Sakyamuni (sage of the Sakyas), because he belonged to the Sakya clan.

The lion is a very important symbol in Buddhism. It is associated with royalty, strength and power. The teachings of Buddha are sometimes referred to as the 'lion's roar of dharma'. In Buddhist art, lions are often depicted as the protector of dharma, supporting the throne of the Buddha. Four lions, or even eight, support the four corners of his throne.

Simhamukha is a Buddhist dakini with a lion face.

## Jainism

The emblem of the twenty-fourth and last Tirthankara Mahavira was the lion, representing his royal birth.

## Lion Pillars

The famous pillar capitals of Emperor Ashoka, found all over northern India, were topped by four majestic lions or bulls seated back to back, carrying a large wheel, the wheel of dharma.

*Mahavira*

On the capital of the Ashoka pillar at Sarnath, Uttar Pradesh, which was erected by Emperor Ashoka to mark the site where Lord Buddha delivered his first sermon to his five disciples, four lions face the four cardinal directions and carry the dharmachakra above them. The pillars and their lion capitals carried Ashoka's message of non-violence all over India and Asia.

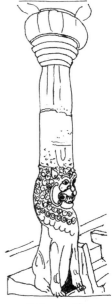

The selection of the heraldic animals is significant. The lion was alien to eastern India or Pataliputra (present-day Patna), where Ashoka's capital was situated. While the bull was a continuum of the Vedic period, when the gods themselves were called bulls, the lions obviously a result of Persian influence, being similar to by the heraldic lions of Persepolis in ancient Persia. But the same capitals have a ring of lively animals—bull, elephant, deer, horse and geese—at the base, obviously inspired

*Pallava pillar*

by Indian traditions and in a state of happiness resulting from a royal policy of ahimsa.

The Pallava pillars of Mamallapuram (seventh century CE) are supported by lion bases, while several Indian dynasties used lion motifs to embellish their buildings. Later dynasties like the Vijayanagara also built pillars supported by lion bases.

Yet there is no evidence of the lion either in north or south India. With the exception of Gujarat, India was the home of the tiger.

### Singh

The title Singh dates back to the Vedic period and means lion. It was originally only used by the Rajputs, a Kshatriya or military caste, but after the creation of the Sikh Khalsa brotherhood by Guru Gobind Singh in 1699, the Sikhs also adopted the name Singh.

### Ecological Role and Current Status

The Asiatic lion ranged once from the Mediterranean to India, covering most of south-west Asia where it was also known as the Persian lion. The historic distribution included the Caucasus to Yemen and from Macedonia to present-day India through Iran (Persia), Pakistan till the borders of Bangladesh. Today they are extinct from all these areas except the Gir forest in Gujarat. The current wild population in India is restricted to the Gir National Park and Wildlife Sanctuary of western India, which had about 359 lions as in April 2006, in a 1,412 sq. km sanctuary covered with scrub and open deciduous forest.

Compared to their African cousins, Asiatic lions have shaggier coats, a longer tassel of hair on the end of the tail and long tufts of hair on their elbows. Males are 1.6 to 2.2 m long and weigh 125 to 225 kg, while females are 1.4 to 1.7 m in length and weigh 100 to 150 kg. Asian lions are highly social animals, living in units called prides, although these are much smaller than those of African lions. The males only associate with the pride when mating or on a large kill. It has been suggested that this may be because of their prey animals being smaller than those in Africa, thus requiring fewer hunters to tackle them.

India's lions are highly endangered. They are poisoned for attacking livestock, while floods, fires and epidemics threaten to wipe out large numbers at a time. Their restricted range makes them especially vulnerable. Nearly 15,000 to 20,000 open irrigation wells dug by farmers in the area have also drowned many lions. Farmers on the periphery of the Gir forest frequently use crude and illegal electrical fences powered by high voltage overhead power lines, which kill the lions and other wildlife.

The biggest threat faced by the Gir lions is from the Maldhari tribe, who do not poach as they are vegetarians, but graze their cattle in the forest, causing habitat destruction, and collect firewood, thereby reducing the natural prey base and endangering the lions. The lack of natural prey forces the lions to kill cattle instead, making them a target for poisoning by the local people.

$\sim$

# Lizard

*Bengal Monitor Lizard*

| | | |
|---|---|---|
| Scientific Name | : | *Varanus bengalensis* Daudin |
| Common Name | : | Common Indian monitor |
| | | Gho (Hindi) |
| | | Udumbu (Tamil) |
| | | Ghorpad (Marathi) |
| | | Godha (Sanskrit) |
| Distribution | : | Throughout India and Bangladesh |

According to a popular legend in Maharashtra, Tanaji Malusare, general of Chhatrapati Shivaji Maharaj, founder of the Maratha kingdom, used a monitor lizard, with ropes attached to it, to climb the walls of the fort of Kondana in the Battle of Sinhagadh. The fort, on the outskirts of present-day Pune, was then an outpost, strategically placed in the centre of a string of forts of Raigadh, Purandar, and Torna, and overlooking Pune and the surrounding countryside. The recapture of Kondana (which had earlier belonged to Shivaji but was captured by the Mughals) was essential to re-establish control over the Pune region. The Mughals had maintained a battalion of 5,000 troops led by Udai Bhan, a relative of Mirza Raja Jai Singh. The fort was built in such a way that all its approaches were covered by cannon fire. Only one turret was not well defended as it was at the top of a vertical overhanging cliff.

In 1670, Tanaji Malusare swore to recapture the fort. He used Chhatrapati Shivaji's pet monitor lizard, a Ghorpad named Yeshwanti, with a rope tied around its shoulder for climbing up the walls of the fort from its steepest and the least guarded side. In the dead of a moonless night, Tanaji and 300 brave followers scaled the cliff using ropes tied to the reptile. The Ghorpad can stick fast to any surface and with one end of a

*Sacred lizard*

rope tied to it several adults can use this force to scale a vertical cliff,. Once he had scaled the fort after the giant lizard, Tanaji threw down rope ladders for the others to climb. Seeing Tanaji, Udai Bhan cut off the hand with which Tanaji was holding his shield. Undaunted, Tanaji used his turban to ward off Udai Bhan's sword and continued fighting for two hours with his wristless left arm bleeding profusely. It is for this feat of Tanaji that he is called Narvir—A Brave amongst Men. At the end of this ordeal, the exhausted Tanaji fell to his death, while Udai Bhan too lost his life at the hands of the Maratha soldiers.

Shivaji Maharaj is said to have said on this occasion 'Gadh aala pan simha gela' (We have won the fort but have lost the Lion—Tanaji). The fort of Kondana was renamed 'Sinhagadh' in honour of Tanaji's brave deed.

Unfortunately, criminals subsequently started misusing the monitor lizard to climb the walls of houses they were burgling.

### Ecological Role and Current Status

The Bengal monitor lizard measures up to 75 cm in body length with 100 cm long tail. It feeds on small terrestrial vertebrates, ground birds and their eggs, arthropods and fish. Monitor lizards are killed for their meat and skin and are threatened in many places by hunting. Famous for their ability to cling to smooth surfaces, they were traditionally reared and trained for this purpose by herders in Maharashtra. Being cold-blooded reptiles, monitor lizards often cling to vertical rock faces and old walls to warm themselves in the morning sun.

### Gecko

| | | |
|---|---|---|
| Scientific Name | : | *Hemidactylus frenatus* Schlegel |
| Common Names | : | Common house gecko |
| | | Chhipkali (Hindi) |
| | | Palli (Tamil) |
| | | Griha godha (Sanskrit) |
| Distribution | : | Human habitation structures in the tropics and subtropics |

The golden gecko or common house lizard is found along the Eastern Ghats. It is revered in the east and south as an animal whose mere touch assures a person of moksha (liberation) of the soul.

As it is not possible to touch a live gecko, several temples keep a golden replica to be touched for good luck.

At the Varadaraja Perumal temple in Kanchipuram, Tamil Nadu, gold and silver geckos are fixed on to the ceiling to be touched by devotees in search of good luck. According to local legend, the two sons of sage Shringabera were the disciples of sage Gautama. One day, when they brought water for their guru's puja, he found two lizards in the water. The angry sage cursed the two students to become lizards. When the contrite students begged his forgiveness, he advised them to pray to Lord Varadaraja of Kanchipuram who gives a thousand times more than is asked of him. The disciples did so and were blessed with the liberation of their souls, while he turned their bodies into gold and silver. The gold and silver lizards were kept in the temple with the promise that all those who came to worship Lord Varadaraja at Kanchipuram should also touch and worship the two lizards, thereby relieving themselves from all sins and illnesses.

Similarly, a golden gecko could once be touched for good luck at the Venkatesha temple in Tirumala, Andhra Pradesh. This practice has now been discontinued in view of the crowds that throng the pilgrimage town.

*Ecological Role and Current Status*

Geckos are small- to average-sized lizards that make chirping sounds when they interact with other geckos. The name stems from the Malay word *gekoq*, derived from cry. Many species have specialized toe pads that enable them to climb smooth vertical surfaces and move across ceilings. They are common in the tropics and subtropical regions where several species of geckos live inside human habitations.

The house gecko is never killed because it feeds on insects and other pests. This provides it protection with the threat that bad luck will follow—in the form of disease and illness—if a gecko is killed.

∿

# Mite

*Velvet Mite*

| Scientific Name | : | *Trombidium grandissimum* Koch |
|---|---|---|
| Common Names | : | Arudrapurugu (Telugu) |
| Distribution | : | Widely distributed in India |

The velvet mite is commonly believed to herald the rains. Farmers in Andhra Pradesh consider it to be a messenger of the rain gods.

*Ecological Role and Current Status*

The velvet mite is not a spider. But both spiders and velvet mites belong to the class of Arachnida, derived from the Greek word *arachnae*, which means spider. Velvet mites are akin to spiders, with adults having eight legs. They are slow-moving parasites with big appetites. Even the young prey upon insects many times their size. They also consume insect eggs. Some mites are used for controlling many kinds of insect pests, and so are considered beneficial to the environment.

Unfortunately, the velvet mite is also believed to be an aphrodisiac, because of which it is caught for the extraction of its oil, which is believed to increase sexual desire and cure paralysis.

∿

# Mongoose

| Scientific Name | : | *Herpestes edwardsi* Geoffrey |
|---|---|---|
| Common Names | : | Mangus, Newal, Newara (Hindi) |
| | | Keeree (Tamil) |
| | | Nukula (Sanskrit) |
| Distribution | : | Throughout India |

The mongoose is often depicted on the lap of Kubera, a yaksha and a receptacle of treasures. The mongoose as a treasure probably results from his role in killing the much feared snake.

## Buddhism

The Buddhist equivalent of Kubera is Jambhala, who holds the mongoose in his right hand and a citrus fruit in the left. It is believed that when Jambhala presses the two sides of the animal, it vomits treasures. Jambhala's consort is Vasudhara, whose vehicle is the mongoose (Majupuria 2000).

## Ecological Role and Current Status

A mongoose is a small cat-like carnivore. The word mongoose is derived from the Marathi word mangus. There are more than thirty species, ranging from 30 cm to 120 cm in length. Some species of mongooses lead solitary lives, seeking out food only for themselves, while others travel in groups, known as mongaggles, sharing food amongst themselves. Mongooses feed on insects, crabs, earthworms, lizards, snakes, chickens, and rodents. However, they also eat eggs and carrion. The Indian mongoose is popularly used to fight and kill venomous snakes, even king cobras. They are able to do this because of their agility and cunning, thick coat and high

*Kubera*

resistance to the venom. However, they prefer to avoid the cobra and do not consume their meat. Mongooses have receptors for acetylcholine that, like the receptors in snakes, are shaped so that it is impossible for snake neurotoxin venom to attach to them.

The mongoose is the natural enemy of snakes and is native to the Indian subcontinent. It is easily caught and tamed. Unfortunately, this has resulted in its capture and exploitation by snake charmers who organize snake–mongoose fights for entertainment. It is also killed for its furry tail, which is used to make paint brushes. The unchecked killing of mongooses has depleted their numbers considerably.

Some species of mongoose can be easily domesticated, for they are very intelligent animals and can even be taught simple tricks. They are often kept as pets to protect houses from rodents and snakes. Rudyard Kipling's story of Rikki Tikki Tavi is not far from the truth.

⌇

# Monkey

*Grey Langur*

| Scientific Name | : | *Semenopithecus entellus* Dufresne |
|---|---|---|
| Common Names | : | Grey Langur (all seven species) |
| | | Hanuman langur (Hindi) |
| | | Kurangu (Tamil) |
| | | Kapi, vanarah (Sanskrit) |
| Distribution | : | Throughout India |

*Rhesus Macaque*

| Scientific Name | : | *Macaca mulatta* Zimmermann |
|---|---|---|
| Common Names | : | Rhesus monkey |
| | | Bandar (Hindi) |
| | | Kurangu (Tamil) |
| | | Kapi, Vanarah (Sanskrit) |
| Distribution | : | Throughout India |

There are several terracotta figures of monkeys in the Harappan sites. Several species are found in India.

The Sanskrit word for primate is kapi. However, the word vanara is used for monkey in the *Ramayana*—it is derived from the two words vana (forest) and nara (man), meaning 'people of the forest' or forest dweller, and probably never meant monkey. This is confirmed by the Jaina *Ramayana*, which calls the Vanaras a tribe of brave forest-dwelling warriors, and the *Mahabharata*, which describes the Vanaras as a forest-dwelling tribe. Thus the so-called 'monkey' tribe was obviously one that either worshipped the monkey or used the monkey symbol (or totem), or maybe neither. Even Jambavan the bear, whose daughter Jambavati (a human) marries Krishna, is called a vanara, proving the point that the word originally meant forest-dweller.

The poet Valmiki obviously preferred to treat them as monkeys: a keen observer of animals, he brought several animal species, including the bear and squirrel, into his epic, besides describing in loving terms the flora and fauna of the Dandaka forest. Thus Rama, a hunter and non-vegetarian, became responsible for the veneration of several species.

However, over the centuries, the term vanara has become an umbrella for all the primate species of India, giving them a special status and protection. Later writers of the *Ramayana* described the vanaras as monkeys and the association has come to stay in popular culture. While the grey langur is actually identified with Hanuman and his Vanaras, the rhesus macaque is also associated with the monkey tribe of the *Ramayana* and accorded equal status in places where the grey langur is missing.

The sanctity accorded to Hanuman has penetrated so deep into Indian culture that all monkeys are protected by the common people and given a special status. In fact, temple towns are populated by large troupes of monkeys whom the pilgrims feed in order to earn merit. Even Buddhist and Jaina temples protect monkeys. The Buddha is believed to have taken an earlier avatara as a monkey, while the emblem of the fourth Jaina Tirthankara Abhinandanatha was a monkey. Elaborate funeral rites are held for dead langurs and rhesus monkeys, whose bodies are garlanded and buried or cremated in a sitting position, as befits a sanyasi.

Vanaras play an important role in the *Ramayana*, where they are described as amusing and childish, honest and loyal, courageous and kind. They were volatile, indisciplined, vacillating—even fickle-minded, rough, emotional, inquisitive, gullible and gregarious, living in groups. They lived in Kishkindha, present-day Hampi in Karnataka, in the aranya (forest) of Dandaka, where Rama met, sought and received their help in his war against Ravana.

On the wall of the temple of Angkor Wat in Cambodia is found an enormous relief of the war between the Vanaras and the rakshasas. Using sticks and stones, the monkey army was able to decimate most of the rakshasas. But the hero of the war was undoubtedly Hanuman, the greatest and most famous of the vanaras and a warrior who could not be defeated. His fame and veneration have spread far and wide, wherever the story of Rama travelled. In fact, his image is used as a good luck charm in many parts of South and South-East Asia.

*Hanuman*

Hanuman was a loyal devotee of Rama, one of the ten incarnations of Lord Vishnu. Some even see Hanuman as an incarnation of Lord Shiva. An army of monkeys or the Vanara sena (army) under the leadership of Hanuman was instrumental in the defeat of the demon king Ravana of Lanka, when he fought against Lord Rama.

*Hanuman*

Hanuman's other names are Hanumat, Anjaneya (son of Anjana) and Pavanasuta (son of the wind). Because, as a child, he swallowed the sun, Indra threw his vajra at him, hitting him on the jaw (hanu), hence his name Hanuman or Hanumat. He was fast as the wind, his father, and had great physical strength, which makes him the favourite deity of wrestlers.

According to the *Shiva Purana*, Hanuman was the son of Shiva and Vishnu's feminine form of Mohini (or, according to other sources, Parvati), whose embryo was deposited in Anjana's womb. Thus Hanuman's mother was Anjana, giving him the name Anjaneya. His foster father was Kesari, another vanara.

Hanuman is the devotee par excellence, a monkey and a god, the unquestioning ambassador of Rama. He was a great warrior and an immortal, yet he stands out because of the rare quality of humility he possessed, being totally unaware of his strength and divinity. He acquires divinity by his absolute faith in his Lord Rama.

When Sugriva is banished from Kishkindha, Hanuman remembers that rishi Matanga's ashram was out of Vali's jurisdiction and helps Sugriva find asylum there.

The distraught Rama, searching desperately for his wife Sita who was carried away by Ravana, the wicked Rakshasa king of Lanka, arrives at Kishkinda (Vijayanagara or contemporary Hampi). He is recognized by Hanuman who gives him Sita's jewels, which she had thrown away as Ravana carried her off. Hanuman introduces Rama to the exiled Vanara king Sugriva, who is helped by Rama to regain his kingdom. (See VALI and SUGRIVA later in this section). Hanuman was Sugriva's minister, and used to see Vali kick Sugriva every day, which bothered him very much. He waited for an opportunity to kill Vali, and this came in the form of Rama, who was searching for his spouse Sita and required an army to fight Ravana. He introduced the two, made an alliance between them and then waited for Rama to finish off Vali.

After the death of Vali and the coronation of Sugriva, Hanuman was sent by Sugriva to look for Sita. He reached Lanka by growing to his full size. His shadow, says the epic, was ten yojanas broad and thirty yojanas long. In one leap, he crossed the straits separating the island from the Indian subcontinent and found Sita in a grove of ashoka trees. He allowed himself to be caught and tied up. His tail was set on fire, but he escaped and set Lanka on fire.

Hanuman returned to Rama and mobilized an army of monkeys who built a bridge (setu) to cross over from south India to Lanka. He led the rag-tag monkey army, armed with sticks and stones, and killed some of the greatest rakshasa warriors. He defeated the demoness of Mount Mainaka, who guarded the island.

Hanuman brought life back to both Rama and Lakshmana. Rama and Lakshmana were badly wounded at the beginning of the war by Ravana's son Indrajit, a great rakshasa warrior, and nearly died, tied up by the demon's snake arrows. Then Sushena, father-in-law of the vanara king Sugriva, told Hanuman to fetch the life-saving herbs that grew on the Drona and Chandra mountains, which lay in the ocean where the nectar of immortality (amrita) was churned. However, Garuda appeared and saved the brothers.

Hanuman was a tiger among monkeys and the monkeys' best friend, who alone had the power to save the brothers, continued Jambavan. Jambavan then instructed Hanuman to fly over the ocean and go to Himavat (Himalayas) where, between the golden peaks of Kailasa he would find four herbs unmatched in shining splendour: mritasanjivani, vishalyakarani, sauvarnakarani and samdhani. Hanuman expanded himself till the earth and ocean trembled, and flew off in the direction of Mount Meru. He found the mountain of herbs shining like fire because of the plants that grew on it. He began plucking them, but the herbs, knowing his intent, made themselves invisible. Furious, he uprooted the mountain itself and took it back to the vanara army in Lanka. And Rama, Lakshmana and the monkeys were restored to life and health by inhaling the sweet-smelling medicinal herbs. Thereafter, Hanuman took the mountain back to the Himalayas and returned to the war in Lanka.

Hanuman challenged Indrajit to battle and took care of the demon hordes, thereby permitting Lakshmana to have the satisfaction and honour of killing the demon. Later, when Ravana nearly killed Lakshmana, Hanuman went back to bring the mountain again, and Lakshman was revived.

Hanuman could have killed Ravana, but he left that privilege to his lord Rama, whose wife had been abducted by the evil demon and whose Dharma required him to kill him. After the death of Ravana, Hanuman was sent to inform Sita of Rama's victory, then again to tell her to bathe and dress and bring her back to Rama. He was sent ahead of Rama's return to Ayodhya to inform Guha, king of the Nishadas, and Rama's brother Bharata of Rama's successful return to Ayodhya.

When Rama's exile was over and he returned to Ayodhya, Hanuman followed him. Rama gave Sita a necklace of pearls to give to whoever she liked for possessing the qualities of 'lustre, courage, good name, efficiency, capability, humility, refinement, manliness, achievement and wisdom'. She naturally chose Hanuman who then also received the gift of immortality from Rama.

Hanuman derived his great strength and his ability to fly from his father Vayu, the wind god. However, he was so modest that he did not know his strength until somebody reminded him of it. He is invoked before a journey, so that his strength, which protected Rama and Lakshmana, may protect the devotee. He is also invoked during a strong wind.

The true hero of the *Ramayana* is Hanuman, who is flawless, with superhuman skill which he uses for the triumph of truth and goodness and the destruction of evil represented by the demons. So popular is Hanuman that he and his exploits have been held up as role models through centuries. The *Ramayana* calls him a perfect being, learned in the shastras and with no equal in understanding their meaning. He is the ninth author of grammar and, in rules of austerity, rivals Prajapati.

Hanuman is the embodiment of dharma, and will never see death, for he is one of the seven immortals (chiranjeevi). He is the only character who appears in both the great epics, the *Ramayana* and the *Mahabharata*. In the later epic *Mahabharata*, Hanuman appears as an old monkey and the elder brother of the great Pandava warrior Bhima, the son of Vayu and Kunti. Bhima asks the old monkey to move out of his way, and the monkey asks him to move his tail, since he is too old to do it. Bhima tries to move the tail but does not succeed. Then he realizes there is more to the monkey than is apparent. Hanuman then reveals his identity and accepts Bhima's request to fly on the Pandava flag during the Kurukshetra war.

In later literature, stories of Hanuman's exploits of immeasurable strength—combined with a total naivety regarding his abilities—captured the popular imagination. According to one legend, as a child, Hanuman swallowed the sun, plunging the whole world into darkness. All the gods prayed to him to spit it out, which he did, saving the world from a catastrophe. He could lift hills, as he did when he was asked to bring the sanjivani plant from the Himalayas. He was as wise as he was strong. When going to Lanka to ascertain the whereabouts of Sita, a demon called Surasa tried to save Ravana by destroying Hanuman. She asked him to enter her mouth. Hanuman agreed, but first expanded his size to make her expand his mouth. Suddenly he shrank himself and darted into her mouth and out through her ear, and sped off on his way. He was a great yogi, a musician and grammarian, possessing the eight supreme powers (ashtha siddhi).

Hanuman became a cult figure in the medieval period, through the works of Tulsidas who wrote the *Ramcharitmanas* and the *Hanuman Chalisa* in Hindi, the language of the common man.

He is held as the portrayal of a true devotee, an image of what every person should be.

The grey langur is also referred to as the Hanuman langur as it is identified with Hanuman and the vanaras. It is said that during the war against the rakshasas in Lanka, Hanuman was trapped in a fire. The other monkeys went to help him. All their faces got burnt, hence the langur has a black face.

## Totem

It is likely that Hanuman was the god of the totemic Vanara tribe, more so since there are records of a Vanara tribe having existed in central India. However, he grew beyond that association to become a divine person in his own right.

When the British arrived in India and went to the islands in the Bay of Bengal, they named them the Andaman Islands after the Hanuman tribe, a tribe that dressed like monkeys, with a tail, and called themselves the Hanuman.

While the other animal deities are worshipped and revered, the rest of their species are not given special privileges. The case of the much-abused elephant is one such example, in spite of the popularity and status of Ganesha, the elephant-headed god. Only monkeys are treated on par with people, talking to humans, fighting alongside humans and making friends with and enemies of human beings. It is interesting to note that Hindu religion and its adherents recognized the similarity of humans and other primate species, and refrained from killing the latter.

## Icon

The monkey appears among the terracotta figurines of the Indus Valley. In Bharhut the monkey makes an offering to the Buddha.

Hanuman appears in various forms: as the devotee with his two hands clasped together as in prayer; standing or kneeling before his beloved Rama; holding the mace (club) in one hand

and Mount Kailasa in the other, even as he is either flying or starting to fly; tearing open the skin over his heart to reveal the image of Rama and Sita seated within. The image that is worshipped is invariably in the form of a devotee or as the son of the wind taking off into the skies.

Hanuman images are protectors keeping out evil spirits and dangers. Often the images are depicted with a demon underfoot, representing the rakshasas that he destroyed in such large numbers.

Small Hanuman figures are kept as good-luck talismans even among non-Hindu populations in South-East Asia.

### Symbolism

Hanuman remained a bachelor all through his life, dedicating himself to Rama and Sita and symbolizing absolute and total devotion to one's Lord. Although the other monkeys are described as childish and irresponsible, playing pranks and not concentrating, in typical monkey behaviour, Hanuman is a role model of how one can rise above one's birth and environment to evolve into a perfect being. He is strong, but is unaware of his strength or physical prowess and uses it sparingly, only in the service of truth.

Hanuman is popularly called Bajrang Bali in north India and is a symbol of strength. Wrestlers and warriors often chant 'Bajrang Bali ki jai' to spur their followers. The militant Hindu organization Bajrang Dal is named after Hanuman or Bajrang Bali, to evoke the strength of Hanuman.

### Hanuman Chalisa

In the sixteenth century Sant Tulsidas wrote the *Hanuman Chalisa*, a hymn of forty verses praising and invoking Hanuman. This hymn celebrates Hanuman as the godhead and is very popular all over north India.

## Anjana

Anjana the Vanara performed severe austerities sitting on a hill at Kishkindha in order to produce a son. The foetus produced by Shiva and Vishnu as Mohini (or, say some sources, Shiva and Parvati) was given to Vayu, the wind god, who gave it to Anjana to hold in her womb. The child who was born to Anjana and her vanara husband Kunjara (also known as Kesari) was Anjaneya or Hanuman, the greatest of the vanaras.

## Vali and Sugriva

These are two Vanara brothers, chiefs of their tribe. They were fathered by the gods with Vanara women, as was the rest of the Vanara tribe.

Vali was the son of Indra and ruler of Kishkindha. Later Puranas say he was born of Aruna, the male charioteer of Surya. His wife was Tara and his younger brother was Sugriva.

Sugriva's wife was Ruma. Vali had received a boon that anyone who came before him lost half his strength to Vali, thereby making Vali virtually unconquerable. This was used by Rama to kill Vali with an arrow aimed at his back.

*Vali and Sugriva*

One day, the demon Mayavi challenged Vali to a battle. Vali accepted, but the demon disappeared into a cave, followed by Vali. When he did not return for a year and blood oozed out of the cave's entrance, his brother Sugriva, mistakenly taking the blood for Vali's, concluded that his brother was dead, and sealed the mouth of the cave to prevent the demon from coming out. He took over the kingdom and Vali's 'widowed' wife Tara. However, Vali returned and, believing that Sugriva sealed the mouth of the cave because he coveted the kingdom, took back his wife and Sugriva's, and banished Sugriva, in spite of the latter's efforts to explain his role. The two brothers became bitter enemies and Sugriva wandered the forest with his small band of supporters, which included Hanuman.

When Rama entered Kishkindha in search of Sita, he met Hanuman who took him to Sugriva. Rama and Sugriva conspired to kill Vali and take over Kishkindha, thereby placing the Vanara army at Rama's disposal in his coming fight against Ravana and his rakshasa army of Lanka.

Sugriva challenged Vali to battle and the latter was killed by Rama, who hid in a bush behind Vali, thereby leaving a question mark over his reputation of being the perfect human being. Vali asks Rama to justify his act, for he killed from the back in an ambush. Rama justifies his act by saying that Vali had taken away Sugriva's wife, even though Sugriva was still alive, and Vali needed to be punished for violating dharma.

In spite of Rama's justification of killing Vali as a punishment for adharma, the killing of Vali is the single most reprehensible action by Rama,. The death of Vali is one of the most moving sequences of the *Ramayana*. In retribution, Rama grants Vali instant moksha or liberation of the soul.

Sugriva married Tara, as per the Vanara custom by which a widow is married to her husband's brother, and became the king of the Vanaras.

Valmiki has been described as a great observer of India's geography. But he was also a great observer of animal life. His descriptions of Sugriva and the warrior brigade, Sugriva's and Vali's defeat and the taking over of the females are typical langur behaviour. The bachelorhood of Hanuman and the other Vanaras is again typically langur—only the strongest male maintains a harem.

As the son of the sun, Sugriva is also called Ravinandana. He was a dissolute and womanizing monkey, unlike his disciplined elder brother. However, he collects the Vanara army and leads them to battle against the rakshasas of Lanka. The Vanara army builds the bridge connecting Rameshvaram (at Dhanushkodi) with the island of Lanka. The bridge is known as Rama Setu (the bridge of Rama) or Adam's bridge in English.

The battle between the brothers was a favourite theme of the Khmer sculptors. A relief in Angkor Wat and Banteay Srei depicts the killing and the death of Vali, surrounded by the Vanaras.

### Angada

Angada is the son of Vali and Tara, who is declared to be the heir apparent of Sugriva. The Vanaras were on his side and against Sugriva, obviously a legacy of Vali who was preferred by the Vanaras over Sugriva. In fact it was Hanuman who had to play the diplomat to prevent the Vanaras from abandoning Sugriva.

*Angada*

In order to avoid a war, Rama sent Angada to the court of Ravana, to plead with him to release Sita. Ravana was amused at the monkey messenger and refused to even offer him a seat. So Angada made a seat out of his own tail and sat at a level higher than Ravana. Then he said that if anybody could lift his foot, Rama would accept defeat and depart. No Rakshasa, not even Ravana's mighty warrior son Indrajit could do so. Ravana began to abuse Angada, but Angada hit the ground, causing tremors in the earth and knocking off Ravana's crowns, which Angada threw towards Rama, waiting on the other shore of the straits. It was caught by Hanuman who handed it over to Rama. This story illustrates Angada's great strength. Ravana ordered his men to kill Angada but the latter laughed and escaped.

The scene of Angada Shistayi, when Angada visited Ravana's court as Rama's messenger and sat on a seat higher that Ravana's throne, on his own coiled tail, was a favourite theme of medieval Indian artists.

In the war Angada killed Ravana's son Devantaka.

## Nala

He was the son of the divine architect Vishvakarma, and had the ability to make stones float in the water. He built the Rama Setu or Nala Setu, the bridge connecting India to Sri Lanka, which Rama, Lakshmana and the Vanara army used to cross over to fight Ravana and his rakshasas of Lanka.

## Malekudiya Rituals

In the village of Naravi, Belthangadi taluk of Dakshin Kannada district, Malekudiya tribals perform an annual ritual to propitiate the monkeys. They visit Pingar Koni on the periphery of the forest with jaggery, beaten rice and coconut and spread it over a flat rock, praying for the monkey to come and eat the food. By doing so, the tribals believe, monkeys will not invade their orchards and will leave them alone for the rest of the year (Ardhya 2005). The word Malekudiya means mountain habitations, which these tribes inhabit. Rhesus monkeys also inhabit the same hills.

## Buddhism

The *Mahakapi Jataka* is named after the monkey. According to Buddhist tradition, the Buddha was born eighteen times as a monkey. As king of his herd, he built a bridge to enable his monkeys to cross over to safety, away from the murderous king Brahmadatta and his warriors.

## Jainism

As mentioned earlier, the Jainas regarded the Vanaras as a great warrior tribe whose flag bore the monkey emblem.

Abhinandananatha, the fourth Tîrthankara, is identified by the monkey symbol on his pedestal.

*Ecological Role and Current Status*
The grey langur is identified with the Vanara hero and is thus also known as the Hanuman langur. The Vanaras of the *Ramayana* are generally identified with the grey langur, but the rhesus monkey is given an equally sacred status in and around temples, particularly where the grey langur is not found. The Hanuman langur inhabits the tropics, including the dry, thorny scrub, pine and alpine forests. They generally stay on the ground, except when they sleep.

*Jaina Tîrthankara
Abhinandananatha*

There are seven species of grey langurs in India. They are large terrestrial animals, inhabiting open wooded habitats and urban areas. Males are up to 75 cm tall, and females 65 cm. Langurs from the south are smaller than those from the north. Grey langurs feed on leaves, fruit, buds and flowers, supplementing their diet with insects, tree bark and gum. Although they sleep in trees, they spend more time on the ground than any other known colobine species.

Langurs live in medium to large groups, usually with one dominant male. Males do not hold the dominant position for long in a group, the average time being about eighteen months. Adolescent males who are expelled from the group form 'bachelor' packs that harass the group that expelled them, and challenge the alpha male for leadership of the pack. If an attack by a bachelor pack is successful and they are able to kill the alpha male, they will then engage in a power struggle, where first all of the infants fathered by the previous alpha male are killed, and then the bachelors fight among themselves, killing each other until only one remains, who then becomes the leader of the pack and takes over all the females.

This behaviour is interestingly manifested in the story of Vali and Sugriva in the *Ramayana*. The only female monkeys mentioned in the Ramayana are Tara and the harem females, first belonging to Vali then Sugriva, then Vali again and Sugriva again (after Vali's death). All the others are males, such as Hanuman, Nala the architect and so on, and live as bachelors. Valmiki was obviously a good observer of natural life and knew the habits of the grey langur.

An interesting relationship has been observed between the chital deer and the grey langur. Chital deer benefit from langurs' good eyesight and ability to post lookouts on treetops, so that an alarm can be raised when a predator approaches. For langurs, the chital's superior sense of smell assists in early predator warning, and it is common to see langurs foraging on the ground in the presence of chitals. Chitals also benefit from fruits dropped from trees by langurs. Alarm calls of either species can be indicative of the presence of a predator such as the tiger

The other species of monkey that is revered in India, the rhesus monkey, is one of the best-known species of monkeys. Adult male rhesus macaques are 53 cm and females about 47 cm tall. They are brown or grey with pink faces without fur. The rhesus macaque may be found in grasslands, woodlands and mountainous regions up to 2,500 m high. They are good swimmers and easily move from rural to urban areas, relying on handouts from humans.

Rhesus macaques are both arboreal and terrestrial; they are mostly herbivorous and feed on leaves and pine needles, roots, and the occasional insect or small animal. The rhesus monkey has the widest geographic range of any non-human primate, occupying a great diversity of altitudes throughout South and South-East Asia.

Although the langur is identified with Hanuman, the monkeys that surround temples and pilgrimage centres and are fed by pilgrims in the hope of divine blessings are the rhesus. India used to export rhesus monkeys for research purposes to Europe and the USA. This was banned in 1977 after a sustained campaign by the Blue Cross of India, Chennai, and an article by this author in the *Illustrated Weekly of India*. However, there is a thriving black market, which catches and smuggles rhesus and bonnet monkeys to Bangladesh, from where they are shipped to the USA and Europe.

Unfortunately, the rhesus monkey has become a pest in some areas, even perceived as a possible risk to public safety. Delhi is so overrun by rhesus monkeys that the larger and stronger langurs have been brought in to control them by frightening them away.

Even if monkeys—langurs or macaques—raid crops and fruits they are not killed. At the most they may be caught and relocated to forest areas. If a monkey dies near a human habitation, it is buried in a samadhi and a temple is built over the body.

~

## Mouse

| Scientific Name | : | *Suncus murinus* Linn |
| --- | --- | --- |
| Common Names | : | House musk shrew |
| | | Chachundar/chuha (Hindi) |
| | | Moonjoor/mookeli (Tamil) |
| | | Mushakah (Sanskrit) |
| Distribution | : | Throughout India |

The mouse is the vahana or vehicle of Lord Ganesha. In Hindu mythology, Lord Ganesha is accompanied by the mouse wherever he travels. An offering to Lord Ganesha and his small companion forms an important part of Hindu worship.

The story goes that the world was harassed by Gajamukha, an elephant-faced evil demon. The gods rushed to Ganesha for help. Ganesha broke off his right tusk and threw it at the demon, even while cursing the demon to change into a rodent. The demon became a rodent and Ganesha sat on him, keeping him under control.

According to another story, the Deva Krauncha had been cursed by Vamadeva to become a rodent. The animal entered the ashrama of the sage Parashara and caused great havoc. The sage requested Ganesha to help him. So Ganesha appeared, sat on the mouse and made it his vehicle, bringing him under control.

*Mouse vehicle of Ganesha*

The mouse is also Ganesha's friend and advisor. According to one story, Lord Shiva once decided to hold a contest between his two sons to see who could encircle the world first. The winner would receive the sacred jambu fruit from Shiva's hand. Kartikeya set off on his peacock which could even fly. Ganesha consulted his mouse vehicle, who advised him to encircle his parents Shiva and Parvati and tell them they were the universe. Ganesha did so and was granted the fruit and the title Vighneshvara, or lord (remover) of obstacles.

It may appear odd that such a tiny animal was chosen to be the vehicle, but this was a tribute to the elephant who keeps the mice away from the rice fields, for the elephant is the only animal the rats are afraid of. The common factor in both stories is that Ganesha brought the mice under control, an animal that threatened (and continues to threaten) food security. However, sometimes the icons look very odd, with a huge, fat Ganesha seated on a tiny mouse.

# Owl

| | | |
|---|---|---|
| Scientific Name | : | *Strix leptogrammica* Temminck |
| Common Names | : | Brown wood owl |
| | | Ullu (Hindi) |
| | | Aandai (Tamil) |
| | | Ulukah (Sanskrit) |
| Distribution | : | Throughout India |

The Zoroastrians of India, who leave their dead bodies in the Towers of Silence to be consumed by vultures, consider that if the owl eats the dead body, the soul will rest in heaven.

Among the tribes of the Garo Hills of Meghalaya, in north-east India, the cry of the owl means that a person is going to die. When heard in cemeteries, the owl's hoot signifies that the spirit of a departed soul has been captured by the owl.

Lakshmi

The owl is very sacred in Bengal, where the white owl is described as the vehicle of goddess Lakshmi, the Hindu goddess of wealth and prosperity. The Bengalis believe that the hooting of an owl brings wealth and happiness. The entrance of a white owl in the home is regarded as a very good omen.

During the festival of lights or Dipavali, owls are sacrificed on behalf of industrialists by Tantriks in Ludhiana in the Punjab to appease goddess Lakshmi. Dried flesh, beak, claws, feathers and blood of owls were 'ingredients' used for black magic (Vasdev 2005).

The owl is also the vehicle of Chamunda, a form of Durga.

However, in spite of the association with Lakshmi, owls are considered to be bad omens and messengers of ill luck elsewhere in India. The hooting of an owl at night is considered to be an ill omen.

*Ecological Role and Current Status*

The brown wood owl is a medium to large bird, with dark brown upper parts and white spots on the shoulders and a white neckband. The eyes are large, rounded and dark brown. It is a nocturnal bird, which feeds mainly on small mammals, birds and reptiles. It is a great pest controller and a friend of the farmer, hence its association with the goddess of prosperity.

The brown wood owl nests in a hole in a tree or on a forked trunk, laying two eggs. In a 400-year-old rain tree in the garden of the C.P. Ramaswami Aiyar Foundation in Chennai, there is a hole which has been continuously habited by owls for the last few centuries. It is not known whether the same family or a new owl takes over when the previous chicks have grown up and flown away. But it is always the same species that inhabits the tree.

Today, the owl is an endangered species, its numbers reduced thanks to the ill effects of the pesticides used to control rodents, which are eaten by owls, who then suffer a slow and lingering end.

In Hindi the word for owl—ullu—means fool. Surprising, for the bird is hardly foolish.

∽

# Parakeet/Parrot

| | | |
|---|---|---|
| Scientific Name | : | *Psittacula krameri* Scopoli |
| Common Names | : | Indian ring-necked parakeet/parrot |
| | | Tota (Hindi) |
| | | Pachai killi (Tamil) |
| | | Shukah (Sanskrit) |
| Distribution | : | Throughout India |

Although it is commonly referred to as parrot, it is the parakeet that is commonly seen in most parts of India.

The parakeet is sacred to goddess Meenakshi, who is depicted holding a parrot in her right hand. The famous Meenakshi temple at Madurai in Tamil Nadu has a separate killigoondu (parrot cage) mandapam. The parakeets in the mandapam were trained to repeat goddess Meenakshi's name. Many devotees would buy and gift a parrot to the temple in fulfilment of a vow. Earlier, they were kept locked and died in six months to a year. In response to a sustained campaign by the Blue Cross of India, the temple released the birds in 2005, with an assurance to refuse the gift of any more birds.

*Meenakshi*

The parakeet is also associated with Andal, the only female among the twelve Alvars or saints of Tamil Vaishnavism. According to legend, the bird is Sri Suka Brahma Rishi, who Saint Andal sent to Lord Ranganatha as her messenger (dhootu).

Rati, wife of Kama, the god of love, is depicted seated on a parrot vehicle.

Unfortunately, parakeets are caught by fake astrologers who train them to pick a card which is then used to tell the future.

The wings of these parakeets are clipped and they spend their entire lives alone, imprisoned in the cage.

*Ecological Role and Current Status*
This non-migrating bird is one of the few parrot species that has successfully adapted to living in 'disturbed habitats', and has survived urbanization and deforestation. Parakeets usually feed on buds, fruits, vegetables, nuts, berries and seeds. Wild flocks fly several kilometres to forage in farmlands and orchards.

*Andal*

In the wild, this is a noisy species with an unmistakable squawking call. The adult male has a black neck-ring and pink nape-band while the female and immature birds of both sexes either show no neck rings, or display shadow-like pale to dark grey neck-rings.

*Rati*

In India, the birds were first kept as pets at least 3,000 years ago. Later, they were also bred with colour mutations. They were prized as pets and for their ability to talk, and a status symbol among the aristocracy to have a caged parakeet. They are very intelligent birds, requiring a large amount of mental stimulation.

The Indian parakeet is commonly but incorrectly called the parrot. The same word is used for both birds in the Indian languages, hence the confusion.

～

# Peacock

| | | |
|---|---|---|
| Scientific Name | : | *Pavo cristatus* Linn |
| Common Names | : | Indian peafowl or Blue Peafowl |
| | | Mor or mayur (Hindi) |
| | | Mayil (Tamil) |
| | | Mayurah (Sanskrit) |
| Distribution | : | Throughout India |

The peacock is the national bird of India. Its association with Indian life and literature may be attributed both to its beautiful appearance as well as to its intelligence and abilities. Unfortunately, the beauty of its feathers has led to its killing on a mass scale, as people aspire to own the beautiful peacock feathers, especially as fans and in native medicine.

Whenever Indra, lord of the heavens, transformed himself into an animal, he is believed to have become a peacock. Later, this story was changed to Indra giving the gift of beautiful colour to the peacock.

According to legend, when Indra was battling Ravana, the rakshasa king of Lanka, a peacock raised its tail to form a protective screen behind which Indra could hide. As a reward, Indra granted the bird the beautiful blue-green plumage and the exotic feathered tail. When it rains—another gift from Indra, the god of rain and thunder—peacocks are believed to dance in happiness.

When the poison was churned during the samudra manthana, the peacock is believed to have absorbed its negative effects. Thus the peacock is regarded as a protector.

The peacock is an enemy of snakes, thus representing the victory over evil or poisonous tendencies such as human anger, greed and ignorance.

The peacock is very sacred to Hindus. The vehicle of Lord Kartikeya—also known as Skanda or Muruga—is a peacock named Paravani.

In Tamil tradition, it is believed that during a battle between Lord Muruga and a demon named Surapadman, the demon assumed the form of a big mango tree. This tree was split into two by Lord Muruga's spear. From one half emerged a rooster and from the other a peacock. Lord Muruga took the peacock as his vehicle and the rooster as the symbol on his flag. Devotees of Lord Muruga carry a kavadi (arched sticks resembling a hill) made of peacock feathers and dance the kavadi attam annually on their way to Palani Hill in the Western Ghats.

*Murugan (Kartikeya)*

The bird is sometimes associated with goddess Sarasvati, as her vehicle.

The crown of Lord Krishna is usually adorned with a peacock feather, and is called the mormukuta (peacock crown). The fact that it is a single feather means that it could be picked up only during the moulting season, when the peacock drops a single feather. Unfortunately, this has given licence for the bird to be killed in large quantities for its feathers, although only fallen feathers may be collected both by tradition and by law.

The peacock appears in nearly every work of Indian literature and art, as a symbol of beauty and sylvan surroundings. Kalidasa (fifth century CE) was enamoured of its beauty. In his *Ritu Samhara* (Round of the Seasons), he describes the bird through six seasons and its joy when the rains arrive (II.6). Kalidasa's *Raghuvamsha* (Lineage of Raghu) and *Meghaduta* (Cloud Messenger) also contain beautiful descriptions of the bird. Several writers, including Valmiki in the *Ramayana*, Shudraka in *Mrichchhakatika* (Clay Cart), Udaya in the *Mayura Sandesha* (Message of the Peacock), and Munidhurandhara in the *Mayuraduta* (Peacock Messenger), describe the peacock in loving detail and attribute several abilities to the bird.

At temple festivals, peacock feathers are made into large fans which are used to fan deities.

The mayuri is a musical instrument shaped like a peacock, decorated with feathers. However, it is no longer in use. The rudra vina is sometimes depicted in the shape of a peacock.

### Peahen

There is a later belief that Sita, heroine of the *Ramayana*, was born from the egg of a peahen. However, this does not appear in Valmiki's *Ramayana*.

According to popular legend, Parvati manifested herself in the form of a peahen in the ancient village of Mylapore, now a part of Chennai. She prayed to the Shiva linga, called Kapalishvarar. Shiva married her and their wedding is celebrated annually, in the Tamil month of Panguni (March–April) on the day of the asterism Uthiram, in the form of a grand, colourful ten-day festival. Shiva and Parvati are carried each day by a different animal or human vahana or vehicle. Mylapore and

*Krishna*

the legend are over two thousand years old. The Pallava ruler Nandivarman III was known as Mylai Kavalan or the Protector of the City of Peacocks.

There is an ancient stone statue in the northern side of the Kapalishvarar temple compound of the Mylapore temple of a peahen garlanding the linga. In fact, the word Mylapore itself means 'town of the peafowl', and the area was renowned for its peacocks. By making the animal a divine incarnation of the goddess, she was protected for millennia. Unfortunately, under British rule, religious sentiment was brushed aside and the peacocks were gradually wiped out as Mylapore grew from a village to a city.

The Mori clan of the Bhil tribe of central India worships the peacock as a totem. They believe that if they even step on a peacock's tracks, they will get sick. A Mori woman hides her face if she sees a peacock.

Similarly, the peacock is the sacred totem of the Jat community of north India.

The bird is also sacred to the Ahir and Khand tribes, while the Koyis of the river Godavari in Andhra Pradesh tie peacock feathers to Sitalamata (also Mariamma), the goddess of smallpox.

The Warli tribesmen of Maharashtra fix peacock feathers in a pot to represent their god Hirva, and dance around it.

*Family and Place Names*

The king Chandragupta, founder of the Mauryan Empire in the fourth century BCE had the peacock in his clan name, Maurya.

More (pronounced moray) is the totemic name of a Maharashtrian clan derived from the word mor, which means peacock in Marathi.

In Morachi Chincholi, named after the peacock, the birds are protected by the villagers.

Morgaon is the 'peacock village' on the banks of river Karha in Baramati taluk of Pune district.

Apart from Mylapore, several villages and towns in Tamil Nadu are named after the peacock. Mayiladuthurai (near Kumbakonam) means 'shore of the dancing peacocks', while Mayilam (near Tindivanam), and other villages are named after the bird. Nemili, Nenmeli and similar Telugu names for the peacock are used in villages of northern Tamil Nadu and Andhra Pradesh. While peacocks have disappeared from all these places, only Viralimalai in Pudukottai district still abounds with peacocks.

The district of Mayurbhanj in Orissa is named after the peacock.

### Buddhism

The Jataka story of Mahamor narrates how the Buddha was a golden peacock in a previous birth. In Buddhist mythology, the peacock is a symbol of compassion and watchfulness. The *Nachcha Jataka* describes the peacock's wedding.

In Vajrayana (Mahayana) Buddhism, Mahamayuri, the 'Great Peahen' or Peacock Wisdom Queen—the Mother of Buddhas— is depicted riding a peacock.

The Amitabha Buddha (Buddha of Eternal Light) is seated beneath a tree, his throne supported by eight peacocks. Six peacock feathers arranged as a fan decorate the vase and sprinkling utensil used for distributing the purifying water in Tibetan Buddhist ritual. They symbolize compassion, immortality and the universal antidote against poisons such as human anger, greed and ignorance.

### Jainism

It is believed that the feathers of the peacock ward off evil, so Jaina sages carried fly whisks made of peacock feathers. Munidhurandhara, the pre-eminent sage says that there is no place for serpents or paramours in the peacock's kingdom for, hearing its voice, they fly away. If one wears the peacock's feathers, one would be free of all fear.

### History

The peacock is mentioned in the Bible, as an import by King Solomon from Muziris (on the Malabar, Kerala coast) via Judea. They wandered around the grounds of his famous temple. In fact, the Hebrew word for peacock—*tuki*—is believed to be derived from the Tamil togai.

Alexander, who invaded the Punjab in 326 BCE, took back 200 peacocks from India and sent them to Macedonia. From there they were was taken to Rome where they were bred and slaughtered for their meat and plumes.

The peacock has played a prominent role in history. The Mauryan dynasty, founded by Chandragupta Maurya, is named after the peacock, their clan emblem. Chandragupta's grandson Ashoka (304–232 BCE), who was responsible for spreading the message of the Buddha to the world, forbade the killing of the peafowl for food. Some of his stone edicts, which display his message of dharma, bear the peacock prominently.

*Goddess Parvati as a peahen*

The seal of the Kushana emperor Kanishka was the peacock.

The Gupta rulers (320–550 CE), who reigned during what is known as the classical age of Indian history, issued several coins depicting the peacock. The bird also appeared prominently in the art of the period.

In the medieval period, the Tughlak rulers (CE 1320–1414) adopted the peacock's feather as their state symbol and used it for the headgear of their soldiers.

The grand Mughal, Shah Jahan (1592–1666), builder of the Taj Mahal, commissioned the Peacock Throne, made of gems and jewels that was the envy of the medieval world. The top had two peacocks facing each other, not unlike the peacock guardians of the Islamic gates of paradise and recreating the Persian belief that two peacocks facing each other symbolize the duality of nature. In 1739, Nadir Shah, a Persian king, invaded India and took away the throne to Teheran where it survived for over two hundred years till it mysteriously disappeared in the twentieth century. In 1857, the last Mughal king of Delhi, Bahadur Shah, sat on a silver peacock throne.

*Ecological Role and Current Status*

Peafowl are best known for the male's beautiful tail, which it displays during courtship. The peacock has iridescent blue-green or green coloured plumage. The tail of the peacock, also called the train, is not the tail quill feathers but highly elongated upper tail coverts. The train feathers have a series of eyes that are best seen when the tail is fanned open. The peahen has a mixture of dull green, brown, and grey in her plumage. She lacks the long upper tail coverts of the male but has a crest. Females display their plumage to ward off danger to their young.

In the past, peacocks were found in and around wetlands. Their beautiful feathers and habit of foraging in the ground for insects have made them an easy prey for hunters who catch them for their beautiful feathers, which fetch a good price in the market, and their meat, which is regarded a delicacy.

~

# Pheasant

| | | |
|---|---|---|
| Scientific Name | : | *Ithaginis cruentus* Hardwicke |
| Common Names | : | Blood pheasant |
| | | Chillimey or semu (Sikkimese) |
| Distribution | : | The mountains of Nepal and Sikkim |

The blood pheasant is sacred to the Lepchas who are the aboriginal inhabitants of Sikkim. For the Lepcha hunter-gatherers of Sikkim, the blood pheasant is part of a sacred myth. According to the Lepchas, when a terrible flood devastated the earth, the bird saved the Lepcha ancestors by guiding them to the safe environs of Mount Tendong. Hence this species, along with its forest patch is well-protected, leading to the conservation of several species (Jha, 1998).

The blood pheasant is the state bird of Sikkim.

*Ecological Role and Current Status*

The blood pheasant's name comes from the fact that the males have vivid red colouring on the feathers of the breast, throat and forehead. Females are more uniformly coloured with duller shades of reddish brown. Both males and females have a distinct ring of bare skin around the eye that is crimson in colour, in addition to red feet.

The bird's habitat is coniferous or mixed forest and scrub areas at the snowline. The pheasants move their range depending on the season and, during summer, are found at higher elevations. Populations move to lower elevations as the snow increases in the fall and winter.

~

# Porcupine

| | | |
|---|---|---|
| Scientific Name | : | *Hystrix indicus* Kerr |
| Common Names | : | Indian porcupine |
| | | Sayal, sahi (Hindi) |
| | | Mullam panni (Tamil) |
| | | Sallakah (Sanskrit) |
| Distribution | : | Throughout India |

The most popular use of the porcupine's quill was as a pen, dipped into Indian ink. It is hard and sharp, and is suitable for painting letters on dried palm leaves.

In the upanayanam (investiture of the sacred thread) ceremony, the hair of the brahmachari was separated into three portions using the quill. It marked his initiation into education.

During the simantam ceremony of a pregnant woman, her hair was parted with a porcupine's quill.

Fortunately, the use of the quill in religious ceremonies has been replaced by a wooden or plastic comb, a more appropriate tool for parting the hair.

*Jainism*

The porcupine is the emblem of the fourteenth Tirthankara Anantanatha.

*Ecological Role and Current Status*

The sanctity of the porcupine comes from its unique association as the source of the quill. However, this sanctity did not prevent its capture and destruction in order to produce quills. The quills are actually modified hairs

*Jaina Tirthankara Anantanatha*

coated with thick layers of keratin, leaving them as sharp as needles. It grows to about one metre in length and weighs about 15 kg. The most common use of the quill was as an instrument to write with. These were supplied to schools and universities until other writing materials were invented.

This nocturnal animal is actually a rodent and lives in different habitats.

~

## Praying Mantis

| | | |
|---|---|---|
| Scientific Name | : | *Mantis religiosa* Linn |
| Common Names | : | Devil's riding horse |
| | | Khandobache ghoda (Marathi) |
| Distribution | : | Throughout India |

The insect's resting posture—ostensibly in prayer—has given it the image of a pious and gentle creature, hence its name.

Its strange shape and posture has perpetrated the belief that it is a soothsayer. In Maharashtra, Khandoba (see DOG) is regarded as an incarnation of Shiva. He rides a horse and is accompanied by a dog. The Marathi word for the insect means the horse of Khandoba, but the reason for this strange name is not known.

In Arabic and Turkish cultures, the insect was believed to point to Mecca.

Among the Gonds of Vidarbha (Maharashtra), the vaid or medicine man keeps a praying mantis as a pet. He worships the insect and uses it for fortune-telling. This is a very unusual practice and its origin and significance are unknown.

*Ecological Role and Current Status*

They are named for the typical 'prayer-like' stance, and the word *mantis* derives from the similar Greek word for prophet or fortune-teller. Their diet usually consists of living insects, including flies and aphids, while larger species have been known to prey on small lizards, frogs, birds, snakes, and even rodents. Mantises are masters of camouflage and use protective colouration to blend in with the foliage, both to avoid predators and to catch their victims. Various species have adapted to even mimic the foliage, appearing as leaves, sticks, bark of the tree, grass, flowers and even stones. Mantises are the farmer's favourite, since they prey upon many crop-damaging insects.

$\sim$

# Rat

| Scientific Name | : | *Rattus rattus* Linn |
| Common Names | : | Black rat |
| | | Kala chuha (Hindi) |
| | | Yeli (Tamil) |
| | | Unduruh (Sanskrit) |
| Distribution | : | Throughout India |

In the town of Deshnoke, 30 km from Bikaner in Rajasthan, the Karni Mata temple is devoted to the worship of rats. The 600-

year-old temple is dedicated to Karni Mata, a famous mystic of her times, believed to be an incarnation of goddess Durga. The holy rats are called kabas and many people undertake pilgrimages from distant places to see them. It is believed that the rats will reincarnate as sadhus or holy men in their next birth. The priests feed milk and grain, of which the pilgrims also partake, to the animals. Eating food that has been touched by the animal is considered a blessing. The souls of Karni Mata's devotees are meant to reside in rats, which is why they are allowed to roam free. White rats earn even more luck as they are supposed to be future incarnations of mystics or sadhus. Devotees feed the rats, believing that they will be reincarnated as holy men. The temple has a silver door and a wire mesh over the courtyard to protect the rats from birds. The image of Karni Mata holding a trishul (trident) surrounded by rats is accompanied by the images of her sisters and the sisters of Avad Mata. If a rat is injured in the temple, a gold or silver replica must be presented to the temple. The rats eat from huge metal bowls filled with milk, sweets, and grains donated by devotees.

According to legend, a woman brought the body of her dead son to Karni Mata and asked her to restore the boy to life. Karni fell into a deep trance and encountered Yama, the lord of death, who told her that the boy had accepted another body and could not be recalled. Karni refused to accept this and said that Yama would no longer govern her tribe of Charans. At death they would enter the bodies of kabas, or sacred rats, and when the rats died they would be reborn as Charans. Karni Mata was an ascetic who led a righteous life dedicated to the service and upliftment of the poor and downtrodden. It is believed that she possessed supernatural powers. She laid the foundation of Deshnoke and her principal followers, Charans, as well as the rulers of Bikaner worship her as a goddess.

The Karni Mata festival is held in the months of Vaishakha (April–May) and Kartika (October–November).

The Karni Mata temple at Deshnoke is a stone-and-marble structure, also known as Madh. Rajputs bring their children here for their first hair cuts and place them at the deity's feet for blessing. Charan priests perform mangla-ki-arti and offer bhog (special food) as worship.

### Ganesha's Vehicle

Sometimes the rat, rather than the mouse, is considered to be the vahana of Ganesha. This is probably derived from the Maharashtrian tradition of depicting a large mouse, not unlike the rat, on which Ganesha is mounted.

### Ecological Role and Current Status

Due to the Hindu reluctance to kill animals, mice and rats are generally caught in live traps and, rather than being killed, are released in the wild, away from homes. The dwindling snake populations, the breeding of mice and rats for research purposes and the poor storage systems of grains have resulted in an explosion in their population in recent years. The plague which broke out in 1994 in Surat is a pointer to the growing problem of rodents. They breed in the garbage of urban India and the grain stocks of rural India.

~

# Rhinoceros

| | | |
|---|---|---|
| Scientific Name | : | *Rhinoceros unicornis* Linnaeus |
| Common Names | : | Great Indian one-horned |
| | | Rhinoceros (English) |
| | | Gainda/Gonda (Hindi) |
| | | Ganda (Sanskrit) |
| Distribution | : | North-east India |

Figurines and seals of the one-horned rhinoceros, with its distinctive horned snout, is found in the Indus Valley sites.

Although the rhinoceros is no longer found in the region of the Indus river, rhinoceros bones have been found at Harappa. Some figures wear collars and, while they could not have been domesticated, they may have been held captive.

## Buddhism

The Buddhist *Khaggavisana Sutta*, literally 'Rhinoceros Horn' and better known as the *Rhinoceros Sutra*, is one of the earliest and most authentic expressions of original Buddhist thought. It is written in the Kharoshthi script, describing the virtues of solitude and the dangers of attachment, prescribes a solitary spiritual life and discusses the nature of friends and friendship. The message of the sutra is to 'wander alone, like a rhinoceros'. The Asian rhinoceros has one horn and folklore attributes to it a solitary life in the forest. This sutra is appropriately titled to present what the translator calls an essay 'on the value of living the solitary wandering life', or to the life of a lonely wandering Buddhist monk.

The British Library contains a remnant of a scroll that originally contained the complete text. A Gandhari language version of the sutra examines in detail the literary and textual background of the sutra, describes the condition of the scroll and its reconstruction, analyses the text, compares it with other extant versions and presents a literal English translation. The sutta is from the Pali collection of texts better known as the *Kuddhaka Nikaya*, the fifth division of the *Sutta Pitaka*. The *Khaggavisana Sutta* is contained in verses 35 to 75 of section one, called the 'Uragavagga' or 'The Snake' chapter.

Although the original provenance of the British Library's scroll is uncertain, it probably came from Hadda in the Jalalabad Plain of eastern Afghanistan, west of the Khyber Pass, and was most probably written during the reign of the Saka rulers in the early first century AD, making it the oldest Buddhist text ever found, as well as the earliest surviving manuscript in an Indian language.

## Jainism

The emblem of the eleventh Tirthankara Shreyasanatha is the rhinoceros.

*Rhinoceros emblem
of Jaina Tirthankara
Shreyamsunatha*

## Ecological Role and Current Status

The Indian rhinoceros was once widespread, found in northern Pakistan, north India, Assam, Nepal, northern Bangladesh and Myanmar. It lived mainly in grasslands where the grass grew up to 8 metres in height, as well as swamps and forests. The one-horned rhinoceros is a grazer, associated with waterbodies for feeding, wallowing and resting.

The accounts by Al Beruni and Ibn Batuta, two historians and scholars of the medieval period, and the Mughal emperors Babur, Akbar and Jehangir, record their existence in regions of modern Uttar Pradesh.

The decline of the rhino population was caused by habitat destruction and fragmentation for extension of agriculture and, later, tea gardens; poaching of rhino for horns, which are much in demand in the Middle East, and other parts believed to have medicinal value; and hunting of rhino for sports during the Mughal and British periods. Rhinos were wiped out from most of their range of distribution in the last four hundred years, except in the states of Assam and West Bengal, and Nepal, where the terai is the last home of the rhino.

In 1975, only 600 individuals survived in the wild in India and Nepal. By 2002, conservation efforts resulted in an increase of their numbers to 2,400 in the terai region of India and Nepal and the grasslands of Assam, north Bengal and north-east India. At least half of the total population is found in India's Kaziranga National Park, which remains the main reserve for this species. About 500 animals are found in the Royal Chitwan National

Park in Nepal (www.hermitary.com/solitude/rhinoceros.html, www.washington.edu/uwpress)

~

# Rooster

| Scientific Name | : | *Gallus gallus murghi* Linn |
|---|---|---|
| Common Names | : | Rooster/cock (m) and hen (f), |
| | | Murga (m)/murgi (f) (Hindi), |
| | | Koli (f)/seval (m) (Tamil) |
| | | Kukkutah (Sanskrit) |
| Distribution | : | All over the country |

The bird heralds the rising sun and is hence a symbol of the sun.

In Tamil tradition, during the battle between Lord Muruga (or Kartikeya, son of Shiva) and the demon Surapadman, the demon assumed the form of a mango tree. The tree was split into two by Lord Muruga's spear. From one half emerged a rooster and from the other a peacock. Lord Muruga took the

*Murugan (Kartikeya) with rooster flag*

peacock as his vehicle and the rooster as the symbol on his flag.

The rooster is also worshipped by rural people as Kukkuteshvara.

The bird is associated with goddess Kamakhya of Assam.

Sadly, the rooster or hen is commonly used in sacrifices because of its easy availability, lower cost in comparison to animals like the goat and buffalo

*Kamakhya*

(other sacrificial animals) and easy manageability, which makes it a favourite sacrificial animal.

~

## Sheep

| | | |
|---|---|---|
| Scientific Name | : | *Ovis aries* Linn. |
| Common Names | : | Bharal (Hindi) |
| | | Chemmari aadu (Tamil) |
| | | Mesha (Sanskrit) |
| Distribution | : | Throughout India |

The animal is considered sacred by the Kurubas of Karnataka who depend on the sheep for their livelihood (Ardhya 2005).

Often, the sheep and goat are interchanged for the sacrifice. The sheep is more expensive, as it also provides wool, and is only sacrificed by rich farmers.

Domestic sheep are cloven-hoofed mammals kept as livestock. One of the earliest animals domesticated for agricultural purposes, they were primarily reared for their fleece and meat. Sheep's wool is the most widely used hair of any animal. The sheep is deeply entrenched in human culture. It is a key animal in the history of farming and finds representation in most languages and symbolism. Sheep figure in many mythologies—for instance, the golden fleece—and major religions, especially the Semetic traditions. In both ancient and modern religious rituals, sheep are used as sacrificial animals.

~

# Snake

| | | |
|---|---|---|
| Scientific Name | : | *Naja naja* Linn |
| Common Names | : | Cobra, Indian cobra |
| | | Saap (Hindi) |
| | | Nalla paambu (Tamil) |
| | | Naga/sarpah (Sanskrit) |
| Distribution | : | Throughout India (excluding the north-east), at habitats from sea level up to 2,000 m. |

Of all the animals, few have held as much fascination, fear and respect as the cobra. Its spectacled hood suggests a divine origin, while its secret life in dark holes under the ground has spun exotic stories. It is regarded as the custodian of buried treasures, the guardian of a secret subterranean world of strange mysteries.

The earliest appearance of the snake is an amulet from the Indus Valley (3000 BCE) of an eagle flanked by a snake on either side, probably anticipating the antagonism between the two and the later story of the sons of Kadru and Vinata (described later in this section). Clay figurines depict a seated deity with attendants on either side, flanked by an erect cobra.

While there is no reference to serpents or serpent worship in the Rig Veda, Ahi Budhnya, who dwelt in the fathomless depth of the aerial ocean, was a snake (Rig Veda, I.186.5; II. 31.6). Vritra, the Rig Vedic demon of drought, was sometimes depicted as a snake.

The *Atharva Veda* refers to the sarparaksha mantra to cure snake bites, addressed to Vainateya (son of Vinata) or Garuda, who was the enemy of snakes; and snake skin as a protection against theft. Kadru, the mother of all snakes, symbolizes mother earth.

Mahanaga in the *Shatapatha Brahmana* (XI. 2. 7. 12) is the only early reference to a great snake.

The popularity of the Nagas from the epic period onwards makes it clear that the cult of the snake belonged to the non-Vedic people of ancient India. Even today, snake worship is more common in rural areas than in urban. The terms sarpa and naga are interchangeable, while the Nagas were worshippers of the snake who left their imprint all over the country, from place names to local traditions.

The *Grihyasutras* recommend elaborate rituals, called sarpa bali, to propitiate the snake.

Ptolemy the geographer refers to the south Indian city of Uraiyur as Orthoura or Uragapura, snake city, and says there were Nagas in and around Nagapattinam in his time (150 CE). The Tamil epics *Silappadigaram* and *Manimekalai* refer to Naga cults and Naga cities.

The ancient Nagas were snake worshippers who were often identified with the animal. They must not be confused with the Nagas of Nagaland in north-east India, who are not snake worshippers.

Snakes, especially cobras, have been one of the most significant symbols in Hindu religion and mythology. Their worship evolved mainly due to human fear of the reptile. It is commonly believed that snakes will never harm those who worship them.

The snake symbolizes the waters, and the snake on which Vishnu reclines symbolizes primordial wisdom and the origin of all life symbolized by the waters.

The naga is associated with almost every deity. One of the most common iconographic forms is the snake hood over every deity.

Ganesha wears a snake as a belt coiled around his stomach.

Goddess Durga used snakes as weapons to destroy the demons Chanda and Munda.

Later, when Varuna became the god of the oceans, he was regarded as Nagaraja or the king of the Nagas.

### Shiva and the Snake

The cobra is most commonly associated with Lord Shiva, who wears a cobra coiled around his neck and body, as his sacred thread and anklets, particularly in his more fearful forms like Aghora, Bhairava and Virabhadra. The association is mentioned in the *Yajur Veda* (3.61) where he is called ahisanah or associated with the snake.

*Shiva*

Shiva neutralized the poison of the snake by swallowing it and holding it in his throat, which became blue—hence Shiva's name Nilakantha (blue throat). Thus Shiva is worshipped as the healer of snake bites, and symbolizes the power he has over what is believed to be the deadliest of creatures.

### Vishnu's Snake Couch

Vishnu, the Preserver, is usually portrayed as sitting or reclining on the enormous coiled body of Adi Shesha or Ananta, a giant snake deity with multiple cobra heads.

*Vishnu on Adi Shesha*

He was one of the nine snake-sons of Kadru, the other eight being Takshaka, Vasuki, Kambala, Karkotaka, Padma, Mahapadma, Shankha and Kalika. All snakes are believed to be descended from these nine. His half-brother was Garuda, son of Vinata. Kadru and Vinata were sisters, married to

Kashyapa. The two took a bet, which Vinata won by cheating, making Vinata her handmaiden. When Garuda learned of it he became the implacable enemy of the snakes and, even though Adi Shesha had refused to heed his mother's order to cheat, the relations between the two were always strained, although both are vehicles of Vishnu (see EAGLE). When Ananta heard his mother's curse on Vinata, he went away ashamed, and practised severe austerities. When approached by Brahma, he lamented that his mother and brothers were envious of Vinata and her son Garuda, so he desired to cast off his body and live a virtuous life forever. Brahma granted his desire and gave him the task of holding the world steady. Ananta was so powerful that he alone was able to uproot Mount Mandara for the samudra manthana (see TORTOISE/TURTLE).

Ananta means infinity and represents the endlessness of cosmic time. His thousand hoods represent the innumerable divisions of time. The word shesha means remainder and signifies that which is left over from the previous creation and forms the seed of the next.

The avataras or human manifestations of Adi Shesha include Lakshmana and Balarama, who were the brothers of Rama and Krishna respectively. When Balarama died, his spirit left his body through his mouth as a white serpent and was welcomed into the netherworld by the nagas.

The association of the snake with Vishnu was a result of the association of Vishnu worshippers with the snake worshippers.

The remaining eight brothers were banished by Brahma to the subterranean world, where they built their exotic cities in the hells of Atala, Patala and Sutala, which belong to the snakes.

The snake Ananta canopied the baby Krishna, protecting him from the rain when his father smuggled him out of the prison in Mathura where he was incarcerated and crossed the river Yamuna in full spate, in order to take the baby to the house of Nanda in Gokul.

### Takshaka

Takshaka was one of the sons of Kadru and chief of the snakes. He was also known as the son of Bharata, Rama's brother. He bit Parikshit to death, leading to Janmejaya's sacrifice.

Takshaka was the founder-ruler of the ancient city of Takshashila, now known as Taxila and situated in Pakistan. The Greek writer Arrian described Taxila as 'a large and wealthy city, and the most popular between the Indus and Hydaspes'.

### Vasuki

When the devas (gods) and asuras (demons) churned the ocean (in the episode of the samudra manthana) for the nectar of immortality or amrita, Vasuki, a brother of Ananta was chosen to be the churning 'rope' for the mountain Mandara which was

*Samudra manthana*

the churning rod, borne on the back of Vishnu as the Kurma or tortoise incarnation (see TORTOISE/TURTLE). Dhanvantari, the divine physician, appeared with the jar of nectar, which Garuda stole to free his mother Vinata from her sister Kadru's curse. While Indra took it away before the nagas could drink it, a drop fell on a blade of dry grass, which was licked by the nagas, splitting their tongue. It is said that because of this, snakes have had forked tongues since then.

### Kaliya

The five-headed serpent king Kaliya lived in the river Yamuna with his wives, thereby poisoning the river. One day, while the child Krishna was playing, he fell into the river and was caught by Kaliya in his coils. But Krishna expanded his body until Kaliya was forced to let him go. Then Krishna started dancing on the snake (Kaliya mardana) and would have killed him, but the many wives of Kaliya begged Krishna to spare their husband's life. Krishna conceded their wish, but banished Kaliya far away to Ramanaka Dvipa in the Bay of Bengal. Thus the waters of the Yamuna became fit for drinking and bathing.

*Kaliya mardana Krishna*

Kaliya, living in the river, was obviously a poisonous water snake, unlike the heroic cobra.

*Rahu, the eclipse*

### Rahu

Rahu is believed to cause the eclipse. The lower half of his body is represented as a snake.

### Vritra

Vritra, the demon of drought defeated by Indra in the Rig Veda, is represented as a mighty serpent in later literature.

## Buddhism

When Maya, mother of the Buddha, gave birth to the baby Gautama, two Nagas, Nanda and Upananda, gave the newborn a ritual bath by pouring streams of warm and cold water.

The serpent-king Muchalinda protected Gautama from a raging storm, as he meditated beneath the bodhi tree, by spreading its hood while he was meditating. In fact many of his early converts were Nagas (Agrawal 1970).

The Buddha confined his esoteric doctrine of Prajnaparamita to the Nagas for safe keeping. Centuries later, they revealed it to the half-Naga philosopher Nagarjuna, who taught it to other people (Sivapriyananda 1992).

Like Hindu deities, Buddhist stupas are often canopied by multi-hooded snakes.

The Nagas were a snake-worshipping tribe of ancient India who have been depicted with one, three or five hooded snakes over their heads in the carvings of Bharhut, thereby establishing their identity as Naga kings and queens. Several major dynasties were associated with them through marriage and other alliances. In the early Buddhist art of Bharhut and Sanchi, where the Buddha is still represented by symbols, Nagas—men and women hooded by snakes—are represented worshipping Buddhist symbols. These were probably the Nagas, members of an ancient tribe that ruled over much of India and from which several Indian dynasties, especially in south India, claimed descent.

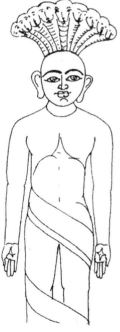

*Parshvanatha*

## Jainism

Parshvanatha, the twenty-third Tirthankara, was protected from the wrath of the demon Samvara by a giant Naga called Dharanendra. The icon of Parshvanatha is identified by the cobra behind his head or at the base of his pedestal (Sivapriyananda 1992).

## Yogic Symbolism

The kundalini, the latent primodial energy of the universe, is believed to lie dormant at the base of the human spine, like a coiled serpent. When awakened by yogic and spiritual practices, it ascends, passing through six spiritual centres or chakras, until it reaches the top of the head, at which point is the thousand-petalled chakra of total awareness and spiritual realization. This energy that animates the universe is always represented as a serpent.

## Nagas

As in the Buddhist sculptures, Nagas appear repeatedly in folklore, Jataka tales and the Sanskrit *Kathasaritsagara* (Ocean of Tales). They were well versed in medicine and could even restore life. They were craftsmen, sculptors and painters. They married human beings and gods.

Rama's son Kusha married Kumudavati, daughter of a Naga king.

Arjuna, the Pandava prince, married Ulupi, daughter of Kauravya, king of the Nagas of Manipur. The royal family of Manipur still claims descent from the snake.

Arjuna's grandson, king Parikshit, once insulted the sage Angirasa, who was meditating, by putting a dead snake around his neck. The sage's son cursed the king to die within seven days. The king renounced his kingdom and awaited his death, which happened as predicted, while listening to the *Bhagavata*

*Purana*. Parikshit's son Janmejaya swore to avenge his father's death and started a naga sacrifice where thousands of snakes were killed every day. Eventually, Astika, son of Jaratkaru and the snake goddess Manasa Devi (or Nageshvari Devi), sister of Vasuki, persuaded Janamejaya to stop his sacrifice, and thus saved snakes from total annihilation.

## Nagas in Kashmir

The word for 'spring' in the Kashmiri language is naga, and this is confirmed by geological reports that state that the land was once 'a vast span of water . . . walled in by high mountains. The valley was elevated out of water and left under the care of the Nagas, of whom Nila, son of Kashyapa, was the chief.' This is probably the reason why the nagas came to be identified with water. Every naga or spring has a snake as its deity, and fishing is restricted, helping to preserve the water ecology. Many festivals in Kashmir relate to Naga worship, including the first snowfall and the propitiation of the ancient Naga king Takshaka. The *Nilamata Purana* lists 527 Nagas that were worshipped in Kashmir. Even Muslims show their respect for the nagas or springs by desisting from catching fish. During times of water scarcity or excess rainfall, they offer sacrifices to Vasuk(i) naga (spring), the water of which remains in the valley during summer and disappears in winter.

In fact, Kashmir was regarded as the seat of snake worship from where it spread to the rest of India. It is named after Kashyapa, father of the snakes, and has many places, such as Anantnag, Sheshnag and Verinag, named after snakes.

Writing of Kashmir in the twelfth century, the poet-historian Kalhana says that the Nagas were the original inhabitants of his state. They were protected, he says, by the great Nila Naga. Sushravas and Padma Naga were the tutelary deities of the Wular Lake. The protectors (dikpalas) of the four directions are nagas. Writing in the seventh century CE, the Chinese traveller Hiuen

Tsang saw temples dedicated to the snake in Kashmir. Abul Fazl, court historian of the Mughal king Akbar, refers to 700 places of snake worship in Kashmir

## Nagas in the Historical Period

The Shishunagas were an ancient Naga clan that ruled from 642 to 372 BCE.

According to Puranic genealogies, one group of Nagas ruled from Vidisha (Bhilsa, in present-day Madhya Pradesh) between 110 and 30 BCE and another group from Padmavati (Pavaya near Gwalior, in present-day Madhya Pradesh). The Kushanas under Kanishka defeated these dynasties and drove them into the forests of Bundelkhand. Around 150 CE, Virasena Nava Naga won back Padmavati and even Mathura in 176 CE from the Kushana king Vasudeva I. The Nagas were now known as Nava Nagas or new Nagas.

A copper plate grant of the Vakataka king Prasavasena I (280–340 CE) describes the Nava Nagas as established along the banks of the river Ganga. Nava Nagas issued punch-marked coins with the Shaivite symbols of Nandi, trishula (trident) and the Trimurti (Trinity of Brahma, Vishnu and Shiva) on a throne with a snake hood, from Vidisha, Padmavati, Kausambi, Mathura and Aichhatra.

Chandragupta II Vikramaditya (385–413 CE) married the Naga princess Kubera Naga.

The Gurjara-Pratihara kingdom (eighth century) of Gujarat was established by Nagabhatta, a Naga prince.

Several south Indian dynasties, such as the Pallava, Chola, Chera, Vijayanagara and Maratha rulers of south India claimed descent from the Nagas.

## Snake Worship

The worship of the snake still continues in south India. Snake stones are popular all through rural India, but more so in the Deccan and the south. Fashioned out of wood and clay, or carved out of granite, they are placed under pipal trees.

In Kerala, every tharavad or matrilineal home has a sarpa kavu or snake grove at the back, where the spirits of the ancestors are propitiated. At Manarshala in the erstwhile Travancore state, now part of Kerala, there is a famous temple of the snake, where kolams (designs) are drawn on the ground of intertwining snakes and an elaborate ritual snake dance, called sarpa bali or thulla is performed. A similar ritual snake dance called naga mandala is performed in coastal Karnataka.

South Karnataka (Canara) is known as the 'land of snakes'. It is said that Sage Parashurama, an incarnation of Vishnu, was searching for a place to do his tapas. He stood on a hill and threw his axe (parashu) into the sea. The area covered by the axe became land and south Canara came into being. When the snakes living in the sea cried at the loss of their home, they were blessed by the sage with the promise that they would be worshipped and would come to no harm. Every Brahmin home has a small shrine called Naga Bana, ceremonially established by a Naga pratishthe (establishment), dedicated to the snake. When one's prayers are answered, they perform a ritual of thanksgiving called thanu or thambila.

The snake in is propitiated in south Canara in several ways: ashlesha bali is one major pooja, when beautiful snake-shaped rangolis called mandalas are drawn and surrounded by 108 lamps. On Naga Panchami, snakes are offered milk and tender coconut. Last rites called samaradhane are performed to dead cobras. The Subrahmanya temple at Kukke in Mangalore is dedicated to the snake-god Subrahmanya.

In Karnataka, on the eve of the paddy festival (kadiru habba) which comes after the rains, the paddy stalks are tied around pipal trees, anthills and groves of snake stones.

In Tamil Nadu and Andhra Pradesh, nagakal or snake stones are consecrated under pipal (*Ficus religiosa*) trees for a boon, especially for the birth of children, and become objects of reverence. Several temples have snake stones placed around the pipal tree or sthala vriksha.

Snakes are associated with Subrahmanya, son of Shiva, and a form of Kartikeya. Snake rituals are performed during Skanda shashthi.

Intertwined snakes are a very popular motif in temple sculpture and painting and in the kolams, designs made on the floor outside the entrance of the house with rice flour. The intertwined snakes keep out evil spirits that may otherwise gain entrance.

Snakes inhabit anthills, making them an object of sanctity and worship. In fact many people leave milk and/or eggs beside anthills to feed snakes and thereby obtain blessings.

In Maharashtra, Nag Panchami is a very important festival when snakes are (force-) fed milk as an offering.

In Bengal, the fifth day of the dark half of the month of Ashadha is dedicated to the worship of the snake goddess Manasa Devi, sister of Vasuki and wife of Jaratkaru.

The companion of Kamakhya, an aspect of Devi, whose temple is in Assam, is the snake. The people of Assam also worship the snake goddess Manasa, a form of Shakti.

The Manasa cult is an ancient folk religion of the east and north-east India. There are two versions of the Manasa story. According to the Puranas, she is the daughter of Kashyapa, who was commanded by Brahma to compose the snake mantras, out of which Manasa was born. She is the sister of Vasuki, wife of Jaratkaru and mother of Astika. She is also known as Jagatgauri, Shaivi, Vaishnavi, Nageshwari, Siddhayogini, etc. She is always dressed in red and rides a swan, flanked by snakes. She protects her worshippers from snake bites and other diseases that come with the monsoon.

A folk story attributes her origin to Shiva and Parvati, who had a daughter named Padma or Manasa, who was sent to the netherworld to rule over and be worshipped by serpents. Not content with her sovereignty over the snakes, Manasa wanted honour and worship from all people earth. Her greatest opponent was Chand Saudagar, a wealthy merchant of Champaka, on the southern banks of the Brahmaputra in the modern Kamrup district of Assam. A devout follower of Shiva, Chand Saudagar refused to worship Manasa. However, his wife Soneka made secret arrangements for worshipping Manasa, and when Chand Saudagar learned about it, he was furious and threw away all the offerings collected for her worship. Manasa was so angry that she caused the death of Chand Saudagar's six sons, sank all his boats, and made him sink into poverty and destitution. Yet, Chand

*Manasa Devi*

Saudagar chose to suffer rather than worship Manasa.

After sometime, a seventh son was born to Chand Saudagar and Soneka, and was named Lakhindara whose death by snake bite on his wedding night was predicted by the astrologers. When he grew up, Lakhindara was married to Bihula. Chand Saudagar erected a meraghara (house of iron) without a single hole in it and made the couple live there. Yet, Lakhindara was bitten to death by a snake on his wedding night. But Bihula was made of sterner stuff and resolved to bring her husband back to life, refusing to part with his body. The next morning, she set out on the river on a raft with the body of her husband. She spent several nights and days on the river and, in spite of men, animals, spirits and goblins trying to frighten and dissuade her, she continued to drift in the water till the raft stopped on the shore, beside Neta, a washerwoman of the gods. Bihula got down, collected a pile of wood and prepared to burn herself on the funeral pyre of her husband. But Neta prevented it and promised to take her to Shiva, who Bihula propitiated with dance and music. Shiva was pleased and restored Lakhindara and his six brothers to life. Bihula, with her husband and brothers-in-law, returned happily to Champakanagara. On her return, Bihula begged Chand Saudagar to worship Manasa and since then goddess Manasa has been worshipped.

During the festival of Manasa, people dance the Devadhvani or Deodhani at the shrine of Kamakhya. The dancer is called Deodha. The dancers live a strict vegetarian life of meditation. It is believed that Manasa appears in their dreams a month before the festival. While dancing, they are unconscious of their surroundings, and walk on the sharp edge of a sword, without any injuries. They make predictions that are regarded as divine. There are two types of Deodhani dance: one is semi-classical and the other is a trance. The Deodhani of Mangaldoi and Kamrup districts of Assam is linked to the Sukanani Oja-Pali form.

The worship of Manasa the snake goddess is also celebrated as the Jhapan festival in the town of Bishnupur in West Bengal. It is a harvest festival, when snake charmers bring cobras, vipers, kraits, pythons, rat snakes, vine and flying snakes in woven baskets, and perform with them while chanting hymns praising Manasa or entering into trances.

The tribes of north-east India have various forms of snake worship. The Khasis of Meghalaya worship U Thlen, a gigantic snake who used to be appeased by human sacrifice, now substituted by animal offerings. Manipur preserves the *Mahabharata* tradition of being the kingdom of the Naga king Chitravahana, whose daughter Chitrangada was married to Arjuna. Even today, the ancestral god of the royal family is a snake called Pakhangba. The Rabhas of Assam worship a snake god who used to live in a cave and was propitiated by the annual sacrifice of a boy and a girl, now replaced by a rooster or goat.

Snake charmers are invariably used as the tourist image of India, although they are a disappearing breed outside tourist centres. It is likely that the original snake charmers were those who used the common fear of the snake to gain control. While fear is a major motivating factor in the worship of the snake, there is also an element of totemism, as seen from the snake-hooded figures in Indian art, particularly of the Buddhist period.

### Snake Festivals

Naga maha, Naga yatra and Naga jatta were ancient festivals conducted by snake worshippers—Hindus, Buddhists and Jains (Agrawal 1970).

Nag panchami is the festival of the snake celebrated on the fifth day of the bright half the lunar month Shravan. Snake stones and anthills are worshipped with offerings of milk, fruits, flowers and incense.

### Ecological Role and Current Status

*Naga worshippers of the Buddha*

Although the term naga or sarpa covers all snakes, it is only the spectacled cobra with its impressive hood that is regarded as sacred.

The Indian cobra is native to the Indian subcontinent and is the most famous of the snakes of India. Like other cobras, it is famous for its threat display, involving raising the front part of its body and spreading its beautiful hood, which has led to its reverence in Indian mythology and culture and, tragically, capture by snake charmers. On the rear of its hood are two circular patterns connected by a curved line, evoking the image of spectacles. The spectacle pattern on the hood is variable as also the ground colour of the snake.

An average cobra is between one and two metres long. Cobras normally feed on rodents, toads, frogs, birds and snakes. Their habitat includes open forest and farmland. However they also thrive in cities, living on rodents in the sewers and underground drains.

The Indian cobra's venom contains a powerful neurotoxin that acts on the synaptic gaps of the nerves, thereby paralysing the muscles and leading to respiratory failure or cardiac arrest. Symptoms of cobra envenomation can begin from fifteen minutes to two hours after the bite, and can be fatal in less than an hour. However, despite its fearsome reputation, only 10 per cent of cobra bites result in death.

The snake is feared more than respected. Its important function as a killer of rats and pests made its preservation essential. But its poisonous fangs which can kill a human being make it a source of fear. Further, it is apparently invisible, appearing suddenly from the undergrowth to catch its prey. All this adds to its mystique, making its subterranean world a haven of jewelled palaces and exotic luxuries.

*Snake deity of Kerala's Sarpa Kavu*

The Indian cobra has been caught by snake charmers, kept in closed wicker baskets and taken out to sway to the tune of a special flute. The cobra is, however, deaf to the snake charmer's pipe, but follows the visual cue of the moving object and the ground vibrations of the snake charmer's tapping foot. Previously, Indian snake charmers also conducted cobra and mongoose fights, in which the snake was either killed or brought to near death, only to be rested to fight again. The mongoose is not known to have any immunity to the venom, but its agility and thick fur helps overcome most snakes. The snake-and-mongoose-fights are now illegal.

The snake is now protected in India under the Indian Wildlife Protection Act, 1972. But the numbers of snakes, especially cobras, are declining rapidly as they are caught and killed for their skin and for their venom, both of which fetch very high prices in the international black market.

~

# Snow Leopard

| Scientific Name | : | *Panthera uncia* Schreber |
| --- | --- | --- |
| Common Names | : | Barafni chita (Hindi) |
| | | Shan (Ladakhi) |
| | | Pani chiruthai (Tamil) |
| | | Hima chitravyaghrah (Sanskrit) |
| Distribution | : | 75,000 sq. km in the Himalayas |

A blue-maned white snow leopard is the national emblem of Tibet.

Achi Chokey Dolma, the Tibetan equivalent of Durga, is the protectoress who rides the snow lion, . She is venerated by Buddhist communities in Ladakh, Sikkim, Tibet and elsewhere in the Himalayas.

*Ecological Role and Current Status*

The snow leopard is a shy animal that avoids human settlements, and is therefore rarely seen.

A large cat, it is native to the cold mountain ranges of southern Asia. It represents an intermediate between the big cats and smaller species, as it cannot roar. Well-known for its beautiful fur, the snow leopard has a whitish-tan coat with ringed spots of dark ash-brown and black spots. The fur turns white in the winter. Its tail is heavy with fur and the bottom of its paws are covered with fur for protection against snow and cold. It weighs between 35 and 55 kg.

Its long tail, which helps it maintain its balance on the rugged terrain and unstable surfaces of its habitat, distinguishes it. It also doubles as a warm cover and is used to cover its nose and mouth in very cold conditions. The snow leopard's big furry feet act as snowshoes. In summer, the snow leopard usually lives above the tree line on mountainous meadows and in rocky regions at an altitude of up to 6,000 m. In winter, it comes down into the forests to an altitude of about 2,000 m.

A loner, the snow leopard's cubs are reared for long periods in the mountains. It eats whatever meat it can find: it can kill animals three times its size, including domestic livestock. It ambushes prey from above, and can jump as far as 14 m. An individual snow leopard lives within a well-defined home range. However, it does not defend its range when encroached upon by other individuals.

The snow leopard is an endangered species whose pelts command a very high price in the fur market. During the 1960s, the snow leopard's population went down dramatically, but has since recovered slightly. Sanctuaries for the snow leopard's protection have been set up at Hemis National Park, Ladakh, in the state of Jammu and Kashmir; Nanda Devi National Park in the state of Uttarakhand, a UNESCO Natural World Heritage Site; and the Valley of Flowers National Park, Uttaranchal, another UNESCO Natural World Heritage Site.

$\sim$

# Spider

| | | |
|---|---|---|
| Scientific Name | : | Araneae (order) |
| Common Names | : | Makda (Hindi) |
| | | Silandhi (Tamil) |
| | | Saalapurugu (Telugu) |
| | | Lootah, ashtapadah (Sanskrit) |
| Distribution | : | Throughout India |

The spider represents the importance of perseverance and hard work. It also represents the essence of existence, for it spins its web and later eats it too, signifying that everything that is produced by Brahman ends in Brahman.

Sri Kalahasti in Andhra Pradesh is named after three animals—Sri or the spider, Kala or the snake and Hasti or the elephant—who regularly worshipped the lingam of Shiva situated at this temple and attained salvation.

The Tamil Shaivite *Periyapuranam* has a story about a spider and an elephant who worshipped a Shiva lingam. The spider would spin a web above it every day to protect it. The elephant thought it looked ugly and removed it everyday. Angry, the spider one day entered the elephant's trunk as it was trying to remove the web, gave it a poisonous bite and caused the elephant's death. Thereafter, the spider continued to weave a protective web over the lingam.

*Shri Kalahasti*

Removing a spider's web is supposed to bring bad luck. However, the untidiness of cobwebs has made it inevitable. Therefore, the number of days for cleaning cobwebs is restricted: it is not permitted on Tuesdays and Fridays, on the full moon or new moon, on festival days and other special constellation days. This is to give the spider time to enjoy its nest and catch and feed on its prey.

*Ecological Role and Current Status*

All spiders produce silk, a thin, strong protein strand woven into webs and used to trap insects, although there are also many species that hunt. The silk woven by the spider can be used for climbing, to form smooth walls for burrows, build egg sacs, wrap prey, and even hold sperm.

Spiders are one of the most important links in the regulation of the insect population. Different spiders perform different roles in the ecology, including malaria control by snaring the malarial anopheles mosquito. Like many other species, spiders are endangered in India due to habitat destruction and pesticides.

~

# Squirrel

| Scientific Name | : | *Funambulus palmarum* Linn |
| Common Names | : | Indian palm squirrel/ |
| | | Three-striped palm squirrel |
| | | Ghilahari (Hindi) |
| | | Anil (Tamil) |
| | | Kalandakah (Sanskrit) |
| Distribution | : | Throughout India |

An interesting legend explains the three stripes on the back of the Indian palm squirrel. During the construction of the Adi setu (bridge) at Rameswaram by Lord Rama and the Vanara army, a little squirrel also contributed in its own little way. It rolled in the beach sand and then ran to the end of the setu to shake off the sand from its back, chanting Lord Rama's name all along, thereby providing the sand required to bind the stones for the bridge together.

Lord Rama, pleased by the creature's dedication, caressed the squirrel's back and ever since the Indian squirrel has carried three white stripes on its back, which are believed to be the mark of Lord Rama's fingers. The squirrel has come to symbolize hard work and selfless service.

*Rama*

As a result, squirrels are considered sacred in India and are not to be harmed. They are fed by many Hindu families. This is mainly because of their association with Lord Rama.

*Ecological Role and Current Status*

The Indian palm squirrel is a species of rodent found in south India and Sri Lanka. An adult squirrel weighs about 100 g. It lives on trees in rural and urban areas and is a very adaptable animal.

~

# Swan

| Scientific Name | : | *Cygnus olor* Gmelin |
|---|---|---|
| Common Names | : | Mute swan |
| | | Hans (Hindi) |
| | | Annaparavai (Tamil) |
| | | Hamsah (Sanskrit) |
| Distribution | : | Throughout India |

The swan is the associate of Lord Brahma, the Creator. It is said to possess the sacred knowledge of the Brahman. The hamsa represents perfect union, balance and life. The constant repetition of the word hamso changes to soham (so-aham from sah aham), which means 'That I am'. Hence the hamsa is often identified with the Supreme Spirit or Brahman.

The flight of the hamsa also symbolizes the escape from the cycle of birth, death and rebirth, or samsara.

The bird also has special connotations in the monistic philosophy of Advaita Vedanta—just as the swan lives on water but its feathers are not drenched by water, an Advaitin similarly lives in this material world, untouched by the material appeal created by maya.

A swan is said to have a sensitive beak, which can distinguish pure milk from a mixture of water and milk. The swan thus symbolizes the ability to discriminate between good and evil. It is often described as the king of birds.

*Vehicle*

Brahma, the Creator, and Sarasvati, the Hindu goddess of wisdom, knowledge and learning, use a white swan as their vehicle and companion, giving Sarasvati the name Hamsavahini (She who has a swan vehicle).

As Sarasvati is dressed in a white sari and is seated on a white lotus, the swan associated with the gods is the white swan, also known as the mute swan. Its height results

*Brahma*

in a goose-like appearance in Indian sculpture and painting.

*Arayanna*

Swans are believed to reside in Lake Mansarovar (a lake in Tibet, sacred to Hindus and Buddhists), from where they migrate to Indian lakes in winter. They were heavenly swans named arayanna: ara means royalty. As the swans did not like rain (or snow), they came to India when it rained and returned to their lake when the rains stopped. They are believed to be descended from the Lord of all Beings, Prajapati, and his wife Tamara (lotus). The *Ramayana* says that this lineage gave the swan divinity.

Swans were originally black-and-white, but were blessed by Varuna, lord of the oceans, to become as white as milk and thus be protected from the demon king of Lanka, Ravana.

According to another story, Prince Nala once freed a swan that was stuck in a water tank, but seeing the bird tremble with fear, released it at once. The Arayanna was so happy that it flew to the next kingdom and narrated stories

*Sarasvati*

about Nala's beauty and goodness to Princess Damayanti, and thus helped the two to get married.

Persons of great spiritual abilities and grace are given the title Paramahamsa or the supreme swan, for they can see the Divine and leave the rest. The hamsa mantra indicates the sound made by the exhalation (ha) and inhalation (sa) of the breath.

Ramakrishna, the great nineteenth-century mystic, after whom the Ramakrishna Mission is named, was called Ramakrishna Paramahamsa.

*Mythical Bird*

The hamsa was used extensively in the art of Gandhara, along with images of the Buddha. The bird is as sacred to the Buddhists as it is to the Hindus.

Later, as the depiction of the swan became highly stylized in art, hamsa ceased to resemble the beautiful swan. It was given a plump body, a short neck and a long, flowery beak. This motif

became so popular that we see
the mythical hamsa everywhere: as
decorative motifs on lamps, saris, in
sculpture and painting and so on.

Today the word hamsa means
the swan, which is depicted as a
mythical bird, even as the mute
swan has disappeared from India.

*Kama*

*Ecological Role and Current Status*

The hamsa (hansa) is the mute
swan, a symbol and a decorative
element of Indian religion and
art. It can grow up to 127 cm tall, which results in a goose-like
appearance in some works of Indian sculpture and painting. Hansa
also refers to the goose, flamingo and even other waterbirds.
This may be because Indian swans are never found in feral
populations, domesticated flocks or zoos. But ornithological
checklists about India clearly state that swans winter in India,
although not regularly.

This species of bird is found mainly in temperate areas of
Europe, across western Asia, and as far east as Siberia. It is a
migratory bird throughout the northern latitudes in Europe and
Asia and as far south as north Africa. Mute swans nest on large
mounds that they build in shallow water in the middle or at the
edge of a lake. These monogamous birds reuse the same nest
each year, restoring or rebuilding it as needed. Male and female
swans share the care of the nest, and once the cygnets are fledged
it is not uncommon to see whole families looking for food. They
feed on submerged aquatic vegetation, reached with their long
necks. Although this bird can be tame, especially to those who
feed it daily, it is aggressive in defence of its nest, and its size
and impressive hissing make it a formidable adversary for animals
as large as a fox.

The most familiar sound associated with mute swan is the whooshing of the wings in flight once this bird has laboriously taken off from the water. The word swansong refers to this moment of passage, and to the legend that it is utterly silent until the last moment of its life, and then sings one achingly beautiful song just before dying; in reality, the mute swan is not completely silent, but has a kind of guttural warning call it will give when approached.

Unlike black swans, mute swans are strongly territorial. The male curves its neck backwards in a threat display. The mute swan is a protected bird, but this has not prevented illegal hunting and poaching in many places.

~

# Tiger

| | | |
|---|---|---|
| Scientific Name | : | *Panthera tigris* Linn |
| Common Names | : | Bengal tiger |
| | | Bagh (Hindi) |
| | | Puli (Tamil) |
| | | Vyaghrah (Sanskrit) |
| Distribution | : | Originally throughout India, now limited to a few reserved forests and national parks. |

The tiger is the national animal of India.

*Vehicle*

If Vishnu Durga rides the lion, Shiva Durga or Shakti rides the tiger. In places like Nepal, her battle with Mahisha takes place on the back of the tiger (Singh 1996). While Durga is the destroyer of evil, her tiger mount represents power and immortality. The more ferocious forms of Durga—Shakti and Kali—ride the tiger. In Andhra Pradesh, for example, the tiger is an integral part of goddess Durga's iconography.

There are parallels in Siberia, where the tiger spirit is a woman who appears as a winged tiger during the initiation of a shaman, while Tibetan frescoes depict goddesses riding tigers.

The tiger is the vahana of Rahu, the serpent or eclipse, one of the navagraha or nine planets of Indian mythology.

*Shakti*

## Ayyappa

The tiger is associated with Lord Ayyappa of Sabarimala, who was born from the union of Lord Shiva with Mohini (incarnation of Lord Vishnu) who appeared at the samudra manthana. According to legend, Ayyappa was found by a king and queen on the banks of a river and they brought him to their palace. When the queen had a child of her own, she became jealous of Ayyappa and planned to get him killed. She pretended to be ill and sent Ayyappa to fetch tiger's milk to cure her illness. She expected him to be killed by the tigers and was surprised to see Ayyappa return to the palace riding on a tiger, with the other devas following him in the form of so many tigers. The terrified king begged Ayyappa's forgiveness, but the latter said it was time for him to leave. When asked where his temple should be built, he fired an arrow which fell on the hill called Sabari.

*Ayyappa*

Every year on Makara Sankranti day, a mysterious light appears on the hill. It is believed that Ayyappa has returned to bless his faithful devotees.

The tiger is the vehicle of both Ayyappa and Male Mahadeshvara.

### Vyaghranatheshvara

Lord Shiva is often depicted wearing or seated on a tiger skin. Shiva also bears the name Vyaghranatheshvara (Lord of the tiger), because he once had slain a demon who had taken the form of a tiger.

*Shiva*

Shiva in the Rig Veda was known as Rudra. The *Yajur Veda* describes Rudra as clothed in a tiger skin. This prompted sages and yogis to sit on tiger skin while meditating. This was done at a time when tigers roamed the subcontinent in large numbers.

### Bengal and the North-East

The region is steeped in tiger worship. In northern Bengal the tiger god was worshipped by both Hindus and Muslims. Scroll paintings depict a Muslim holy man riding a tiger, carrying a string of prayer beads and a staff.

In another story, a man and a woman were in the jungle, but were prevented by the presence of the Asur Dano from making love. Then the woman took a branch of an ebony tree, cut it into pieces and threw the pieces at the Asur. They turned into bears, tigers and hyenas which kept the Asur away. Then they copulated and there was seed and fruit (Thapar 1995).

A legend from Nagaland narrates the story of the first spirit, the first tiger and the first man, all of whom came out of the pangolin's den, born of the same mother. The man stayed at home, the tiger went to the forest. One day the man went into the forest where he met the tiger, and the two began to fight. The man tricked the tiger into crossing a river and then killed the tiger with a poisoned dart. The tiger's body floated down the river till it lay among the reeds. The god Dingu-Aneni saw that the bones had come from a human womb and and sat on them for ten years, as a result of which hundreds of tigers were born and went to live in the hills and plains. Naga folklore invokes the tiger as a guardian of the region, who ensured human fertility. Oaths were taken over a tiger's tooth or skull and tiger spirits were invoked to cure illnesses. Nagas only killed tigers on ceremonial occasions and strict taboos governed the cutting, skinning and eating of tiger's flesh. The head was put in water or the mouth propped open to allow the spirit to escape and prevent the tiger god from avenging his wrath on his killer. The Lhota Nagas put leaves in the tiger's mouth for the same purpose while the Lephori kept tigers heads in trees and used them for taking oaths. The eclipse is explained as the attempt by the tiger to eat the moon or sun, which could be prevented by the loud beating of drums (Thapar 1995).

## Karnataka

The tiger is worshipped as Betaraya in the inland districts and Huliraya (tiger king) in the sacred groves of the Western Ghat region.

Hulideva is the popular Tiger deity of North Canara, where the forests are called Hulidevaruvana or 'forest of the tiger god'.

The tiger was the emblem of the Hoysala kings of Karnataka, while Tipu Sultan, an erstwhile ruler, was known as the 'Tiger of Mysore' (Ardhya 2005).

## Maharashtra

Wagh is the Marathi word for tiger and the tiger is a popular deity in rural Maharashtra. It once roamed the Western Ghats, but was killed in enormous numbers for its beautiful skin and head to be hung up as trophies in the palaces of vain maharajas, British bureaucrats and army officers.

Waghoba is the forest deity whose festival is celebrated in the month of Chaitra (March–April) with the sacrifice of hens and goats. He is worshipped to ensure that tigers do not attack people or farm animals. An image of the tiger is made out of clay and worshipped. At Pench National Park, the tiger's pugmarks in clay are worshipped.

Waghya is the god of the Warli tribe, represented as a shapeless stone. He is also the main deity of the Dhangers and Bapujipoa of the Kolis (Gadgil and Malhotra 1979).

Wagle is a totemic family name, while Waghmare is yet another family name once borne as a title of a tiger killer.

*Tiger Dance*

Mimicking the tiger, or the tiger dance, is very popular in several parts of India. It is called puliyattam in Tamil, puli vesham in Andhra Pradesh, puli kali in Kerala, bagh nritya in Orissa and huli kunita/huli vesha in Karnataka. It is generally performed during Dussehra in honour of goddess Durga who rides a tiger or lion. Young men paint their bodies yellow with black stripes to resemble tigers. They pretend to catch deer, or flee from a hunter or may even convey the

*Puliyattam*

motions of being hunted and killed. The dance and movements are accompanied by the loud beating of drums.

The puli kali of Thekkinkadu Maidan in the centre of Thrichur town in Kerala is particularly famous. Performed on the fourth day of Onam, to the accompaniment of drum beats and the encouraging shouts of the onlookers, tigers of every shape, size, colour and decoration dance and perform impossible feats. Puli kali celebrates the annual return of the dethroned king of Kerala, Mahabali, in the form of the harvest during Onam, with performers and fans cutting across barriers of religion, caste and creed. Interestingly, the dance owes its origin to the Muslims who originally introduced it during Muharram, the recollection of the murder and martyrdom of Ali, Prophet Mohammed's son-in-law, who was a great warrior and thought to have possessed the strength of a tiger. Gradually, other communities, particularly the Tamil Konars and Chettiars with the Tamil tradition of puli atam, took it over and organized it during the Pongal festival. Whether it is puli atam or puli kali, the dance primarily mimics a tiger moving on its hind legs to the rhythm of the drums. There is a strong influence of kalaripayattu, the martial art of Kerala. Climbing bamboo poles and accomplishing acrobatic feats, the dancers are an awesome sight, with beautifully painted bodies and faces recreating the feared predator (Paul 2005).

## Ecological Role and Current Status

The Bengal tiger is a subspecies of tiger found primarily in South Asia. It is the second largest and the most common tiger subspecies and lives in a variety of habitats, including grasslands, subtropical and tropical rainforests, scrub forests, wet and dry deciduous forests and mangroves. Male Bengal tigers measure 275 to 310 cm, with their tail weighing between 180 and 270 kg. Females are much smaller and weigh between 141 and 180 kg. The fur is generally orange-brown with black stripes, although there is a mutation that sometimes produces white tigers.

Bengal tigers hunt medium-sized and large-sized animals such as wild boar, deer and water buffalo. They sometimes prey on smaller animals like hares, monkeys, langurs or peacocks. Bengal tigers have also been known to attack young Asian elephants and rhino calves and other predators such as leopards, wolves, jackals, foxes, crocodiles and dholes, although these predators are not typically a part of the tiger's diet. Bengal tigers prefer to hunt mostly by night, but are awake in the daytime. During the day, the cover of the tall elephant grass camouflages the animal. They kill their prey by overpowering it and severing the spinal cord, or by biting the throat of large prey, thereby suffocating it to death. A Bengal tiger will usually drag its kill to a safe place to eat away from other predators. Despite their size, Bengal tigers can climb trees effectively, but they are not as adept as the smaller leopard, which hides its kill in the trees. Bengal tigers are strong swimmers, often chasing their prey into the water. The Bengal tiger can consume up to about 30 kg of meat at a time and then go without eating for days. Bengal tigers normally hunt large animals, but, when driven to hunger, will eat anything, such as frogs, fowl, crocodiles and domestic livestock.

At the turn of the twentieth century, the tiger population in India was estimated to be around 40,000. The first-ever all-India tiger census was conducted in 1972 which revealed the existence of only 1,827 tigers. Project Tiger is a wildlife conservation project initiated in India in 1972 to protect the Bengal tiger by conserving it in specially constituted tiger reserves, representative of various biogeographical regions throughout India. The project was launched in 1973, and nine tiger reserves were created in the country based on a 'core-buffer' strategy. Today there are twenty-nine tiger reserves in India. The main achievement of this project was an increase in the tiger population in the reserve areas, from a mere 268 in nine reserves in 1972 to above 1,000 in twenty-eight reserves in 2006. In 2007, there were twenty-eight Project Tiger wildlife reserves covering an area of 37,761 sq. km. Project Tiger helped increase the population of these tigers from 1,200 in the 1970s to 3,500 in the 1990s. Since the early 1990s, the tiger population suffered a setback due to habitat destruction and large-scale poaching of the animals for their skins and bones.

It was recently discovered that tigers had been wiped out of Sariska, a Project Tiger sanctuary in Rajasthan. The current population of wild Bengal tigers in the Indian subcontinent is estimated to be around 1,300.

Tigers, being at the apex of the food chain, are indicators of the stability of the ecosystem.

The Bengal tiger probably entered India through Burma from Siberia at the end of the last Ice Age. The tiger once roamed the entire Indian subcontinent, from the cold heights of Kashmir to the tropical and dry deciduous forests of the south, from mangrove swamps to evergreen forests, living in an extraordinary variety of temperatures, altitudes and climates. The animal was held in high esteem and rural Indians recognized they had to share the same space with this majestic animal. From a population of between 50,000 and 100,000 in the nineteenth century, their population has dwindled to less than 2,000 today. Records show that at least 20,000 were killed by the British and the Indian maharajas between 1860 and 1960 (Thapar 1995). Hunting was banned too late in India—the tigers had lost the battle against the gun.

Habitat loss and poaching are important threats to species survival. Poachers kill tigers not only for their pelts, which are in great demand in Tibet, but also for components to make various traditional East Asian, especially Chinese, medicines. Other factors contributing to their loss are urbanization and revenge killing. Farmers blame tigers for killing cattle and shoot or poison them. The beautiful skin of the tiger has sounded its death knell. It is being hunted to extinction for its skin and body parts, which are used in Chinese medicine.

Will the tiger survive? It is doubtful. Its numbers are decreasing rapidly and its habitats are shrinking. The recent Scheduled Tribes and Other Traditional Forest Dwellers (Recognition of Forest Rights) Act, 2006 (2 of 2007) envisages handing over landownership to individual tribals and others in forest areas, which will lead to the end of the forests. The tiger will be pushed out.

~

# Tortoise/Turtle

| | | |
|---|---|---|
| Scientific Name | : | *Testudinidae* (family) |
| Common Names | : | Kachua (Hindi) |
| | | Aamai (Tamil) |
| | | Kurmah (Sanskrit) |
| Distribution | : | Coastal areas |

*Vishnu's Incarnation—Kurma*

> *Glory to you, O Lord of the universe,*
> *Who took the form of a Tortoise;*
> *When the ocean of milk was churned,*
> *You were the pivot beneath the churning rod that was Mount Mandara,*
> *Which left a beautiful impression on your back.*

*Gita Govinda* by Jayadeva

Kurma was the second incarnation of Lord Vishnu, when he incarnated in the form of a gigantic tortoise and sat at the bottom of the ocean. He helped the devas attain amrita or the nectar of immortality from the celestial ocean by holding the mountain Mandara on his back.

The story of the tortoise incarnation of Vishnu first appears in the epic *Ramayana*. Due to the curse of the sage Durvasa, all the devas or celestial beings lost their powers. They were afraid that the forces of evil, the asuras, would destroy them. So they rushed to Brahma the Creator who sent them to Vishnu the Preserver. Vishnu advised them to collect all the plants and herbs and put them into the Ocean of Milk. Then, using Mount Mandara as the churning stick and the snake Vasuki as a rope, they had to churn the ocean, along with the asuras, each holding one end of the rope. The churning would bring out the nectar of immortality. The devas and asuras started churning the ocean of milk, but the mountain began to sink. So Vishnu incarnated himself as a tortoise and bore the mountain on his back. The marks on the tortoise's shell are attributed to the movement of the mountain on Kurma's back.

This is an important incident, for many important things came out of the ocean. Poison was the first to emerge, which was drunk by Shiva to save the world. The rest of the items came out one after another: Lakshmi, goddess of prosperity and Vishnu's consort, seated on a lotus; Dhanvantari, physician of the gods, holding the nectar of immortality;

*Kurma*

Surabhi, the cow; Varuni, goddess of wine; Parijata, the tree of paradise; apsaras, celestial nymphs; Chandra, the moon; Uchchaishravas, the divine horse; Kaustubha mani, the divine jewel; Airavata, the divine white elephant; Visham, the poison of the snakes; Shankha, the divine conch used in religious ceremonies; Dhanus, the divine bow. The last item to emerge was Amrita, the nectar of immortality.

The above sounds like a shopping list—many of the items were those to be imported by Indian states, like wine (from Arabia), 'white' elephants (from Burma), the conch shell (from Gujarat and Kanyakumari), horses (from Arabia and central Asia) and so on.

Both groups—gods and demons—wanted the amrita, and began to quarrel. So Vishnu took the form of a beautiful woman called Mohini, to distract the demons, so that the devas could take away the nectar without sharing it with the demons. Seeing that they had lost the nectar a terrible battle took place in which the gods were victorious.

The tortoise was the pivot on which the ocean was churned. The tortoise is an ancient mariner, with a long life, who travels over thousands of miles from one continental shelf to another. He is the best example of seafaring.

The temple of Mallikarjuna or Shrikurmam in Srisailam, Andhra Pradesh is the only existing temple of Kurma. It was once a Shiva temple that was converted to a Vaishnava temple by the medieval philosopher Ramanuja. It contains a very unusual image of a tortoise, with an upraised tail and its back to the worshipper. According to a local legend, the image was regularly worshipped by a Bhil king from behind the back wall of the shrine. Seeing his devotion, Kurma turned around to face the king. It is more likely that this story was invented to explain the absorption of a Bhil deity by the Hindu pantheon.

*Vishnu on Tortoise (Cambodia)*

The story of the churning of the ocean is very popular in the Hindu art of ancient Cambodia, where Vishnu stands on the tortoise, rather than taking on the incarnation of the tortoise. The samudra manthana story is carved on the walls of Angkor Wat, while devas and asuras flank the gates of Angkor Thom, in a replication of the churning of the ocean with the aid of the snake Vasuki, where the earth below the gates symbolizes the tortoise, an incarnation of Vishnu whose spouse is Mother Earth.

Like Matsya, the image of Kurma is depicted on sculptures and paintings of Vishnu temples as a half-man half-tortoise, the lower half with a tortoise shell, the upper half human and four-armed, holding the attributes of Vishnu: conch (shankha), discus (chakra) and mace (gada), the fourth hand in the abhaya ('be without fear') mudra (position).

The churning of the ocean by the devas and asuras represents the struggle between the opposing forces of good and evil. The victory of the devas, made possible by Vishnu, reflects the fact that the Lord always stands by good. The simple tortoise—ridiculed for his slowness and the apparent weight on his back—is the Lord's choice to carry the sacred mountain for this world-shattering event.

The tortoise's qualities of perseverance, steadfastness, silence and longevity are replicated in the earth. His strong shell, which bears the heavy load of the mountain, represents the strength of the earth which carries all creation on her back. Like the tortoise retracts into his shell when he senses danger, human beings too must retract their senses in the cover of knowledge. Thus the tortoise represents the earth itself.

### Vehicle

The tortoise is the vahana of Goddess Yamuna, who personifies the holy river Yamuna.

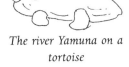

*The river Yamuna on a tortoise*

### Buddhism

Saturn or Shani, in the Buddhist tradition, rides a tortoise. The slow-moving animal is appropriately matched to the slow-moving planet.

The tankhas of Mahayana Buddhism often depict the body of the tortoise as the cosmic cycle, with the various worlds contained within.

## Jainism

The emblem of the twentieth Tirthankara, Munisuvrata, is a tortoise. Sometimes the sixteenth Tirthankara uses the tortoise, at other times the deer.

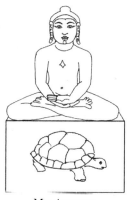

*Munisuvrata*

## Ecological Role and Current Status

The tortoise is an amphibious species. Some are very strong and are the largest animals in their environment, felling plants and creating pathways, used by other animals, as they search for food.

The tortoise is under extreme threat by fishing nets, high-speed trawlers and poachers who hunt it for its flesh on the east coast, particularly in Andhra Pradesh and Orissa.

~

# Vulture

| Scientific Name | : | *Gyps bengalensis* Gmelin |
|---|---|---|
| Common Names | : | Asian white-backed vulture, |
| | | Gidh (Hindi) |
| | | Kazhugu (Tamil) |
| | | Gridhah (Sanskrit) |
| Distribution | : | Throughout India |

Jatayu and Sampati were the two sons of Aruna, chariot driver of Surya, the sun, and Shyeni, a divine bird. Sampati was very fond of Jatayu. Once, when the brothers were young, they tried to fly close to the sun. Jatayu almost got his wings burnt. Seeing his brother in distress, Sampati flew higher and shielded his brother from the sun's ray and in the process burnt his own wings.

According to the epic *Ramayana*, when Ravana was abducting Sita to his kingdom of Lanka, a fierce battle took place between him and the vulture king Jatayu. The bird was fatally wounded in his attempt to rescue Sita from Ravana. He lived long enough to inform Rama and Lakshmana about Sita's abduction by Ravana. Jatayu died chanting Rama's name and the brothers performed the funeral rites for the bird. Jatayu was released from the bondage of karma and reached heaven in a chariot of fire. This has sanctified all vultures.

*Jatayu*

Sampati played his role in the epic by confirming Sita's abduction to Lanka and her imprisonment in the forest of ashoka (*Saraca Indica* or *Jonesia Ashok*) trees.

Once again, there is confusion with this bird of prey. Jatayu and Sampati are sometimes described as the sons of Garuda, who is actually an eagle, but is also identified with the Brahmani kite. Now there is one more bird of prey in the reckoning: the vulture. The two brothers are always regarded as vultures, but their Puranic association with Garuda creates yet another problem, for a school of belief identifies Garuda with the vulture.

The vulture is also the vehicle of the constellation Ketu.

*Two Immortal Vultures*

At the Vedagirishvarar Temple in Tamil Nadu, situated on top of the Thirukalukunram Hill, two vultures—*Neophron percnopterus Gingianus*—have been appearing every day from the northern sky. They descend on the hill, are fed rice gruel and then take off towards the south. This tradition has survived for centuries—nobody knows when it began—and has given the hill the title of Pakshitirtha (the sacred place of the birds). It is believed that two rishis, in the form of these two birds, fly from Kashi (or

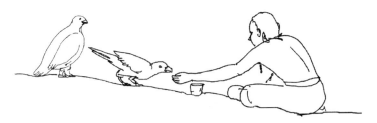

*Feeding vultures at Thirukalukunram*

the Himalayas) to the south every day, and return to Kashi/the Himalayas by evening. Never are there more or less: always only two. It is one of those phenomena that defy explanation. It is also surprising that carrion eaters have opted for vegetarian food (Siromoney, 1977).

However, in recent years, the vultures have not been appearing. There are many theories for this absence but the most probable and least discussed is that they have fallen a victim to the drug diclofenac found in the carcasses of cattle (see the following story).

### Zoroastrianism

In the tenth century, a small group of Zoroastrians (better known in India as Parsis), fire-worshipping followers of the Persian philosopher Zoroaster, landed as refugees from Muslim conquest and conversion in Gujarat, on the western coast of India, and were given sanctuary by the local Hindu king Jadi Rana. In the seventeenth century, when the British trade commenced, many of them migrated to Bombay, where they built the Towers of Silence to dispose of their dead by exposing the bodies to the sky, where they are eaten by vultures. The Towers are situated at Dongarwadi, the highest point on Malabar Hill in Bombay (now Mumbai). They are known as the dakhma.

As the four elements—earth, air, fire and water—are considered to be sacred by the Zoroastrians, the Parsis cannot bury, cremate or throw dead bodies into the river (as is done by Hindus, Buddhists, Jains and Sikhs). The bodies are first washed and perfumed by the nasasalars and blessed by the dastoor (priest). The bodies are then placed on one of the three tiers, depending on whether it is the body of a man, woman or child. Once inside, vultures and other carnivorous birds dispose of the body. It is a very clean and sanitary disposal as the carrion birds cannot fly for at least one hour after they feed and therefore no bones are dropped from the air. Most importantly, this form of disposal ensures food for the carnivores, especially the vultures, which is in keeping with the Zoroastrian requirement of charity, which they perform even after death by feeding their corpses to the vultures.

Since the 1990s, an alarming decline in the population of vultures—nearly 95 per cent—particularly the slender and the long-billed white-backed vulture, was observed. The villain, it was discovered, was diclofenac, a non-steroidal anti-inflammatory drug widely used for cattle, because it is cheap and prevents afflictions like lameness and fever. The dead bodies of the cattle are left to rot in the open, due to the Hindu disinclination to kill cattle. The vultures then dispose of them. Unfortunately, it causes kidney failure in the great birds, leading to death within a few days of consumption. The Government of India banned the sale of diclofenac on 11 May 2006, but the ban has yet to be made effective by state governments. Meanwhile the Bombay Natural History Society (BNHS), along with the Royal Society for the Protection of Birds, has set up two vulture breeding centres in Haryana and West Bengal.Unfortunately, vultures are slow breeders, each producing just one offspring a year. While a modelling study showed that even if one per cent of cattle had diclofenac, it could lead to a decline in the vulture population, sampling studies showed that up to ten per cent of cattle carcasses had traces of diclofenac. The alternative drug for cattle could be Meloxicam, which could save the vultures for their religious role as disposers of the Parsi dead and ecological role as scavengers (Surya Narayan 2006).

*Ecological Role and Current Status*

Vultures are scavenging birds, feeding on the carcasses of dead animals which they find exclusively by sight. They are found in every continent except Antarctica and Oceania. A particular characteristic is the bald head, devoid of feathers. This is likely because a feathered head would become spattered with blood and other fluids, and thus be difficult to keep clean.

Vultures seldom attack healthy animals, but may kill the wounded or sick. Thus battlefields and scenes of floods and droughts are their favourite haunts. They gorge themselves till their crop bulges and sit sleepily to digest their food. They do not carry food to their young, but disgorge it. Vultures are excellent scavengers, especially in hot countries. They can eat rotten flesh containing various bacteria, which are destroyed in their stomachs.

~

# Yak

| Scientific Name | : | *Bos grunniens* Linn |
|---|---|---|
| Common Names | : | Yak (English, Hindi and all languages), Yak/Drong (male), Dri/Nak (female) (Tibetan/Ladakhi) Chamarah (Sanskrit) |
| Distribution | : | Throughout the Himalayan region, primarily Ladakh (Jammu and Kashmir) |

While the yak itself is not sacred, its bushy tail is in great demand as a fly whisk (fan) in many Buddhist monastries of Ladakh and Tibet, and north Indian temples and palaces. Women fanning deities or rulers with the chamara is a common image in Indian art, appearing as early as the Mauryan period.

*Ecological Role and Current Status*
The yak is a long-haired bovine animal. Apart from the large domestic population, there are a few endangered wild yaks. Yaks, both domestic and wild, are herd animals. Wild yaks stand about two metres tall at the shoulder and can weigh up to 1,200 kg. Domesticated yaks are about half the height and weight of wild yaks. Often, the pack animals are actually cross-breeds of the yak

*Chauri (fan) made of yak hair*

and *Bos taurus* (common domestic cattle). Both types have long shaggy hair to insulate them from the cold. Wild yaks can be either brown or black, while domesticated ones can also be white. Both males and females have horns. They eat grasses, lichens and other plants.

Both wild and domesticated yaks are killed for food in Ladakh. Domesticated yaks are kept primarily for their milk, fibre (used as knitting wool), skin (used for coats and as floor rugs), meat, and as beasts of burden. They transport goods across the mountains.

Yak fibre is soft and smooth, in shades of gray, brown, black and white. The length of yak fibre is about 3 cm. It is combed or shed from the yak and then dehaired. The result is a lovely downy fibre that is spun into yarn.

# Conclusion

The philosophers of yore were canny people. They realized that man's apathy and the belief that the life and blood of one creature could compensate for another would result in unnecessary cruelty and large-scale decimation of animals, including ecologically important species. While man had to struggle to survive, he equally required the biological diversity of the planet for his survival.

They also realized that animals had a life and a soul no less than that of a human being and that all are intricately involved in a web of interdependence that we, today, call biodiversity. They realized that the karmic cycle involved animals as much as it did humans, from the lowly ant to the magnificent tiger to the human being.

And thus an elaborate mythology was evolved to protect each species and honour it. It worked for a while—for as long as good values remained important and greed was regarded to be a vice.

Unfortunately, the success of greedy colonial powers in the eighteenth and nineteenth centuries reversed this trend. First, people watched with horror as values were overturned. Then, in the twentieth century, when post-colonial governments learned that evil was profitable, they jumped on the bandwagon and decided to follow suit.

*The Future*

Ancient India used religious sentiment to protect animals, and it worked: animals survived.

Modern India has enacted laws and acts to protect animals, and it has not worked: domestic animals are suffering unbelievable acts of cruelty while wildlife is getting wiped out.

Some cults have grown in strength and stature. Ganesha is among the most popular of deities. Shiva without Nandi and Durga without the lion or tiger is inconceivable. Yet this has not translated to protection for the animals on the field. The elephant is still poked and prodded by cruel mahouts and circus owners; the plight of the bullock in life and death is awful; and the tiger and lion are being poached to extinction.

Unless the ancient respect for all creations returns, unless India restores and respects her tryst with the biological diversity of creation, the sacred animals of India will remain sacred only in name.

Over two thousand years ago, the great Tamil philosopher Thiruvallur wrote extensively about kindness to animals and ahimsa in his epic *Kural*. He said: 'Those who treasure all living things do not need to fear themselves being harmed by any evil deed' (25. 244); 'those who have realised what is suffering must refrain from inflicting it on others' (32. 316); and 'all suffering falls on those who caused others suffering. Those who don't want it must stop from causing it' (32. 320).

Respecting these sentiments would certainly improve the lives of domestic animals and the chances of survival of India's endangered wildlife.

# Appendix

## Sacred Animals and Animal Divinities of Ancient Mesopotamia and Egypt

The earliest forms of religion all over the world must have included animals. Stone Age paintings contain many animals, from combined human–animal figures as seen at Dordogne, to scenes of the hunt found in different places, which probably represented some form of magic to overpower the animals ancient people were hunting, or fighting against for their survival. All ancient civilizations portray aspects of nature worship, be it the worship of the earth mother or plants or animals.

### Mesopotamia[*]

Ancient Babylon had more animal demons than gods. Animals were seen as a threat to life and survival. Yet a few were worshipped, even as they were sacrificed to the gods. As in India, most were vehicles of the gods, rather than gods themselves. In addition, the similarity to many Indian deities is quite remarkable. Where they differed was that they had human heads and animal bodies, unlike Indian (and Egyptian) animal deities who had animal heads and human bodies.

Each deity was identified by his attributes and weapons, as well as his animal. Sometimes they were natural, often they were hybrid. Sometimes they symbolized the gods and often they

[*] Source: Black and Green 1992; Kramer 1994; 1956.

were the vehicles on which the deity stood, or the companion to their special god. Some animals guarded the entrances to temples while others held up the altars.

### Birds

Depictions of a walking bird are common in all periods, but in the Kassite and Neo-Babylonlian periods the walking bird was regarded as a religious symbol of the minister god Papsukkal or Ninshubur.

Ninurta was the avian war god who also represented agriculture. He is a warlike figure who defeats the Anzu bird Imdugud.

The Sumerian goddess Nanse was also associated with birds.

### Bull

He was the vehicle of Ishkur or Adad, who held a two-pronged fork as a symbol of lightning. On an Old Assyrian seal, a god on a bull holds a trident, representing lightning, while another god on a lion also holds the trident. The bull was also the symbol of Nanna-Suen or Sin, the moon god.

### Bull-Man

He appears as an attendant of the sun god Samas or Utu. In a Neo-Babylonian tablet, a pair of bulls with human heads supports the god's throne.

A human-headed winged or wingless bull was a common motif in Mesopotamia and, later, in Neo-Babylonian, Achaemenid and Assyrian periods. Later, these were adopted as Zoroastrian symbols as well.

The god Lahmu, meaning 'hairy', is a benevolent deity often associated with the bull-man Kusarikku.

## Centaur

A popular figure, human above the waist and with the body and legs of a horse, he represented the god Pabilsag, associated with the city of Larag.

## Cow and Calf

This theme appears frequently and represents the mother goddess Ninhursaga.

The name of the goddess Ninsun means 'lady wild cow' and it is possible that she was originally associated with wild cattle. She is the mother of the hero Gilgamesh.

## Dog

The canine was sacred to Gula (Ninisina), goddess of healing. In the Assyrian period, dogs became protective figures flanking gateways.

## Donkey

The animal is the vehicle of Lamashtu, a demoness. Sometimes Lamashtu was depicted with the head of a lion with the teeth and ears of a donkey. She was the daughter of the supreme god An or Anu, and practised evil for evil's sake.

## Dragon

While the dragon as a whole is not to be seen, hybrid creatures like snake-dragons and lion-dragons are not uncommon.

## Eagle

King Etana of Kish travels to heaven on the back of an eagle. The bird is constantly at war with the serpent.

An eagle-headed staff was the symbol of Zababa, local god of Kish.

## Fish

Enki, god of Eridu, was the god of the waters and Eridu was situated close to the marshes. The fish was associated with Enki and offerings of fish were made regularly to him.

The Sumerian goddess Nanse was associated with fish.

Generally, figures dressed in the bodies of fish are described as exorcist priests.

## Fish-Man and Fish-Woman

The merman and mermaid had a human head and a fish's body. Associated with the water god Ea or Enki, they were creatures of the subterranean waters or apsu.

## Fly

The tiny insect has been compared to the flood waters in the Mesopotamian story of the Great Flood. However, the image of the fly on Babylonian seals has been identified as a symbol of Nergal, the god of disease and death, thereby indicating that the Sumerians were aware that the fly was a carrier of disease.

## Frog

The amphibian is a symbol on cylinder seals of the Kassite period.

## Goat-Fish

This hybrid animal was also associated with Ea or Enki, god of the ocean in the Neo-Assyrian period.

## Griffin

This is the European name for a fabulous animal which was a combination of a lion and an eagle. Its significance is not known.

## Horse

The animal was ridden by and sacred to the sun god Shamash, as in India where the sun was drawn in a chariot by seven horses.

A winged horse or centaur is sometimes seen on Middle Assyrian seals.

## Lion

Lions were common in ancient Mesopotamia and appear in the art of all the dynasties of the Iraq–Iran region. In fact the last lion in the region was killed in the twentieth century.

The king of the jungle has been associated at different times with different deities: Ningirsu, god of Lagash; Ninlil (Mullissu), the mother goddess who was seated on a lion; Ishtar (Inana), a warrior goddess whose vehicle-companion was the lion; and Damkina (Damgalnuna), a mother goddess. Ishtar probably influenced the later iconography of Durga, the Hindu mother goddess.

## Lion-Bird

This composite creature with a lion's head and the body of Imdugud, the Anzu bird, was identified with Ningirsu, the warrior god of Lagash, worshipped by Gudea.

## Lion-Centaur

A lion's body and a man's head, upper body and arms made up Urmahlullu, who wore the horned cap of divinity. The motif passed into Achaemenid and then Seleucid art.

## Lion-Dragon

With a lion's forelegs, bird's hindlegs, tail and wings, he was the vehicle of god Ishkur and was later transferred to several Assyrian deities, including Ashshur, Sin (moon god) and Adad.

## Lion-Fish

This unidentified motif is often found on old Babylonian seals.

## Lion-Man

A lion-headed human figure represents the god La-tarak or Lulal, a protector against witchcraft.

## Mongoose

This palm-rat, found in southern Mesopotamia, was connected with the goddess Ningilin, associated with magic.

## Pigeon

The Sushuru was a type of pigeon associated with Enmesharra, a god connected with the underworld.

## Shakkan

He was the son of the sun god Shamash and the protector of wild animals, for whose fertility he was responsible.

## Seven Sages

Like the seven rishis or sages of Indian lore, represented as human beings or heavenly bodies, the seven sages of Babylon were represented as birds or fish in ancient Assur.

## Scorpion

Ishara's companion in the late Kassite period was the scorpion. Neo-Assyrian cylinder seals depict different kinds of scorpion men. The scorpion people, identified by their prominent tails, appear frequently in the art of several periods of Babylonian history.

## Snake

The snake gods 'seem to be the only fully animalian, non-anthropomorphic deities'. The snake god Nirah was worshipped as the symbol of Ishtaran, the local god in the northern city of Der, and at E-kur, the temple of Enlil in Nippur, where he was regarded as a protective deity.

The snake was the companion of the goddess Ishara in the earlier period.

The motif of the two intertwined snakes was very common from a very early Sumerian and Neo-Sumerian periods, while the seven-hooded snake depicted in early dynastic art may be the seven-headed Ningirsu or Ninurta.

### Snake-Dragon

With a snake's body, horns, a lion's forelegs and bird's hindlegs, this composite creature guarded the shrines of Marduk, the patron god of Babylon. He was the vehicle of the scribal god Nabu of Babylon, Assur of Assyria, and Marduk and was associated with Ningishzida and his son Ninazu, gods of the underworld, before his association with Marduk.

### Turtle

He was associated with the water god Ea or Enki.

# Egypt*

Of all the ancient civilizations, animals were revered and sanctified in ancient Egypt more than in any other culture. Most of the Egyptian gods had heads of animals and birds. They are shown receiving the adoration of mortals and kings, they are painted and sculpted on sarcophagi and mummy cases and on the walls of temples and tombs.

The earliest representations of gods in Egypt appeared around 3500 BCE, when the inhabitants of the fertile lands adjoining the river Nile lived in tribes. Each tribe had its own god, who was

* Source: *New Larousse Encyclopedia of Mythology*; *Funk & Wagnalls Dictionary of Mythology*; Farid Atiya 2006.

either an animal or bird or fetish. In early representations, the chief of the clan held a staff with the totemic animal or bird seated on it, sometimes holding a weapon.

Later, when the tribes settled and turned to food production, the animals became gods and their heads were transferred to the part-human part-animal deities. Thus we have falcon-headed or jackal headed divinities. Once the gods were installed in a temple, they became the local deities of a particular city. As in India, the artistic abilities of the ancient Egyptians made the transition from the animal or bird head to the human body so perfect that it appeared to be perfectly natural.

Sometimes live animals themselves were worshipped and given offerings by the kings, priests and common people. When a sacred animal died, it was mourned, mummified and entombed. As soon as a substitute was found, there was much rejoicing.

Most temples maintained animals in whose form the local god was incarnated, such as cats in the temple of Bast or a falcon or ibis in the temple of Horus. The animal was regarded as sacred and it was forbidden to kill or eat it, and any violation could even result in a death sentence. Cats were so venerated that, according to Herodotus, when a building caught fire, Egyptians would neglect the fire in order to save the cats. When a sacred animal died, providing for its funeral was regarded as an act of great merit.

However, it also resulted in the animal being hunted down or killed mercilessly in an enemy province, leading to wars. According to Plutarch (first century CE), when the Cynopolitans ate an oxyrhynchites (spider crab), the oxyrhynchites were so angry that they sacrificed dogs, sacred to the former, and ate their flesh. This started a bloody war which had to be ended by the Romans who punished both severely.

While the animal head, or the animal's emblem which surmounts the head, identifies the deity, Egypt has the advantage in that its hieroglyphics have been deciphered and the gods are identified and their roles described by the accompanying explanation. The undeciphered seals in the Indus Valley civilization of the same period make the role of the animals impossible to understand. However, the animal-headed deities of ancient Egypt are earlier than those found in India or elsewhere in the Middle East and this appendix has been placed at the end in order that the main subject of the book is not diluted.

These, then, are some of the sacred animals and animal-headed gods of ancient Egypt, who represent the lives and concerns of the Egptians and their rulers.

## Birds

The bird Bennu has been identified with the phoenix, lapwing or heron. He was a legendary figure, although his existence was never doubted. He was worshipped as the soul of Osiris and was also connected with the cult of Ra.

## Bull

The bull was the most sacred of animals and was the reincarnation of the gods themselves. All the dynasties of Egypt had temples dedicated to the sacred bulls who were given grand funeral rites, mummified and tombed after their lives were over.

Onuphis (Egyptian Aa Nefer*) was the bull in which the soul of Osiris (Egyptian Ousir) was reincarnated. Osiris was primarily a nature god who embodied the spirit of vegetation. Later, he became the god of the dead and the most popular deity of ancient Egypt.

Apis (Egyptian Hapi) was a very popular and much honoured deity throughout Egypt. He was the reincarnation of Ptah, the god of Memphis, who was represented as a mummy holding a

---

* While the Egyptian gods are better known by their Greek names, I have also given the Egyptian names.

sceptre. He was venerated by the Pharaohs and their priests as the creator of the world.

Ptah, in the form of the celestial fire, impregnated a virgin heifer, and was reborn from her as a black bull with a white triangle on his forehead, a vulture with outstretched wings on his back, a crescent moon on his right flank, a scarab's image on his tongue and double the hairs of an ordinary bull on his tail.

The sacred bull lived in the temple of Memphis, opposite the temple of Ptah. He was let loose at a particular hour each day and attracted crowds of devotees and tourists from Greek and Rome. He was allowed to die of old age unless he lived beyond a certain age, when he was drowned in a fountain. During Persian occupation, the sacred bull was assassinated twice.

Vast subterranean chambers have been discovered at Saqqarah containing mummified bodies of sacred bulls that were given a grand funeral and buried in huge monolithic sarcophagi made of sandstone or pink granite. Above rose a huge temple—of which nothing remains today—where the funeral cult of the dead bull, called Osiris Apis, was celebrated.

Buchis (Egyptian Bukhe) was sacred to Menthu (Greek Mont), the Theban god of war. We are told that the hair on his hide changed colour every hour and grew in the opposite direction. Buchis was worshipped at Hermonthis in upper Egypt, while the vaults containing his mummies were discovered at Armant along with the tombs of the cows that gave birth to these sacred bulls.

Later, Menthu himself was represented as a man with a bull's head surmounted by the solar disc and two tall straight plumes.

Merwer (Greek Mneuis) was the sacred bull of Atum, a personification of Ra the sun, at Heliopolis. Later, Horus–Ra–Atum came to represent the three phases of the sun: the rising, midday and setting sun. Atum was the last. He may have been of a lighter colour.

Onuphis was the bull incarnation of Osiris, who was very fond of taking incarnations.

## Cat

Bast (Bastet) was the local goddess of Bubastis, capital of lower Egypt. She was originally a lion goddess who personified the sun's warmth. Later the cat became her sacred animal and she was represented as a woman with a cat's head holding a semicircular breastplate surmounted by the head of a lioness in her right hand. Many statues of the cat were consecrated by her devotees. Further, the sacred cats that had been venerated in her temples were mummified when they died.

Bast was a pleasure-loving goddess who enjoyed music and dance. She beat time with a sistrum (an instrument) decorated with a seated cat.

Another form of Bast was Pekhet, the cat or lion-headed goddess of Speos Artemidos.

## Cow

Isis (Egyptian Ases, Eset) was the wife of Osiris, god of the dead, and mother of Horus, part of the Horus–Ra–Atum triad representing the three phases of the sun. Her headdress was the disc, flanked by the cow's horns, and occasionally by two feathers also. Later, when Isis was identified with Hathor, she was represented with a cow's head on a human body.

But Plutarch has another tale. Isis tried to intervene on behalf of her brother Set, who was also her husband Osiris's murderer, thus cheating her son Horus of his vengeance. Furious, Horus cut off his mother's head. Then Thoth, the moon god, gave her the head of a cow.

Hathor (Egyptian Athyr) was the daughter of Ra and the wife of Horus; sometimes she was called the mother of Horus, for her name also means the 'dwelling of Horus'. She was the great celestial cow who created the world and all that it contains, including the sun. She may be represented as a cow or as a cow-headed goddess or even as a fully human persona with cow's ears or in a human form with the solar disc flanked by the cow's horns surmounting her head.

Mut was Amon-Ra's wife and a sky goddess who remained in the form of a cow.

Nut, the sky goddess, a woman with an elongated body who touched the earth with her toes and fingers while her body was held up by Shu, god of the air, is sometimes represented as a cow, a form she assumed to bear Ra on her back to the sky after the sun god had decided to abandon his subjects. A god was appointed to guard each of her four legs, the four pillars which supported the sky. She is called both the daughter and mother of Ra.

### Crocodile

Sebek (Greek Suchos) was the great crocodile deity of the Nile, represented as a man with a crocodile head or even as a crocodile, who was venerated at Fayyum. It is not inconceivable that the treacherous swamps and the river being the home of this deadly predator, made the people worship and appease the crocodile. He had an evil reputation, for he aided the murder of Osiris when Set took refuge in the crocodile's body. Thus, even as he was venerated in one place, the crocodile was hunted viciously in others.

Sebek's chief sanctuary was in Crocodilopolis, the capital of Arsinoe, in a lake dug out near the great temple, where a real crocodile called Petesuchos (Greek—'he who belongs to Suchos) lived and was worshipped. Petesuchos was an old crocodile, with golden rings in his ears and bracelets in his forelegs. Along with several other crocodiles that lived there, he was regarded as sacred.

Crocodile tombs have been found where the animals were mummified and buried with their newborns and even their eggs.

## Dog

Anubis (Egyptian Anpu), the conductor of souls, was represented as a black-skinned man with the head of either a dog or a jackal. He presided over the embalmment and funeral prayers were addressed to him.

One of the four sons of Horus and Ibis was the dog-headed Hapi.

## Falcon

The falcon is represented from the earliest periods as a totem on a standard, and was always a pre-eminent divinity. The ideogram for god is a falcon on its perch. The falcon was the most sacred of all the gods.

Horus (Egyptian Hor) or Behdety was a falcon-headed solar god. Horus meant sky, which was regarded as a divine falcon whose two eyes were the sun and the moon. His followers were numerous and powerful for, wherever they settled, Horus was worshipped.

Ra Harakhte (Horus of the horizon), the solar god of Heliopolis and the other aspect of the solar triad, is invariably represented with a human body and a falcon's head surmounted by a solar disc encircled by a snake. At Edfu in upper Egypt he is portrayed as a full falcon wearing the double crown of upper and lower Egypt.

Horus the falcon had four sons, born of Ibis, who were appointed by their father to watch over the four cardinal points and the heart and entrails of Osiris. They were

- the human-headed Imsety,
- the dog-headed Hapi,
- the jackal-headed Duamutef, and
- the hawk-headed Qebhsnuf.

Khensu (Greek Khons), whose name meant navigator, seems to have been a moon god represented as a man with a falcon's head surmounted by a disc in a crescent moon.

Menthu, the Theban god of war, had a falcon head surmounted by the solar disc and two tall straight plumes, and a man's body.

### Frog

Heket was a frog-headed goddess who symbolized decomposed grain and its moment of germination.

### Goose

Geb (or Seb, Keb), the earth god and sibling of Nut, the sky, is sometimes depicted with a head surmounted by a goose, which is the ideogram of his name.

### Hawk

Seker was the hawk-headed goddess of the dead of Memphis. One of the four sons of Horus was the hawk-headed Qebhsnuf.

### Hippopotamus

Tauret (Apet, Opet) was the goddess of childbirth of Thebes who was represented as a standing female hippopotamus. She was very popular among the people. Her name was given to children and homes decorated with her images. As an avenging goddess she sometimes appeared as a hippopotamus with the head of a lioness, holding a dagger.

### Ibis

Thoth (Egyptian Zehuti), the moon god, may be represented with the head of an ibis surmounted by a crescent moon, or even as a full ibis. He was the wise one, inventor of the arts and the sciences, hieroglyphs and magic.

## Jackal

Anubis (Egyptian Anpu) was the conductor of souls, who opened the paths to the netherworld for the dead. He is represented as a black jackal with a bushy tail, or as a black-skinned man with the head of a jackal or dog. He presided over embalmments and funeral prayers were addressed to him.

One of the four sons of Horus and Ibis was the jackal-headed Duamutef.

## Lion

Harmakhis (Egyptian Hormakhet) is the name of the Sphinx, the huge lion with a man's head, 18 m high and over 54 m feet long, sculpted 5,000 years ago in the image of King Khapren near the pyramids of Giza at Cairo.

Nefertum is the son of Sekhmet. Sometimes he has a lion head, sometimes he stands on a crouching lion.

## Lioness

Sekhmet (Greek Sakhmis) is the goddess of war, represented as a savage lioness or as a woman with the head of a lioness, whose name means 'The Powerful'. She was the wife of Ptah, and bore him a son, Nefertum. She was worshipped by bone-setters who cured fractures due to her intercession.

Tefnut was worshipped as a lioness or as a woman with the head of a lioness, and was sometimes identified with Artemis by the Greeks. She is both wife and twin sister of Shu, the god of air who keeps apart Nut, the sky goddess, and Geb, the earth god. She supports the sky and receives the newborn sun each morning.

## Ram

Amon (Amun, Ammon) is represented with the head of a ram, with curled horns. A live ram was the sacred animal of Amon at Karnak. Amon became the 'King of the Gods', with several temples dedicated to him at Thebes and elsewhere in Egypt.

Mendes (Egyptian Ba Neb Djedet or Banadad) was the incarnation of the soul of Osiris and Thoth, the moon god. While Thoth was represented as an ibis-headed man or dog-headed ape, the kings were required to give offerings to the living ram. When Banadad died, there was public mourning and public celebrations when his replacement was found.

Efu Ra was the sun at night, believed to be dead. He was portrayed as a man with a ram's head surmounted by the solar disc, drawn in the evening boat throughout the night.

Harsaphes or Hershef, another ram-headed god, was the presiding deity of Heracleopolis Magna in the Fayyum.

Khnum or Khnemu was a ram-headed man with long, wavy horns, unlike the curved horns of the ram-headed Amin.

## Scarab

The sanctity of this little insect in Egyptian culture is well known. Khepera (or Khepri) 'represented the rising sun which, like the scarab, emerges from its own substance and is reborn of itself'. Khepri, representing renewal, was the god of transformations, depicted as a scarab-faced man or as a man with the scarab on his head or even as the scarab itself.

## Scorpion

Selket is depicted with a scorpion's head and a woman's body. Sometimes she was represented as a scorpion with a woman's head. Sometimes she is called the daughter of Ra and was the guardian of marriage.

## Snake

Apep was the great enemy of Ra, the sun. He lived in the depths of the Nile and sometimes—as during an eclipse—succeeded in swallowing the solar boat of Ra. However, he was always defeated by Ra's followers and sent back to the depths of the river.

Metseger (Merseger) was the snake goddess of Thebes. She was represented as a snake with a human head.

Buto (Egyptian Per Uadjit) was a snake goddess represented as a cobra. She was generally portrayed along with the vulture goddess on official documents.

## Vulture

The bird was the sacred animal of Mut, wife of Amon and adoptive mother of Mont and Khons. She was often represented as wearing the headdress of a vulture, which was also the ideogram of her name.

## Wolf

Khenti Amenti was the wolf god of Abydos in upper Egypt. He was later identified with Osiris, the god of the dead, giving the latter the name of Osiris Khenti Amenti or 'Lord of Westerners', since the dead dwelt in the west, where the sun sets.

Upnaut (Egyptian Ophois Wepwawet) is a wolf-headed god who signifies 'he who opens the way'. He could be seen on prehistoric standards, guiding his warriors in war.

# Bibliography

- Agrawal, V.S., *Ancient Indian Folk Cults*, Varanasi: Prithivi Prakashan, 1970.
- Alvares, Claude (ed.), *Fish Curry and Rice*, The Goa Foundation, 2002.
- Amirthalingam, M., 'Sacred Animals of Tamilnadu', *Ecological Traditions of Tamilnadu*, Chennai: C.P.R. Environmental Education Centre, 2005.
- Ardhya, H.S.N., 'Sacred Animals of Karnataka', *Ecological Traditions of Karnataka*, Chennai: C.P.R. Environmental Education Centre, 2005.
- *Atharva Veda*, Hoshiarpur: Vishveshvaranand Indological Series, 1960–64.
- Atiya, Farid, *Ancient Egypt*: Farid Atiya Press, Giza, 2006.
- *Bhâgavata Purana*, Nadiad: Krishnashankar Shastri, 1965.
- *Bhagavat Gita*, Almora: Advaita Ashrama, 1933.
- Biju Kumar, A., 'Snake Worship in Kerala', *Ecological Traditions of Kerala*, Chennai: C.P.R. Environmental Education Centre, 2006.
- Black, J. and Green, A. *Gods, Demons and Symbols of Ancient Mesopotamia*, London: The British Museum Press, 1992.
- *Chandogya Upanishad* Poona: Vaidika Samsodhana Mandala, 1958.
- Coomaraswamy A.K., and Sister Nivedita, *Myths of the Hindus and Buddhists*, New York: Dover Publication Inc., 1967.
- Debroy, Vivek, *Sarama and her Children, The Dog in Indian Myth*, New Delhi: Penguin, 2008.
- Dowson, J., A *Classical Dictionary of Hindu Mythology and Religion*, Rupa & Co., New Delhi, 1982.

- Dwivedi, O.P., *World Religions and the Environment*, New Delhi: Gitanjali Publishing House, 1989.
- Funk and Wagnalls, *Standard Dictionary of Folklore, Mythology and Legend*, New York, 1949.
- Godbole A. and Sarnaik J., Eco Restoration of Sacred Groves in Maharashtra', *Ecological Traditions of Maharashtra*, C.P.R. Environmental Education Centre, 2006.
- Gupta, S.K., *Elephant in Indian Art and Mythology*, New Delhi: Abhinav Pulications, 1983.
- Harris, Marvin, 'India's Sacred Cow', *Human Nature*, 1978.
- Jagannathan, Shakunthala and Nanditha Krishna, *Ganesha—The Auspicious...The Beginning*, Vakils, Feffer & Simons Ltd. Mumbai: 2002.
- Jha, Ajeya, 'Ecological Prudence of the Lepchas', *Development Alternatives*, Vol. 8, No. 6, June 1998.
- Kramer, S.N., *From the Tablets of Sumer*, Colorado: The Falcon's Wing Press, 1956.
- Kramer, S.N., *Sumerian Mythology*, Philadelphia: American Philosophical Society, 1944.
- Krishna N., Amrithalingam M. and Godbole A. 'Sacred Animals of Maharashtra', Ecological Traditions of Maharashtra, C.P.R. Environment Education Centre, Chennai, 2006.
- Krishna, Nanditha *Art and Iconography of Vishnu Narayana*, Mumbai: D.B. Taraporevala Sons & Co. Pvt. Ltd, 1980.
- ———, *Painted Manuscripts of the Sarasvati Mahal Library*, Thanjavur: 1994.
- ——— *Book of Vishnu*, New Delhi: Penguin, 2001.
- ——— *Book of Demons*, New Delhi: Penguin, 2007.
- *Mahabharata*, Calcutta: Asiatic Society of Bengal, 1837.
- Majupuria, T.C., *Sacred Animals of Nepal and India*, Gwalior: 2000.
- *Manusmriti*, Calcutta: Education Press, 1830.
- Marcot, B.G., D.H. Johnson and M., Cocker, 'Owls in Lore and Culture', http://www.owlpages.com/articles accessed on.
- Marimuthu, G., 'The Sacred Flying Fox of India', *Bat Conservational International*, 6 (2), 1988.

- Menon, Shobha, 'The Tale of the Sacred Eagles', *The Hindu*, 18 June 2003.
- *New Larousse Encyclopedia of Mythology*, Hamlyn, London 1989.
- Nair, P.T., 'Peacock Worship in India and Abroad', *The Quarterly Journal of the Mythic Society*, Vol. LXV, January–March 1974.
- Paul, G.S.,'"Mimic the Tiger', *The Hindu*, 11 September 2005.
- Ramanujam, Geetha, *Environmental Awareness in Jainism*, Chennai: Department of Jainology, University of Madras, 2006.
- *Ramayana*, Varanasi: Chowkhamba Sanskrit Studies, 1963.
- Rangarajan, M., *India's Wildlife History*, Delhi: Permanent Black, 2001.
- *Rig Veda*, Hoshiarpur: Vishveshvaranand Indological Series, 1963–66.
- Ritvo, Harriet, 'Beasts in the jungle (or wherever)', *Dedalus*, American Academy of Arts and Sciences, 2008.
- Sarkar, B.K., *The Folk Element in Indian Culture*, New Delhi: Orient Books Reprint Corporation, 1972.
- Sarma, M.V.S., 'Our National Bird: The Peacock', *The Quarterly Journal of the Mythic Society*, Vol. LXI, Nos. 1–4, April–December 1970.
- Sehgal, Narendra, *Converted Kashmir*, Kashmir Information Network, 2001.
- Sharma, Ghildial V. and Ramesh C. Sharma. 'Animals of Early Indian Cultures', *Animal Citizen*, Vol. XXIV, N 0.3 Chennai, 1987.
- Singh, Karan, 'Myth and Reality', *The Tiger Call*, Delhi: WWF India, 1996.
- Sircar, D.C., *Select Inscriptions Bearing on Indian History and Civilization*, Vol. I, Delhi: Asian Humanites Press, 1986.
- Siromoney, Gift, 'The Neophron Vultures of Thirukkalukundram', *Newsletter for Birdwatchers*, Vol. XVII, No. 6, June 1977.
- Sitaramiah, V., *Valmiki Râmâyana*, New Delhi: Sahitya Akademi, 1971.
- Sivapriyananda, 'Serpents in Indian Imagination', *India Magazine*, Vol.12, No.8, July 1992.

- Sivarajah, Padmini, 'Where bats are treated as angels', *Deccan Chronicle*, 24 December 2007.
- Srinivasulu, C.V.N., and Bargavi Srinivasulu, 'Sacred Animals of Andhra Pradesh', *Ecological Traditions of Andhra Pradesh*, Chennai: C.P.R. Environmental Education Centre, 2005.
- Surya Narayan, Deepa, 'Vulture-killing drug banned', http://www.iipsenvis.nic.in/archives.htm *Times of India*, Mumbai, 23 May 2006.
- Thapar, Valmik, 'The Cult of the Tiger', *Sanctuary*, Vol.XV, No.1, 1995.
- Vasdev, Kanchan, 'Divali spells doom for owls in Ludhiana', *Tribune News Service*, Ludhiana, 29 October 2005.
- *Thirukkural*, Ramalinga Pillai, T.S. (trans.), Madras: The South Indian Saiva Siddhanta Works Publishing Society, 1987.
- Vyas, S.N., *India in the Ramayana Age*, Delhi: Atma Ram & Sons, Delhi, 1967.
- Williams, George M., *Handbook of Hindu Mythology*, Santa Brbara, California: ABC-Clio Inc., 2003.
- http://www.animalinfo.org
- www.hermitary.com/solitude/rhinoceros.html
- http://www.indiasite.com/wildlife/mammals
- *ww.washington.edu/uwpress/search/books/SALGAN.html*